STUDIES AND TEXTS

38

PLATE 1

St Bernard praying alongside the reapers.
Jörg Breu (1475-1537). Stift Zwettle, Niederösterreich.
(Reproduced by permission.)

THE CISTERCIANS: STUDIES IN THE GEOGRAPHY OF MEDIEVAL ENGLAND AND WALES

BY

R. A. DONKIN
Fellow of Jesus College, Cambridge

PONTIFICAL INSTITUTE OF MEDIAEVAL STUDIES
TORONTO 1978

ACKNOWLEDGMENT

This book has been published with the help of a grant from the Social Science Federation of Canada, using funds provided by the Social Sciences and Humanities Research Council of Canada.

CANADIAN CATALOGUING IN PUBLICATION DATA

Donkin, R. A., 1928-
The Cistercians

(Studies and texts – Pontifical Institute of Mediaeval Studies ; 38 ISSN 0082-5328)

Bibliography: p.
Includes index.
ISBN 0-88844-038-3

1. Cistercians in England. 2. Great Britain – Economic conditions. 3. Great Britain – History – Medieval period, 1066-1485. I. Title. II. Series: Pontifical Institute of Mediaeval Studies. Studies and texts – Pontifical Institute of Mediaeval Studies ; 38.

BX3416.D65 271'.12'042 C77-001138-1

PONTIFICAL INSTITUTE OF MEDIAEVAL STUDIES
59 Queen's Park Crescent East
Toronto, Ontario, Canada M5S 2C4

PRINTED BY UNIVERSA PRESS, WETTEREN, BELGIUM

*To my mother
and father*

Contents

List of Maps

List of Plates

Abbreviations

1. National and Regional Records

Abb. Plac. Illingworth, William, ed. *Placitorum in domo capitulari Westmonasteriensi asservatorum abbreviatio. Temporibus regum Ric. I, Johann., Henr. III, Edw. I, Edw. II*. London: Record Commission, 1811.

C.A.D. *A Descriptive Catalogue of Ancient Deeds in the Public Record Office*. 6 vols. London, 1890-1915.

Cal. Docs. Scot. *Calendar of Documents Relating to Scotland Preserved in Her Majesty's Public Record Office, London*. Ed. by Joseph Bain. 4 vols. Edinburgh, 1881-88.

Cal. Rot. Ch. Inq. Dam. Caley, J., ed. *Calendarium rotulorum chartarum et inquisitionum ad quod damnum*. London: [Record Commission], 1803.

Cartae Glam. Clark, George T., ed. *Cartae et alia munimenta quae ad dominium de Glamorgan pertinent*. 4 vols. Dowlais, 1885-93.

Cart. Ant. Landon, Lionel, ed. *The Cartae antiquae*. 1: *Rolls 1-10*. P.R.S., Publs., 55., n.s., 17. London, 1938.

C.C.R.(V) *Calendar of the Various Chancery Rolls ... Preserved in the Public Record Office. A.D. 1277-1326*. London, 1912.

C.Ch.R. *Calendar of the Charter Rolls Preserved in the Public Record Office*. 6 vols. London, 1903-27.

C.Cl.R. *Calendar of the Close Rolls ... Preserved in the Public Record Office*. London, 1902-.

C.F.R. *Calendar of the Fine Rolls Preserved in the Public Record Office*. London, 1911-.

C.I.P.M. *Calendar of Inquisitions Post Mortem and Other Analogous Documents Preserved in the Public Record Office*. 14 vols. London, 1904-54.

C.L.R. *Calendar of the Liberate Rolls Preserved in the Public Record Office*. London, 1916-.

C.M.I. *Calendar of Inquisitions Miscellaneous (Chancery) Preserved in the Public Record Office*. London, 1916-.

C.P.R. *Calendar of the Patent Rolls Preserved in the Public Record Office*. London, 1891-.

C.R.R.	*Curia regis Rolls ... Preserved in the Public Record Office.* London, 1922-.
Docs. Eng. Hist.	Cole, Henry, ed. *Documents Illustrative of English History in the Thirteenth and Fourteenth Centuries Selected from the Records ... of the Exchequer.* London: Record Commission, 1844.
E.Y.C.	Farrer, William, et al., eds. *Early Yorkshire Charters.* Yorkshire Archaeological Society, Record Series, Extra Series, 1- (1914-).
Fines	Hunter, Joseph, ed. *Fines, sive pedes finium, sive finales concordiae in curia domini regis ... A.D. 1195-A.D. 1214.* 2 vols. London: Record Commission, 1835-44.
Foedera	Rymer, Thomas. *Foedera, Conventiones, Litterae, et cujuscunque generis acta publica.* Ed. by A. Clarke, et al. 4 vols. London: Record Commission, 1816-1869.
Inq. Dam.	See *Cal. Rot. Ch. Inq. Dam.*
K.F., K.I., and N.V.	Skaife, R. H., ed. *A Survey of the County of York Taken by John de Kirkby, Commonly Called Kirkby's Inquest. Also Inquisitions of Knights' Fees. The Nomina Villarum for Yorkshire.* Surtees Society, Publs. 49. Durham, 1867.
Papal Letters	*Calendar of Entries in the Papal Registers Relating to Great Britain and Ireland. Papal Letters.* Public Record Office. London: HMSO, 1893-.
Parl. Writs	Palgrave, Francis, ed. *The Parliamentary Writs and Writs of Military Summons.* 2 vols. London: Record Commission, 1827-34.
Plac. Quo Warr.	Illingworth, William, ed. *Placita de quo warranto temporibus Edw. I, II et III.* London: Record Commission, 1818.
Register	*Register of Edward the Black Prince Preserved in the Public Record Office.* 4 vols. London, 1930-33.
Rot. Ch.	Hardy, Thomas D., ed. *Rotuli chartarum in Turri Londinensi asservati.* London: Record Commission, 1837.
Rot. Cl.	———. *Rotuli litterarum clausarum in Turri Londinensi asservati.* 2 vols. London: Record Commission, 1833-44.
Rot. Hund.	Illingworth, William, ed. *Rotuli hundredorum ... .* 2 vols. London: Record Commission, 1812-18.
Rot. Oblat.	Hardy, Thomas D., ed. *Rotuli de oblatis et finibus in Turri Londinensi asservati.* London: Record Commission, 1835.
Rot. Orig.	[Playford, and John Caley, eds.] *Rotulorum originalium in Curia Scaccarii abbreviatio.* 2 vols. London: Record Commission, 1805-10.
Rot. Parl.	*Rotuli parliamentorum.* 6 vols. London, 1767-77.
Rot. Pat.	Hardy, Thomas D., ed. *Rotuli litterarum patentium in Turri Londinensi asservati.* London: Record Commission, 1835.

Tax. Eccles. Astle, Thomas, S. Ayscough, John Caley, eds. *Taxatio ecclesiastica Angliae et Walliae auctoritate P. Nicholae IV circa A.D. 1291*. London: Record Commission, 1802.

2. Monastic Records

Account B Hockey, S. F., ed. *The Account Book of Beaulieu Abbey*, Camden Fourth Series (Royal Historical Society), 16. London, 1975.

Ann. Wav. Luard, Henry Richards, ed. *Annales Monasterii de Waverleia.* In his *Annales Monastici*, Rolls Series 36, 2: 127-411. London, 1865.

Book Comb. Hall, James, ed. *The Book of the Abbot of Combermere.* Record Society for ... Lancashire and Cheshire, publs., 31. [London and Manchester], 1896.

Chart. B. Turnbull, W.B.D.D., ed. *The Chartularies of Balmerino and Lindores*. Abbotsford Club, publs., 22. Edinburgh, 1841.

Chart. Bl. Hockey, S. F., ed. *The Beaulieu Cartulary*. Southampton Record Series, 17. Southampton, 1974.

Chart. C. Easson, David E., ed. *Charters of the Abbey of Coupar Angus*. 2 vols. Scottish Historical Society, publs., 3rd ser., 40, 41. Edinburgh, 1947.

Chart. D. Wrottesley, George, ed. "The chartulary of Dieulacres." In *Collections for a History of Staffordshire*, ed. for the William Salt Archaeological Society, n.s., 9 (London, 1906): 291-365.

Chart. Duiske Bernard, John H. and Constance M. Butler, eds. "The charters of the Cistercian abbey of Duiske." *Royal Irish Academy, Proceedings*, 35, sect. C, no. 1 (Dublin, 1918): 1-188.

Chart. F. Lancaster, William T., ed. *Abstracts of the Charters and Other Documents Contained in the Chartulary of the Cistercian Abbey of Fountains*. 2 vols. Leeds, 1915.

Chart Fl. Crawley-Boevey, Arthur W., ed. *The Cartulary and Historical Notes of the Cistercian Abbey of Flaxley, Otherwise Called Dene Abbey*. Exeter, 1887.

Chart. N. Fowler, John T., ed. *Chartularium abbathie de Novo Monasterio Ordinis cisterciensis*. Surtees Society publs., 66. Durham, 1878.

Chart. R. Atkinson, John C., ed. *Cartularium abbathie de Rievalle Ordinis cisterciensis*. Surtees Society publs., 83. Durham, 1889.

Chart. S. McNulty, Joseph, ed. *The Chartulary of the Cistercian Abbey of St. Mary of Sallay in Craven*. 2 vols. Yorks. Arch. Soc., Record Series, 87, 90. 1933-34.

Chart. T. Salter, Herbert E., ed. *The Thame Cartulary.* 2 vols. Oxfordshire Record Society, record series, 25-26. Oxford, 1947-48.

Chart. W. Fowler, G. Herbert, ed. *The Cartulary of the Abbey of Old Wardon.* Bedfordshire Hist. Rec. Soc., publs., 13. Aspley Guise, 1930.

Chron. L. P. Venables, Edmund, ed. *Chronicon Abbatie de Parco Lude.* Lincs. Rec. Soc., publs., 1. Lincoln, 1891.

Chron. M. [Thomas de Burton]. *Chronica monasterii de Melsa.* Ed. by Edward A. Bond. Rolls Series 43. 3 vols. London, 1866-68.

Coucher F. Atkinson, John C., and John Brownbill, eds. *The Coucher Book of Furness Abbey.* 6 vols. Remains ..., n.s., 9, 11, 14, 74, 76, 78. Manchester: Chetham Society, 1886-1919.

Coucher K. Lancaster, William T., and William P. Baildon, eds. *The Coucher Book of the Cistercian Abbey of Kirkstall.* Publications of the Thoresby Society, 8. Leeds, 1904.

Coucher W. Hulton, William A., ed. *The Coucher Book, or Chartulary, of Whalley Abbey.* 4 vols. Remains ..., 10, 11, 16, 20. Manchester: Chetham Society, 1847-49.

Docs. K. Perkins, V. R., ed. "Documents relating to the Cistercian monastery of St. Mary, Kingswood." *Trans. Bristol and Gloucestershire Archaeological Society*, 22 (1899): 179-256.

Docs. R. *Calendar of Charters and Documents Relating to the Abbey of Robertsbridge ... Preserved at Penhurst among the Muniments of Lord de Lisle and Dudley.* London, 1873.

Docs. S. Denney, Anthony H., ed. *The Sibton Abbey Estates: Select Documents, 1325-1509.* Suffolk Record Society, publs., 2. Ipswich, 1960.

Ledger S. Hilton, Rodney H., ed. *The Stoneleigh Ledger Book.* Publs. of the Dugdale Society, 24. Oxford, 1960.

Ledger V.R. Brownbill, John, ed. *The Ledger-Book of Vale Royal Abbey.* Record Society for ... Lancashire and Cheshire, publs., 68. [London and Manchester], 1914.

Liber M. Innes, Cosmo, ed. *Liber Sancte Marie de Melros.* 2 vols. Edinburgh: Bannatyne Club, 1837.

Mem. F. Walbran, John Richard, and J. T. Fowler, eds. *Memorials of the Abbey of St. Mary of Fountains.* 3 vols. Surtees Society publs., 42, 67, 130. Durham, 1863-1918.

Mon. Angl. Dugdale, William. *Monasticon Anglicanum.* New enlarged ed. by John Caley, et al. London, 1830.

Mon. Ebor. Burton, John, ed. *Monasticon Eboracense.* York, 1758.

Recs. K. — Stuart, John, ed. *Records of the Monastery of Kinloss*. Edinburgh: Society of Antiquaries of Scotland, 1872.

Recs. T. — Waller, William Chapman. "Records of Tilty Abbey: an account of some preserved at Easton Lodge." *Trans. Essex Arch. Soc.*, 8 (1900-03): 352-361. "An account of some records of Tilty Abbey preserved at Easton Lodge." Ibid., 9 (1903-06): 118-121.

Reg. Con. — Ellis, Henry, ed. "Register and chronicle of the abbey of Aberconway." *Camden Miscellany*, vol. 1, no. 1: 1-23. Camden Society, publs., 39. London, 1847.

Reg. H.C. — Grainger, Francis, and W. D. Collingwood, eds. *The Register and Records of Holm Cultram*. Cumberland and Westmorland Antiquarian and Archaeological Society, Record Series, 7. Kendal, 1929.

Reg. Newbattle — Innes, Cosmo, ed. *Registrum S. Marie de Neubotle*. Bannatyne Club Publs., 89. Edinburgh, 1849.

Rental C. — Rogers, Charles, ed. *Rental Book of the Cistercian Abbey of Coupar Angus or Cupar-Angus, with the Breviary of the Register*. 2 vols. London: The Grampian Club, 1879-80.

Rental K. — Stansfield, John, ed. "A rent-roll of Kirkstall abbey." *Miscellanea*, pp. 1-21. Thoresby Society, publs., 2. Leeds, 1891.

Rental Kingswood — Lindley, E. S., ed. "A Kingswood abbey rental." *Trans. Bristol and Gloucestershire Archaeological Society*, 22 (1899): 179-256.

Statuta — [Cistercian Order]. *Statuta capitulorum generalium Ordinis cisterciensis ab anno 1116 ad annum 1786*. Ed. Joseph Marie Canivez. 8 vols. Bibliothèque de la Revue d'histoire ecclésiastique. Louvain: Bureaux de la Revue, 1933-1941.

3. Series and Secondary Literature

Ag.H.R. — *Agricultural History Review.*

A.S.O.C. — *Analecta Sacri Ordinis Cisterciensis.*

B.I.H.R. — *Bulletin of the Institute of Historical Research.*

Ec.H.R. — *Economic History Review.*

E.H.R. — *English Historical Review.*

Pat. Lat. — Migne, J.-P. *Patrologia Latina.*

P.R.S. — Pipe Roll Society.

R.S. — Rolls Series: Chronicles and Memorials of Great Britain and Ireland during the Middle Ages.

T.R.H.S. — *Transactions of the Royal Historical Society.*

V.C.H. — *Victoria County History.*

Prologue

For almost 1000 years before the Dissolution, monastic communities were an integral part of English society and of the English economy. Their influence was felt especially in the two centuries or so after the Norman conquest when the number of professed clergy increased much more rapidly than the population as a whole.[1] The first monks of the order of Cîteaux arrived in 1128, and by the middle of the twelfth century two-thirds of the full total of houses had been founded. While the history of the order in England remains to be written, the economic importance of the Cistercians has not been overlooked, rather the reverse. There has been a tendency to exaggerate their contribution to the medieval wool trade and also perhaps their work as depopulators and *défricheurs*. The difficulties in the way of a balanced judgement are formidable in view of the nature of the source material for the first two hundred years. We must rely chiefly on charters conveying land or other property, several thousand documents which are sometimes difficult to date and to locate topographically and which usually tell us little or nothing about how a particular gift or purchase was subsequently used. There are few financial accounts or surveys of property from the twelfth and thirteenth centuries.[2] Distribution maps have to be prepared from lists of items culled from individual references. Such maps can at best show what evidence survives and, in practice, only illustrate the present state of knowledge, much like archaeological maps.

The work of the Cistercian order in England and Wales (and generally throughout Europe) fell into three main phases, the first two each of about one hundred years and the last of about two hundred years. The years ca. 1130 to ca. 1230 saw the emergence of all the main features of the Cistercian economy based on the plan embodied in the *Exordium Parvum*

[1] J. C. Russell, 'The clerical population of medieval England,' *Traditio*, 2 (1944): 177-212. Russell's estimates of a twenty-fold increase in the number of regular clergy and a three- to four-fold increase in the population generally both appear to be too high, but the difference between the two is probably not greatly exaggerated.

[2] The chief exception is the recently published *Account Book of Beaulieu Abbey*, "perhaps the most extraordinary monument to survive of the early history of private accounting in England" (P. D. A. Harvey in *Chart. Bl.*, xvi).

(1119).[3] In both theory and practice the chief characteristic was the direct cultivation of land by lay brothers (*conversi*) and hired workers (*homines mercenarii*) and, initially at least, by the choir monks themselves. During the early and middle decades of the twelfth century this form of exploitation apparently contrasted with a tendency on the part of other landlords to lease out the whole or large portions of their demesnes.[4] The more important donations of land to the Cistercians belong to this period, and from about the middle of the twelfth century the monks also purchased land and other property, indicating a cash income from the sale of agricultural products among which wool came to predominate.

The order of Cîteaux was founded (1098) in reaction to prevailing monastic practices (as exemplified particularly at Cluny) and in an attempt to return to the original Rule of St Benedict.[5] The Cistercians did not regard themselves as innovators, either in terms of religious observance or in matters of economy. The early statutes insisted upon a rigorous asceticism and isolation, so far as possible, from secular activities. Foundation endowments, reflecting the reputation and aspirations of the order, usually included large amounts of reclaimable waste, but these and subsequent grants also conveyed much already cultivated land. One solution to the problems that this posed was to remove the sitting tenants, sometimes after appropriate compensation had been arranged. The general aim was to assemble consolidated properties (*grangiae*) that were independent of communal agriculture and of servile labour. This often proved difficult and in some cases impossible as holdings rapidly increased in size. Already by the end of the twelfth century the order was considered wealthy, fair game for impoverished monarchs,[6] and had departed con-

[3] P. Guignard, *Les monuments primitifs de la règle cistercienne publiés d'après les manuscrits de l'abbaye de Cîteaux*, Analecta Divionensia, 10 (Dijon, 1878), pp. 61-75. See also R. Roehl, 'Plan and reality in a medieval economy: the Cistercians,' *Studies in Medieval and Renaissance History*, 9 (1972): 83-113.

[4] Trends in the management of demesne are summarized in R. A. Donkin, 'Changes in the early Middle Ages,' in *A New Historical Geography of England*, ed. H. C. Darby (Cambridge, 1973), pp. 87-90.

[5] For sources and commentaries concerning the origin of the order, see R. A. Donkin, *A Check-List of Printed Works Relating to the Cistercian Order* ..., Documentation Cistercienne, 2 (Rochefort: Abbaye N.D. de S. Remy, 1969), pp. 11-18, 22-23. The bibliography also has a section on the Cistercian economy in general (pp. 26-28) and attempts to provide a comprehensive list of printed sources and of secondary literature relating to houses in the British Isles. The position of Cîteaux among the new monastic movements is discussed by David Knowles, *The Monastic Order in England (940-1216)*, 2nd ed. (Cambridge, 1963), pp. 208-45.

[6] See C. V. Graves, 'The economic activities of the Cistercians in medieval England (1128-1307),' *A.S.O.C.*, 13 (1957): 37-41.

siderably from the ideals of the founding fathers. At first the monks were widely admired for their self-discipline and willingness to assume the role of backwoodsmen. But after less than a hundred years, admiration had turned to criticism. The monks were then regarded as avaricious[7] and "bad neighbours" and were the object of satirical comment and bitter invective.[8]

The ensuing one hundred years (ca. 1230 to ca. 1330) was a period of consolidation and of change along lines already foreshadowed by the end of the twelfth century. The monasteries continued to acquire property and to farm the bulk of their estates, just as many contemporaries were recovering and working their demesnes. Cistercian estates reached their maximum extent between 1250 and 1300. By then, too, the monks drew a considerable income from various 'feudal' sources, such as mills, churches and markets, that originally had been banned. They also continued to respond to the ever-growing demand for English wool and became deeply involved in marketing operations. The uncertainties of production, the practice of advance selling, and plain business incompetence led to colossal debts, to the point where several houses were taken into royal custody or were temporarily dispersed.[9] The Cistercians, like the Crown, were continually short of capital and they raised large loans on wool and land, through merchants and Jews, to finance ambitious building operations. In 1300 the Cistercian economy was still distinctive, the monks remained active landowners, clearing and draining parcels of land, rounding off the limits of important properties, and raising the output of wool to the highest level ever reached. But, at the same time, the leasing out of land had commenced and new projects were pursued with less determination.

Leasing out, specifically of holdings that were remote and of limited use, was first permitted in 1208.[10] Further concessions by the Chapter General followed in 1220 and 1224. The monks leased out land for several reasons, but chiefly for two: in the short term to acquire ready cash, and, in the long term, to meet the growing shortage of labour.[11] Rationalization of scattered holdings was followed, from about the beginning of the fourteenth century, by the leasing out of portions of granges

[7] *Chronica magistri Rogeri de Hovedene* (ca. 1200), ed. W. Stubbs, R. S. 51 (London, 1871), 4:77. The order acknowledged the charge in 1190 (*Statuta*, 1:177).

[8] Graves, 'Economic activities,' pp. 45-54, has a section on "contemporary social criticism."

[9] Ibid., pp. 33-36, 60.

[10] *Statuta*, 1:346.

[11] See J. S. Donnelly, *Decline of the Medieval Cistercian Laybrotherhood* (New York, 1949).

and then of whole granges. The lessees were chiefly laymen who in turn depended on workers with service holdings. Many granges became hamlets or villages and were organized as manors. By the time of the Dissolution, all that most houses kept in hand was a home farm; other property simply brought in rents in money and kind.

The essays that follow are largely concerned with the period before the Black Death. Furthermore, almost nothing is said about mining, building operations, salt-working and fishing, and large *lacunae* remain to be filled in the topics that are discussed. The first chapter traces the spread of the order throughout Europe and describes the changes that occurred as a result of re-siting by houses in England and Wales. Such re-siting was also common elsewhere but has not, so far as is known, been the object of special study. The following chapter is concerned with the question of depopulation and with the grange, the key to the Cistercian economy. Chapters 3 and 4 focus upon pastoral farming and the winning of new land at the expense of woodland, waste and fen, subjects about which much has been written in general terms. Chapter 5 discusses matters relating to trade, including a hitherto neglected topic, the ownership of markets and urban property. A final postscript refers to the role of the white monks as agents of the diffusion of new ideas and technologies; it also shows how the order became involved in affairs of state when, towards the close of the thirteenth century, abbots in considerable number were called to parliament.

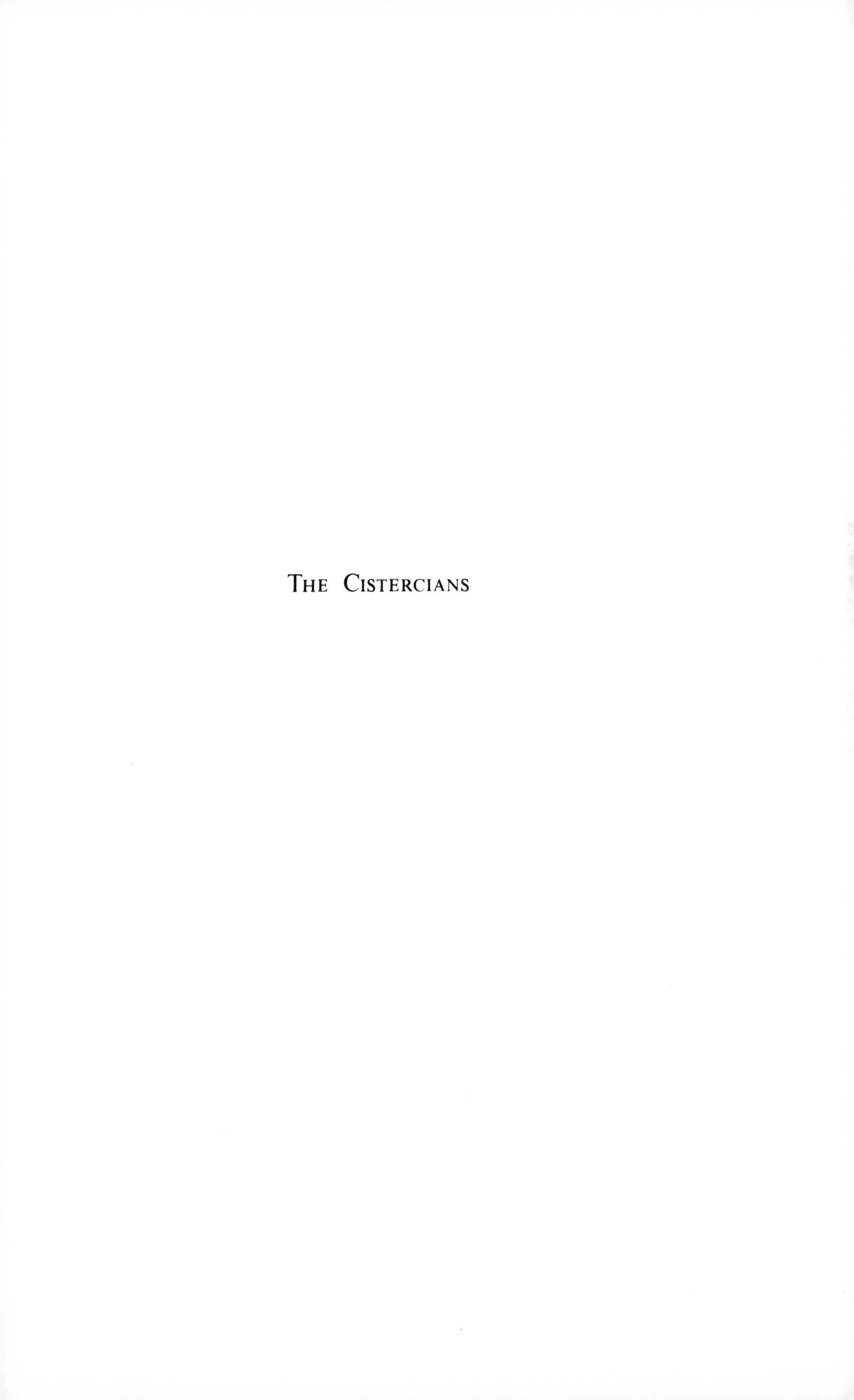

THE CISTERCIANS

1

The Cistercian Plantation

The Order in Europe: *"Omnia Cistercium erat"*

Over ninety per cent of the approximately 740 Cistercian houses founded between 1098 and 1675 were in existence by 1300. Fig. 1 shows the expansion of the order,[1] Fig. 2 the distribution and relative status of the mother houses, Figs. 3 and 4 the five main affiliations.[2]

Expansion 1098-1675

The key to the interpretation of Fig. 1 lies in the date 1152 when the Chapter General called a temporary halt to the founding of new colonies.[3] By the end of 1151, only fifty-three years after the foundation of Cîteaux, some 333 houses had been established, little short of half the final total. The two opening periods — preceding 1152 and each of twenty-seven years — stand in sharp contrast to one another. The first, 1098-1124, witnessed the founding of only twenty-six houses. It was not until 1113, a year after the arrival of Bernard and his twenty-nine companions, that

[1] Foundation dates after L. Janauschek, *Originum Cisterciensium* (Vienna, 1877) unless these have been revised later. D. Knowles and R. N. Hadcock, *Medieval Religious Houses, England and Wales*, 2nd ed. (London, 1971), generally follow Janauschek. Throughout the present work, religious 'house' or 'foundation' refers exclusively to monasteries.

[2] In preparing Figures 1-4, several historical atlases and a larger number of distribution maps have been used. The most serviceable atlas is the *Spruner-Menke Hand-Atlas für die Geschichte des Mittelalters und der Neueren Zeit*, 3rd ed. (Gotha, 1880). The maps are listed in R. A. Donkin, 'The growth and distribution of the Cistercian order in medieval Europe,' *Studia Monastica*, 9 (1967): 276-77. L. H. Cottineau, *Répertoire Topo-Bibliographique des Abbayes et Prieurés*, 2 vols. (Mâcon, 1935-39) has also been consulted on questions of location.

[3] *Statuta*, 1: 45.

Cîteaux dispatched her first daughter colony. The average rate of foundation at this time was approximately one per annum, but there were two years when as many as five houses were founded.

The period 1125-51, years completely dominated by the work and personality of Saint Bernard (who died in August 1153), was undoubtedly the golden age of the order. Mont Peiroux, a grand-daughter of Cîteaux, was founded in 1126, and between this date and the close of 1151, 307 new communities were born, an achievement perhaps without parallel in the history of monasticism. The average rate of foundation, about eleven per annum, was actually reached in 1131, the first of the *anni mirabiles*. Not counting the fifty-one additions of 1147 (largely the result of Savignac houses submitting to Cîteaux), up to nineteen were settled in a single year. After 1151 a number exceeding ten was very rare (1162, fourteen; 1172, eleven). This comparatively short period, 1125-51, secured to the Cistercians an important place in the "Renaissance of the Twelfth Century."

The two following periods, each of a hundred years, brought the order through its prime and middle age to a time, about the middle of the fourteenth century, when its decline was plain to be seen. Between 1152 and 1251 it continued to expand although the rate of foundation dropped steadily and only averaged about three per annum. One hundred and ninety-five new sites were occupied during the remaining years of the twelfth century, and 313 by 1251. The *plantatio* was now virtually complete. A falling off in spiritual fervour was already apparent, and the following hundred years saw a sharp decline in gifts of property of all kinds. Throughout the greater part of Europe, the monks were now *rentiers* rather than farmers. Only sixty-one houses appear to date from 1252 to 1351 and three in any one year was very exceptional. The next 324 years added only thirty-four.

The cradle-land of the Cistercian order lay in Burgundy, on the edge of the Côte d'Or. Cîteaux, *Mater Ordinis*, stood about twenty-five kilometres south-southeast of Dijon, and its first colony, La Ferté, a little further down the valley of the Saone, just below Chalon. Pontigny (1114), Clairvaux (1115) and Morimond (1115) were sited somewhat further afield but still within eastern France; the first two on the margins of the Paris Basin, the last near the headwaters of the Meuse, about thirty kilometres northeast of Langres. These were the senior daughters of Cîteaux and headed separate *lineae*. By 1125 the distribution had widened considerably : one house each in Dauphiné and Languedoc, two in Guyenne, and most of the remainder in a wide arc stretching from the middle Loire (Le Loroux), eastward through the homeland, and then northward as far as Picardy (Foigny). Of Foigny, W.W. Williams has written, "[Its] foundation ... on

11th July of 1121 may be said to have foreshadowed the expansion of the *Cisterciense Institutum* throughout the larger world of Benedictine Europe."[4] Lützel (1124) lay in Alsace, and there were three houses quite outside the limits of present-day France: Tiglieto (1120) in Liguria, Camp (1123) in the lower Rhineland, and Locedio (1124) in Piedmont.

The geographical framework of the order was laid between the years 1125 and 1151, a period which, as has been said, witnessed the birth of no less than 307 foundations. Parts of France were heavily settled, particularly the country between the Garonne and the Pyrenees, an important base for subsequent Spanish colonization; the sea margins of Brittany; the left-bank tributary valleys of the middle Loire, and the Loire itself below Blois; northern France from the base of the Cotentin peninsula to Flanders and thence through the Ile de France to the greatest cluster of all in Burgundy and the borderlands of Germany. There were also a few, more scattered houses in Provence. In 1151 the Cistercian settlement was more complete in France than anywhere else. Only central and eastern England may be compared. Here very few communities were later introduced into a zone extending from the Scottish marches, through the eastern Pennines, the North Yorkshire Moors and the east-central lowlands between Holderness and the Fens, to the Thames estuary. Behind the Wash other colonies carried the distribution into the scarplands and low interfluves of the Midlands and, further west still, to the lower Severn and South Wales. Monasteries in the South-west Peninsula, the march of North Wales, the borders of Cumbria, and the Southern Uplands of Scotland developed in somewhat greater isolation. There was one house in the north of Scotland, Kinloss (1151) on the southern shores of the Moray Firth. The main settlement of Ireland came a little later, but already eight colonies in the South and East formed the nucleus of the final pattern.

In Spain, where, in the wake of the *reconquista*, the northwestern and north-central provinces attracted the bulk of the Cistercian houses, the first was Moreruela (1132) in León.[5] Before 1152 four others came to be sited further to the north-west in the heart of Galicia. Catalonia, on the

[4] *St. Bernard of Clairvaux* (Manchester, 1935), p. 30. He goes on (pp. 30-31): "St. Bernard would seem to have felt that Foigny was a valuable strategic position. For the purpose of establishing and personally supervising in their early days new foundations in Flanders and in districts yet more remote in a northerly direction, such as the Rhineland, he frequently visited Foigny ... ." Nevertheless, Foigny itself established only one daughter house, Bohéries (1141), also in Picardy and but a short distance to the north-west.

[5] A house in Spain was, apparently, first mooted by Preuilly ca. 1129 but Bernard advised against it, probably because (at the time) he feared the development of a thin and very scattered distribution of colonies (Williams, *Saint Bernard*, p. 49).

opposite flank, had one house (Poblet, 1151), and the rest half encircled the Sierra de Guadarrama in high Castile. By 1148, a year after Lisbon was taken from the Moors, the white monks had occupied what was to be their most westerly site, Alcobaça in Portugal. Soon two others lay to the north-east and the final pattern of colonization here began to take shape; it linked up with that of Galicia and formed one arm of the Iberian settlement.

Two groups developed in Italy during the second quarter of the twelfth century. One lay in Piedmont and Lombardy, not far from the two existing houses, the other in middle Italy, from north-west of Rome southward to the hill country behind the Gulf of Gaeta as far as the middle Liri. Sites were also occupied in Sardinia, Calabria, Venezia, and Marche on the Adriatic.

Finally, there is the area particularly associated with the Cistercians as pioneers — northern, central and eastern Europe. There were two main lines of advance eastward. One stretched from Franconia through Bavaria and Bohemia, with, to the south, further colonies in Austria, Slovenia (Sittich, 1136) and Hungary where Czikador (Czikadori apátság) was founded as early as 1142. The other thrust, to the north and pivoting on Camp, penetrated Westphalia and the edge of the Central Uplands as far as the Harz and the Erzgebirge. The North German Plain was left largely untouched, but a few colonies were dispatched to points well to the east of the Elbe — Wagrowice (1143), Lad (1146), and, further east again, Jedrzejów (1149), all in Poland. One is impressed not so much by the scale of penetration (in the north particularly, the lands west of the Elbe were far more closely settled), but by its depth at certain points. Indeed, the outer limits of settlement were never greatly extended beyond those reached in 1151. The Danish houses belong, chronologically and geographically, with those of the North German Plain, but a few places were settled earlier in Norway and Sweden (the first was Alvastra, 1143). Northern Scandinavia, however, was never of much importance so far as the Cistercians were concerned.

The next one hundred years (1152-1251) brought the order to near full strength. In comparison with the years 1125-51, the areas which were now more heavily settled lay, generally speaking, towards the margins of the distribution. This was also the case within France itself where Limousin, the Atlantic coastlands (especially around the Ile de Ré), and the country between Maine and Picardy received important additions. The bulk of the new foundations in the British Isles lay towards the north and west — in Ireland, northern and central Wales, the South-west Peninsula and the West Midlands. About half the Scottish houses date from this time too. The Iberian settlement continued in Galicia and northern Portugal and through Castile to Catalonia. Here and there, advances were made towards the centre of the Meseta, but the existing salients were generally reinforced rather than extended. In Italy, however, the reverse was true; earlier groups were linked up and almost the entire peninsula was affected. This was also the most important period in the settlement of the Baltic lands. A tight cluster in North Friesland formed the western end of a succession of colonies that straddled the Elbe and occupied the coastlands as far as Dünamünde (1208) and Falkenau (1234) in Livonia, the latter furthest of all to the north-east. The Danish settlement virtually completed the pattern. Further south, colonization proceeded between the middle Elbe and the Vistula;[6] and towards the south-east the frontier was quite significantly extended — in Croatia, Hungary, and Transylvania (B. M. V. de Kerz, 1202). Then there were the Eastern houses around Constantinople, in Macedonia, southern Greece[7] and, perhaps most remarkable of all, in Cyprus and Palestine. The first of these was Beaumont (1157) in 'Syria', mother of most of the Cypriot colonies. The rest post-date the fall of Constantinople to the crusaders and the setting up of the Latin Empire in 1204: from 1207 (Daphni) to 1224 (De Saracaz).

Early in the following century (1252-1351) houses were still being sited well towards the eastern frontier of settlement: Koronowa (1256) in Poland; Rauden (1255) and Himmelwitz (1290) in Silesia; Pelplin (1267) in Pomerania; and Erchi (1252) and Abrahám (1263) in Hungary. Many more, however, were placed some considerable distance to the rear — eighteen in a zone extending from the lower Oder to the uplands of Bavaria, Bohemia, Moravia and Austria. Italy also gained a dozen new houses, half of these in or near Tuscany, but there was very little activity elsewhere in Europe. After 1351 the most striking development was the introduction of twenty-one houses into the Low Countries and adjacent parts of Old Germany. The regions more particularly affected (1382-1487) were the Rhineland below Cologne, Hainault eastward as far as the Ardennes, and the marshlands of Holland and the Rhine delta.

The medieval settlement had now run its course. After a hesitant start (Cîteaux stood alone for nearly a decade and a half), the order expanded

[6] However it is not quite true to say (with J. W. Thompson) that Leubus (1175) in Silesia "was the furthest eastern post of German culture in the twelfth century" (*Economic and Social History of the Middle Ages* (New York, 1928), p. 613).

[7] E. A. R. Brown, 'The Cistercians in the Latin Empire of Constantinople and Greece, 1204-1276,' *Traditio*, 14 (1958): 63-120.

gradually until 1130. At this time most of the thirty-nine houses were concentrated in France, but already individual colonies were settled as far afield as Styria and England. Then, for the next most vital twenty years the rate of foundation rarely fell below ten per annum; nearly 300 new sites were occupied, and the outlines of the full distribution clearly emerged. The period ca. 1150-1250, when the order increased by a roughly equal number, was primarily one of consolidation. After this there was a further loss of momentum resulting in sharply reduced settlement between the eastern frontier and the long-established centres of activity.

Mother Houses

Fig. 2 shows the distribution of mother houses graduated in size according to the number of their daughter colonies. The table below contains a chronological analysis of the same material.

TABLE 1: MOTHER HOUSES AND DAUGHTER COLONIES

Period of foundation	Number of houses founded	Number of mother houses founded	Mother houses as percentage of all houses
1098-1124	26	24	92.3
1125-1151	307	150	48.8
1152-1251	314	54	17.2
1252-1351	61	7	11.5
1352-1675	34	—	—
Total	742	235	31.6

Mother Houses														
Period of foundation	Number of houses founded	Eventual number of colonies founded												
		1	2	3	4	5	6	7	8	13	16	23	28	80
1098-1124	24	3	1	1	6	4	1	1	2	1	1	—	2	1
1125-1151	150	69	31	18	12	8	6	1	4	—	—	1	—	—
1152-1251	54	28	12	7	4	—	3	—	—	—	—	—	—	—
1252-1351	7	3	1	3	—	—	—	—	—	—	—	—	—	—
1352-1675	—	—	—	—	—	—	—	—	—	—	—	—	—	—
Total	235	103	45	29	22	12	10	2	6	1	1	1	2	1
% of 235		43.4	19.1	12.3	9.4	5.1	4.3	0.8	2.6	0.4	0.4	0.4	0.8	0.4

In all, 235 houses established colonies. Almost a half sent out no more than one, and there was a steady decline in number between those with two daughters (forty-five, 19.1 per cent.) and those with as many as seven (two, 0.8 per cent.). Six had eight, but most of the rest, with higher numbers still, stood alone: thirteen (Camp, 1123), sixteen (Pontigny, 1114), twenty-three (Savigny, 1147), twenty-eight (Cîteaux, 1098, Morimond, 1115), and, above all others, the eighty houses directly affiliated to Clairvaux.[8] Only La Ferté (five) among the senior daughters of Cîteaux failed to make a really notable contribution to the growth of the order.

Twenty-four of the twenty-six communities established by 1124 were in due course productive. The proportion was still above the average during the period 1125-51 (48.8 per cent.), but thereafter it dropped well below this. Perhaps two points deserve special emphasis: the relatively small number of houses with daughter colonies at all — little more than three out of every ten; and the enormous contribution made by the six leading houses — 188 colonies, or more than a quarter of the entire order.

The principal concentration of mother houses was in eastern and northern France, from Dauphiné through Burgundy and northward almost to the Channel coast. There was also a notable cluster in the South West (Guyenne, Gascony, and the Pyrenean foothills), including one with eight colonies (L'Escale-Dieu, 1137) and three with six (Bonnefont, 1137; Obasine, 1147; and Dalon, 1162). Savigny lay on the borders of Normandy, La Cour Dieu (1119) and L'Aumône (1121), with five each, in central France near Orleans, but elsewhere, and especially in the Massif Central, the distribution was rather thin and largely made up of houses with only one colony.

Within the Iberian Peninsula, Alcobaça alone achieved any great distinction. In the British Isles the great majority of houses, apart from those of Savignac origin, were founded from within, and there was a full proportion of mother houses of moderate standing. Fountains (1135) and Mellifont (1142), each with eight colonies, ranked very high. In Italy, the two centres of early settlement, Liguria-Piedmont-Lombardy and the central provinces, again stand out, but only two houses (one was Sambucina in Calabria) colonized up to six fresh sites. The process of founding new colonies in central and eastern Europe continued among houses well towards the frontier of Cistercian settlement. There were three great houses in the German-speaking lands: Camp (1123), Ebrach (1127) and Heiligenkreuz (1135) in Austria, with thirteen, eight and seven colonies

[8] Already sixty-eight at the time of Bernard's death on 20 August 1153 (Williams, *Saint Bernard*, p. 92).

respectively. Save for these, the distribution between the southern edge of the North German Plain (as already shown, an area of comparatively late settlement) and the high Alps (practically deserted of houses altogether) was fairly uniform. Esrum (1154, six colonies) was the only considerable house in Scandinavia.

Affiliations

All Cistercian houses belonged to one or other of five main families presided over by Cîteaux, La Ferté, Pontigny, Clairvaux and Morimond.[9] In Figs. 3 and 4 mother and daughter houses are connected to show the direction of movement and the distances involved, but, for the sake of clarity, exception is made of colonies immediately subordinate to the five *majores ecclesiae*. Altogether, there were 356 houses under Clairvaux,[10] 214 under Morimond, 109 under Cîteaux, forty-three under Pontigny, and sixteen under La Ferté.

The affiliation of Cîteaux (Fig. 3) belonged chiefly to France, more particularly the less heavily settled areas of the South and Centre. The middle and lower Loire was favoured, also Brittany. On the other hand, Gascony and northeastern France (including Burgundy) had few representatives. Elsewhere, a compact cluster developed in south-central England where Beaulieu (1204) was founded directly from Cîteaux; and Waverley, the first English house (1128), and Tintern (1131) from L'Aumône. Most of the other English houses were related through Waverley. There were also a few members of the affiliation in Spain (three directly from Cîteaux, of which two were unproductive), Italy, Flanders (the group of fifteenth-century foundations was shared with Morimond) and southern Scandinavia.

The houses under Pontigny and La Ferté made no considerable area their own. None spread into England, Spain, the Low Countries, Germany (Stürzelbronn in Lorraine may count as an exception) or Scandinavia. Pontigny did, however, make a contribution to the settlement of southwestern France (from Armagnac northwards) and itself established the Hungarian colony of Egrés, which, in turn, dispatched monks to Transylvania (B. M. V. de Kerz, 1202) and Slavonia (Sancta Crux, 1214). The influence of La Ferté was felt most strongly in northern Italy (nine houses in Liguria alone) whence a colony was sent to Macedonia (Chortaïton, 1214).

[9] Janauschek was doubtful (*matris incertae*) about a few houses.
[10] 159 (out of a total of 340) at the time of Bernard's death.

More than three-quarters of the entire order looked either to Clairvaux or to Morimond (Fig. 4). Their zones of affiliation were largely complementary. Apart from Burgundy and the South — Gascony and the Pyrenees in particular, but also Provence and parts of the Massif Central — Morimond had no great influence in France. Clairvaux settled much of the Paris Basin, Normandy (through Savigny), and the North. It had considerably less interest in other parts of France; and, throughout, a rather high proportion of its progeny failed to send out colonies in their turn. In Iberia, Morimond developed the north-central districts, Clairvaux the northwestern (including Portugal) and Catalonia. Again their respective zones remained generally distinct. In the British Isles the position of Clairvaux was almost unchallenged. Only Dore (1147) and Vale Royal (1274) derived from Morimond. Clairvaux was also responsible for the majority of the Scandinavian colonies; and its affiliation was quite the most important in Italy, particularly in the South and Centre.

Morimond's special province lay to the east, in the German-speaking lands and Poland. The Danish house of Esrum, a daughter of Clairvaux, colonised the southern shore of the Baltic, and there was a notable group of the same affiliation in Hungary-Croatia, two members of which (Zircz, 1182, and Toplica, 1208) were founded directly from Clairvaux. These foundations lay on the margins of Morimond's sphere of influence. The Cistercians in middle Europe formed part of a broad tide of colonization. Its direction, dominantly eastward, is clearly demonstrated by Fig. 4, for the Morimond affiliation, owing much to Camp, Ebrach and Heiligenkreuz, was largely made up of clusters of several generations of colonies. A similar situation, on a smaller scale and with movement westward, developed in the Spanish march. The family of Morimond was more closely associated than any other with the two principal areas of medieval colonisation.

The Order in England and Wales

In all there were about a hundred Cistercian monasteries in the British Isles; seventy-five lay in England and Wales, and two-thirds of these were in existence by 1152, less than a quarter of a century after the first introduction (1128). As many as forty-three belonged to Stephen's reign (1135-54). Colonization was resumed with the foundation of Strata Florida in 1164 and, but for one house, completed before 1300. The general effect was to extend the pattern of monastic settlement, which in 1128 was overwhelmingly Benedictine, towards the less well developed lands of the North and West (Fig. 5).

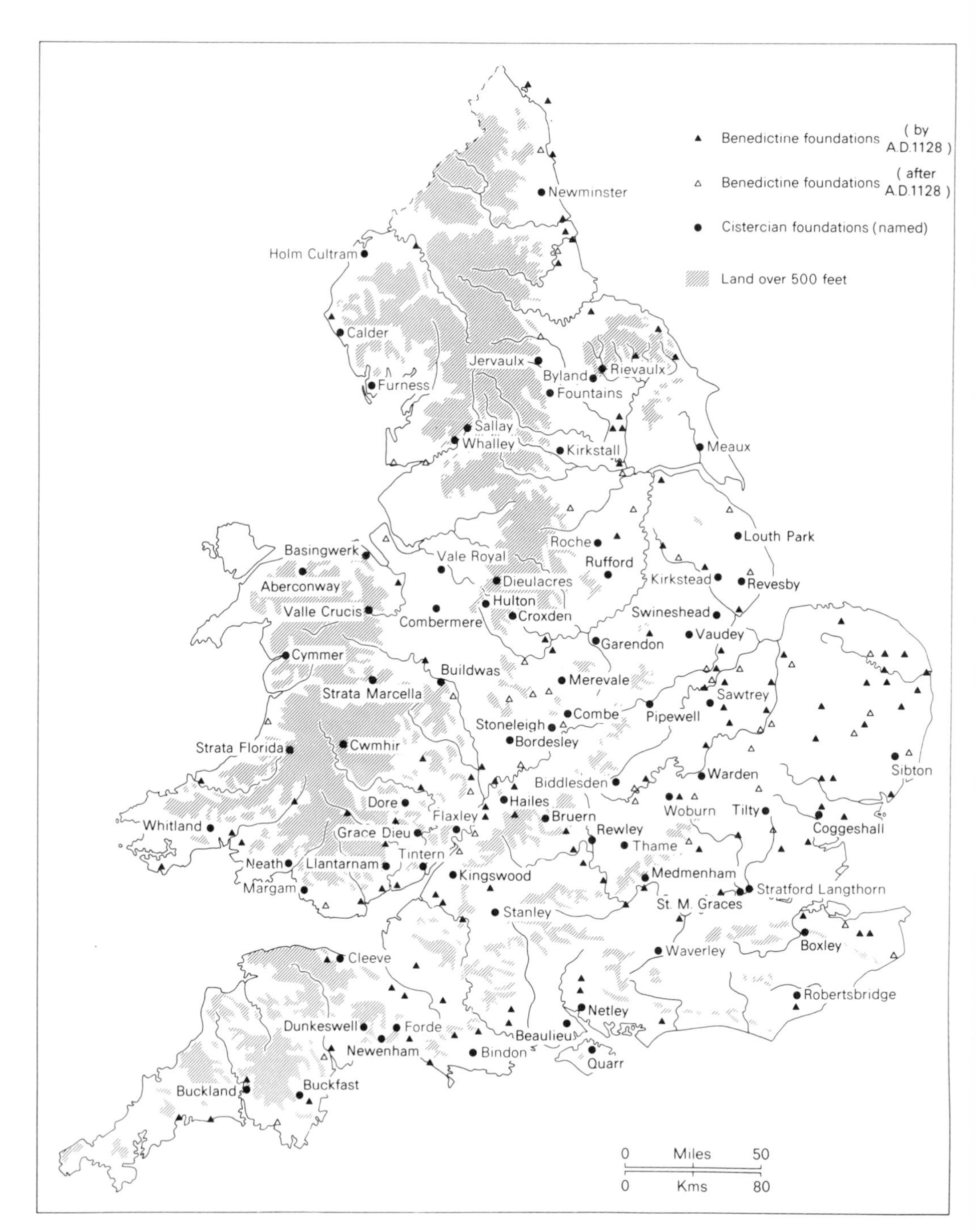

FIG. 5

Benedictine and Cistercian foundations in England and Wales.

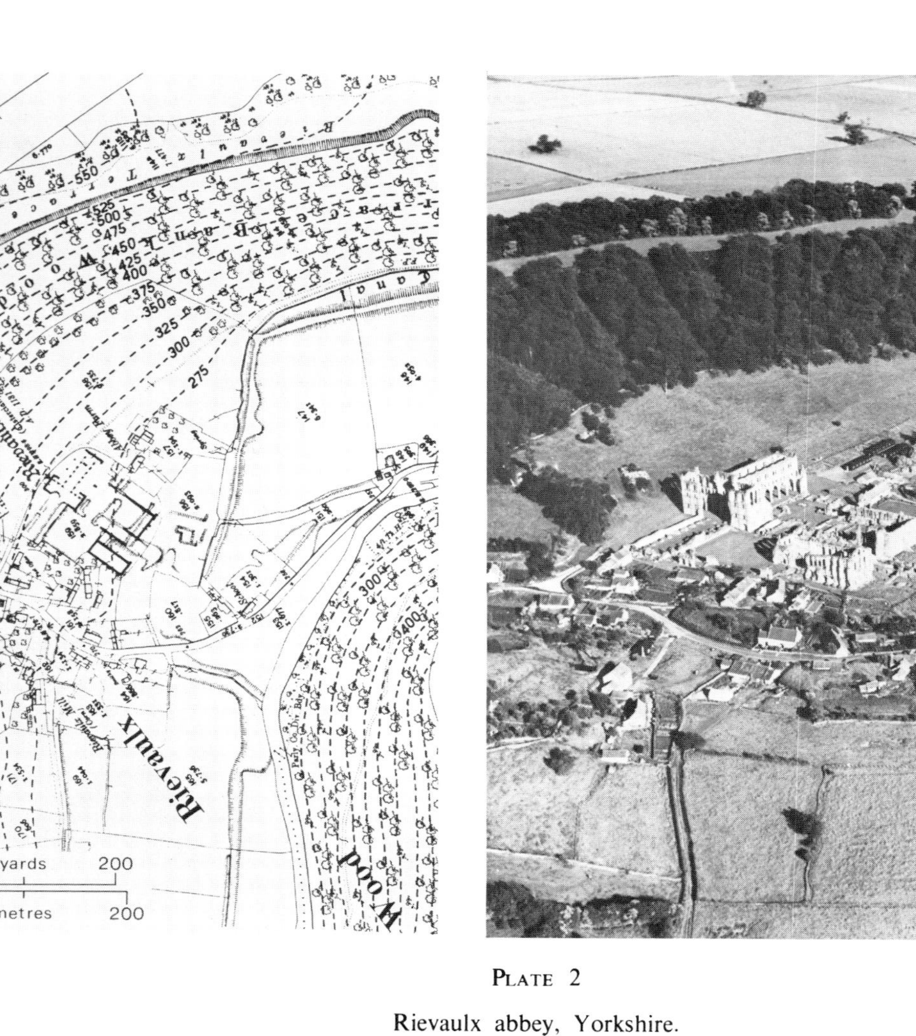

PLATE 2

Rievaulx abbey, Yorkshire.

The church (ca. 1135-1230) lies well back from the river, close to and parallel with the break of slope; it is thus orientated more nearly north-south than east-west.

(The map is based, by permission, on the Ordnance Survey 1:2500 [1912]; the photograph is part of the Cambridge University Collection, copyright reserved.)

During the early years of the order there seems to have been a preference for sites in small, enclosed valleys (Plate 2). But it has to be remembered that establishing a Cistercian community (normally an abbot and twelve monks) was a rather complicated operation, involving a number of interested parties. First there had to be an invitation to settle with the approval of the local diocesan;[11] then, if the Chapter General of the order agreed,[12] the ground had to be inspected and the actual site selected.[13] In view of these precautions, it is surprising to discover just how many communities later decided to migrate to another site — no less than a third of all those in England and Wales. Over the first one hundred and fifty years the pattern of Cistercian settlement changed almost as much through redistribution as by the addition of fresh colonies. This can partly be traced to ignorance of local conditions, as they applied the year round and over a number of years (the preference for secluded sites invited foundation endowments consisting largely of marginal land), and partly to the changing character of the order as the monks relaxed their initial asceticism.

Site Changes

Thirty or more communities in England and Wales changed their site at least once[14] (Fig. 6 and Appendix 1). Ten of these ultimately sent out colonies, but in only two cases before the final site was occupied (Whitland to Cwmhir, and Strata Florida to Caerleon [Llantarnam] and Rhedynog-felen [Aberconway]) and we can probably conclude that poorly judged siting appreciably delayed the progress of colonization.

[11] *Statuta*, 1: xxvi.

[12] Ibid., 22, n. 1. In 1199 the abbot of Revesby was reproved for having sent a colony to Cleeve without permission (ibid., 235, n. 17). Strictly speaking, ten Burgundian leagues had to separate each house (ibid., 32), but this was certainly not always observed.

[13] According to the letter of the statutes the prospective site had to be examined by two abbots who reported to the next Chapter General (ibid., 1: 126, and 2: 54-55). Williams (*Saint Bernard*, p. 76) quotes an instance of Bernard refusing to sanction a request that two brethren of a future convent be sent out in advance to "arrange ... about the site." Cf. C. H. Talbot, 'Two opuscula of John Godard, first abbot of Newenham,' *A.S.O.C.*, 10 (1954): 208-67. Permission to found Newenham was first sought in 1245; a favourable report on the suitability of the site was received in the following year and "two monks were despatched to take possession of the property." The house was founded in 1247.

[14] The pamphlet accompanying the South Sheet of the *Map of Monastic Britain* (Southampton: Ordnance Survey, 1954) lists forty-three "principal" site changes of which nineteen concern the Cistercians. In Ireland only three Cistercian houses changed their site. G. Carville, 'The Cistercian settlement of Ireland (1142-1541),' *Studia Monastica*, 15 (1973): 23.

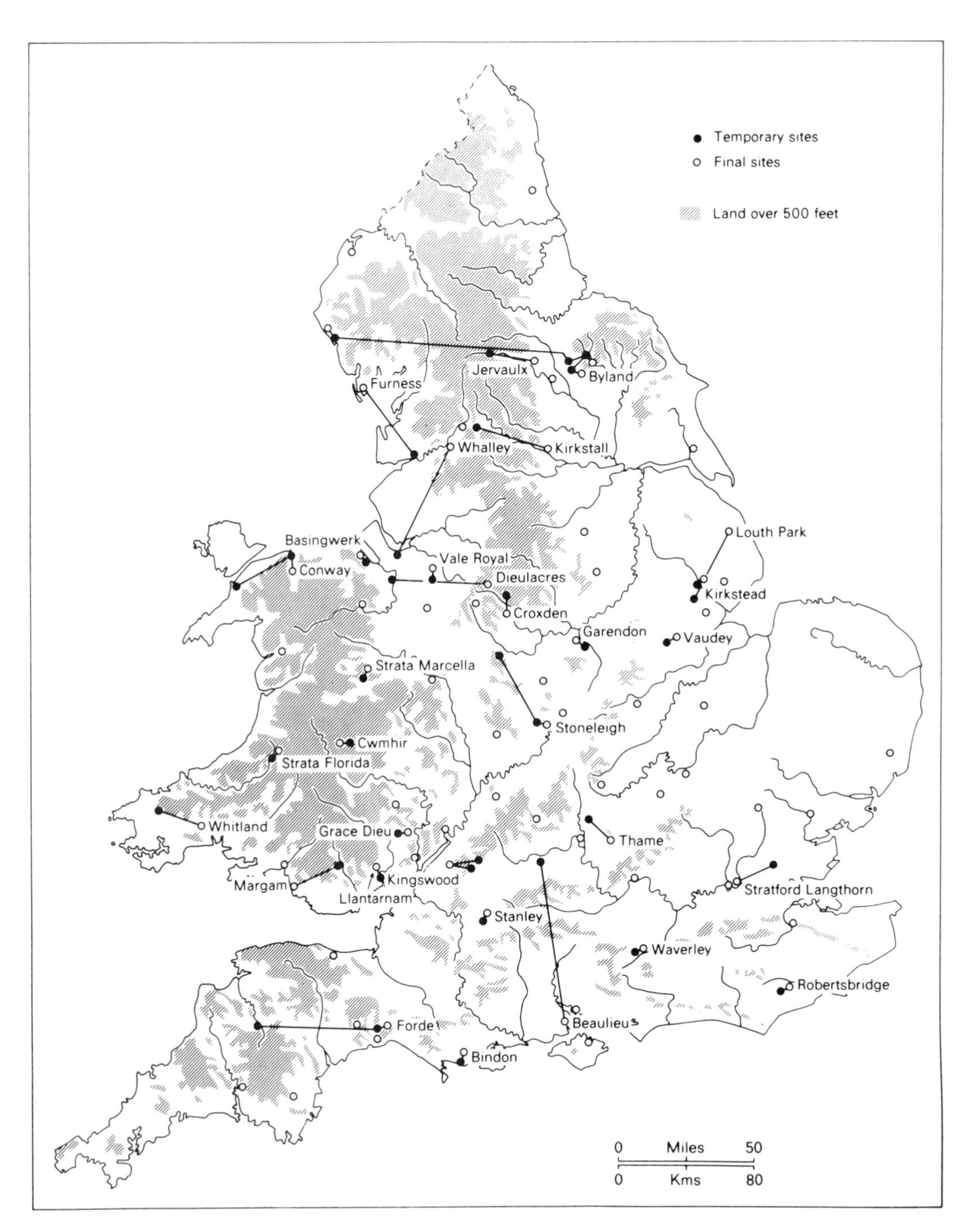

FIG. 6

Sites changes of Cistercian houses in England and Wales (Appendix 1).

Minor changes were almost certainly more common than we can now show. They were probably thought hardly worth recording, and it is sometimes difficult to decide whether a transfer from temporary to permanent buildings alone is implied. The disadvantages to be overcome were plainly local — a question of location rather than situation — but the response was not always immediate. Strata Florida moved two miles after about thirty-six years (1164-ca. 1200), probably to enjoy a better water supply and a more open site. The convent at Ty Faenor (1143) apparently remained thirty-three years before migrating one mile (to Cwmhir). Robertsbridge occupied ground close to the village of Salehurst for more than a quarter of a century (1176-13th century) and then chose a more secluded place on the far bank of the river Rother.

A few high sites within the Pennines and the South-west Peninsula proved unsatisfactory on climatic grounds. Barnoldswick (ca. 500 feet) in the Aire Gap was exchanged for Kirkstall (ca. 200 feet) on the middle reaches of the Aire. The account *De fundatione domus de Kyrkestall* relates that the monks remained at Barnoldswick several years (actually five, 1147-52) in great poverty and discomfort: "*mansibus ibi* [Barnoldswick] *per aliquot annos, multa perpessi incommoda famis et frigoris, tum propter aeris inclementiam et imbrium importunitatem* ... ." The years 1151 and 1152 were notably wet and famine was reported in some areas.[15] Sallay, only six miles to the west in the valley of the Ribble, was also sorely tried and almost decided to seek a new site. Standing "in a foggy and rainy district, [its] crops, white onto harvest, ordinarily rotted in the stalk" (1189).[16] Yet, strangely enough, Robert of Newminster who sent the first colony in 1148 knew the area well, having once been rector of neighbouring Gargrave.[17]

In 1156, when summer rains generally delayed the harvest, Fors in upper Wensleydale was evacuated to a place lower down the Ure (Jervaulx) because of the "intemperance of the air" and the unfruitful environment. Similar conditions probably help to explain the removal of Cotton to Croxden and, in part, Red Moor to the district of Stoneleigh. Cotton occupied a site (ca. 775 feet) near the headwaters of a small stream, Croxden a position more than 300 feet lower on a tributary of the river Dove. Stoneleigh (ca. 200 feet) was built on the banks of the Warwickshire Avon

[15] Unless otherwise stated, references to weather conditions are taken from Charles E. Britton, *A Meteorological Chronology to A.D. 1450* (London: HMSO, 1937).

[16] *Chart. S.*, 2: 128; *Mon. Angl.*, 5: 512.

[17] J. McNulty, 'Sallay Abbey, 1148-1536,' *Trans. Lancs. and Chesh. Ant. Soc.*, 54 (1939): 194.

thirteen or fourteen years after its monks first settled at ca. 600 feet on the slopes of Cannock Chase where the foresters proved troublesome. In the South-West, Brightley, on the Culm Measures at ca. 500 feet, was considered "barren" and in 1141 (which also seems to have been an unusually wet year) the convent moved to Westford and then to Forde, a short distance apart in the valley of the Axe (ca. 200 feet).

An inadequate supply of water could also lead to a change of site, particularly if a monastery grew far beyond what its founders anticipated. The monks who first settled at Kingswood (1139) moved in turn to Hazleton (ca. 1149-50), back to Kingswood, then to Tetbury and finally to the neighbourhood of Kingswood again (1164-ca. 1170). Water was scarce at Hazleton, high on the Great Oolite of the Cotswolds, but, being remote, it had some advantages during the unsettled years of Stephen's reign. Tetbury was probably not much more satisfactory and, in addition, it suffered from a shortage of fuel.[18] Kingswood, however, lay near the spring line of the main scarp. Byland (1177) could look back on four former sites — Calder in Cumberland (1135), Hood (1138), a place by the river Rye below Old Byland (1143), and Stocking (1147). Hood, near the source of a beck and just below the Hambleton Hills, was too "confined": "*locus de Hode nimis arctus fuit ad abbaciam construendam* ... ." Rievaulx forced a withdrawal from Ryedale, and Stocking lacked a good head of water. A similar shortage may also have been one reason for the evacuation of Faringdon (Berkshire), Loxwell (Wiltshire) and West Lulworth (Dorset). Faringdon, where a colony dwelt for less than a year (1203-4) before settling at Beaulieu in the New Forest, lies at ca. 350 feet on a ridge of Corallian limestone.[19] Loxwell (ca. 400 feet), selected in 1151, was served by no more than a brook, but its successor, Stanley (ca. 200 feet), stood by the river Marden, a tributary of the Wiltshire Avon. West Lulworth was occupied for a few months in 1171-72 by monks who, finding it in all probability dry and inaccessible, established Bindon on the Frome. Perhaps the reports of high rainfall in 1151 and 1171 help to explain this and the previous case. Some of the sites which were quickly deserted were probably never intended to be permanent, and temporary buildings alone would be constructed. But when five years or more elapsed, it would seem

[18] E. S. Lindley, 'Kingswood Abbey, its lands and mills,' *Trans. Bristol and Glouc. Arch. Soc.*, 73 (1955): 117-18.

[19] S. F. Hockey (*Chart. Bl.*, xxxiv) rightly questions "whether the manor of Faringdon was found to be sufficiently secluded or remote from the interests of other religious foundations." The Benedictine abbey of Reading, the Cistercians of Stanley and Thame, the abbeys of Bec and Cluny, the canons of Llanthony, and the bishop of Winchester also held lands in the manor.

that the inadequacies of the location only became apparent as numbers grew or new plans were adopted.

Just as a run of wet years might temporarily improve a dry site, the opposite conditions could mask the risks involved in occupying a marshy area, notwithstanding the value placed on isolation and the opportunity to win new land. Such advantages would scarcely compensate for severe flooding such as occurred at Haverholme (ca. 25 feet) in Lincolnshire causing the removal to Louth Park (ca. 50 feet). Oddington Grange (Oxfordshire), which probably marks the site of Otley, lies between two streams and only a few feet above the neighbouring fen of Ot Moor. Otley was "an unsuitable place ... low and unhealthy,"[20] and the monks (later at Thame) remained there only three years (1137-40). After 124 years (1172-1296) persistent flooding (*inundationes*) forced the monks of Stanlaw — on the Mersey estuary and close to the mouth of the river Gowy — to leave their house. "On the day of the Holy Innocents [28 December], 1292, the sea overflowed its bounds and inundated all maritime parts,"[21] and high rainfalls were mentioned in 1290, 1291, 1294 and 1296. Disregarding the objections of Sallay,[22] they chose a sheltered position by the river Calder (tributary of the Ribble) and near the long-established vill of Whalley. By this time the Cistercians were clearly demanding less of themselves and far more of the country.

According to John Leland the grounds of Stratford Langthorn, "sett emonge low marshes" between the Lea and the Thames, were once so threatened that the whole community was temporarily evacuated to the grange of Burstead.[23] Tulketh (1124-7) near the marshes of the Ribble estuary was deserted in favour of Furness. The swollen river Wey endangered Waverley on a number of occasions, and this may have led to limited re-siting. Bytham (Lincolnshire) was soon found to be "inconvenient" and the monks selected the place now known as Vaudey, also on the rim of the Fenland but further from a major stream.

Another group of abbeys suffered on account of their position on the Welsh border or on routes leading into Wales. Conway or Aberconway was transferred to Maenan by Edward I to make room for his castle and town. Grace Dieu, founded in 1226, was re-sited after being destroyed by the Welsh in 1233. Border raids were also given as the reason for the

[20] *Chart. T.*, 1: 5; T. Tanner, *Notitia Monastica* (London, 1787).

[21] *Chronica Johannis de Oxenedes*, ed. Henry Ellis, R. S. 13 (London, 1859), p. 287, as quoted in Britton, *Meteorological Chronology*, p. 128.

[22] *Chart. S.*, 1: 156.

[23] *The Itinerary of John Leland*, ed. Lucy T. Smith (London, 1910), 5 (pt. ix): 5.

removal of Poulton (Cheshire) to Dieulacres after sixty-one years; as the scribe put it, "*maxime propter intrusionem Wallensium, per quos multa perpessi sunt.*" But the earlier site, occupying low ground near the Dee, may not have been altogether satisfactory in other respects. Dieulacres on the river Churnet and a mile north of Leek is, with the possible exception of Whalley, the only instance of a move into the Pennines.

A new site had to be more or less free of the disadvantages of the old, but the actual choice and the distance involved depended on what land was already available, or what, if any, was specially offered. The vacated site was normally the nucleus of an important estate which became a grange when the monks had left.[24]

Most re-siting can be traced, in part at least, to dissatisfaction with environmental conditions. In particular, constricted upland sites were deserted in favour of more spacious surroundings amply supplied with water. There is no exact parallel in popular settlement, however marginal and insecure, for changes there can generally be explained in purely economic terms, whereas the Cistercian site had to match a gradually changing assessment of both material and spiritual needs.

[24] Tetbury (a *grangia* ca. 1291), Faringdon, Hazleton, Westford, Bytham, Loxwell (1304), Otley (ca. 1200), Barnoldswick (1152), Cryfield (ca. 1154), Fors, Pendar, Darnhall, Tulketh (twelfth century), Stanlaw (ca. 1350).

2

Settlements and Estates

Colonization and Depopulation

In the course of the twelfth and thirteenth centuries houses of the Cistercian order both fostered and destroyed village communities. Colonization was attempted where more cultivable land was donated than could be conveniently worked even with many *conversi.*[1] This was especially the case in eastern and central Europe.[2] England, on the other hand, "was already an old country" at the time of the Norman conquest[3] and the opportunities for colonization by the white monks were not great.

Stanlaw in 1209-11 received the vill of Acton (Cheshire) with permission to settle men there to cultivate the ground: "*liceat eis homines laicos si voluerint in villa que dicitur Acton ad terram excolendam ponere.*"[4] Later (ca. 1291) we find the estate described as a grange. Dieulacres had land at Rossal in Thornton (Lancashire) from about 1216. There were

[1] See C. Duvivier, 'Hospites: défrichements en Europe et spécialement dans nos contrées aux XIe, XIIe et XIIIe siècles,' *Rev. d'hist. et d'archéologie*, 1 (1859): 80; L. Champier, 'Cîteaux, ultime étape dans l'aménagement agraire de l'Occident,' *Mélanges Saint Bernard*; *24e Congrès de l'Association Bourguignonne des Sociétés Savantes* (Dijon, 1953), pp. 254-61; L. J. McCrank, 'The Cistercians of Poblet as landlords: protection, litigation and violence on the medieval Catalan frontier,' *Citeaux: Commentarii Cistercienses*, 26 (1975): 255, 274-5.

[2] R. Sebicht, 'Die Cistercienser und die niederländischen Kolonisten in der *goldnen Ave*,' *Zeitschrift des Harz-Vereins für Geschichte und Altertumskunde*, 21 (1888): 1-74. The abbeys of Dargun, Eldena, Kolbatz and Neuenkamp exercised the right to settle Slavs (F. L. Carsten, 'The Slavs in north-eastern Germany,' *Ec. H. R.*, 11 (1941): 62). However, a study of the Cistercians of Obra (founded 1237, diocese of Poznań) produced no evidence of colonization (J. Krasoń, *Uposażenie Klasztoru Cystersów w Obrze w Wiekach Średnich* (Poznań, 1950), p. 173).

[3] R. Lennard, *Rural England, 1086-1135* (Oxford, 1959), p. 1.

[4] *Coucher W.*, 2: 385-86, 392.

probably few inhabitants and little agricultural activity at the time of the Domesday survey[5] and some of the charters to this house — mostly of the first half of the thirteenth century — record grants of villeins (*nativi*) to be removed and settled on the monks' land in and near Rossal.[6] These places lay in the relatively lightly settled North-West, and there is apparently no question of the creation of villages, but simply the resuscitation or extension of old centres.

In a review of Vale Royal's rights in the forest of Delamere in 1375 it was claimed "that the abbot ... has a greater number of men and tenants in the manors of Darnhall, Weaverham and Conwardesley, whom he has put there, than there were at the time of King Edward I."[7] The abbot however denied this. Darnhall was an important estate, part of the original endowment, and Conwardesley ranked as a grange in 1336. The history of Fountains provides a clearer case of the dismemberment of a number of compact holdings and their settlement or re-settlement by lay folk in the middle of the fourteenth century: "*ut predictas grangias in villas construere et redigere possent.*"[8] Permission to lease was obtained after Aldburgh, Sleningford, Sutton, Cowton, Bramley, Bradley, Kilnsey, Clayton and Thorpe Underwood had been ruined in the wars between England and Scotland. Earlier (1336) the granges of Baldersby and Marton le Moor were broken up for the same reason.[9] Aldburgh, Sutton, Bramley, Thorpe Underwood, Baldersby and Marton were completely in the hands of the monks, and all but Kilnsey were mainly arable. Jervaulx in 1342 followed a course similar to that of Fountains, making "towns (*villas*) of the four great granges of Newstead, Rookwith, Aikbar and Didderston."[10] How long it took to establish a village or to enlarge any existing community of peasant workers is not known.[11] The respective estates were certainly run-

[5] Rossal (*Rushall*) was included in a list of places which, taken together, were mostly 'waste' (*V.C.H.* (*Lancashire*, 1906), 1: 288).

[6] *Chart D.*, nos. 56-57, 156, 158-62. The abbey's property at Rossal was assessed ca. 1291 at £6.10.0 (*Tax. Eccles.*, 329).

[7] *Ledger V.R.*, p. 140.

[8] *Mem. F.*, 1: 203-4. At Esrum (Denmark) the conversion of granges to peasant holdings has been traced to about the middle of the thirteenth century (B. P. McGuire, 'Property and politics at Esrum Abbey, 1151-1251,' *Mediaeval Scandinavia*, 6 (1973): 137.

[9] *Chart. F.*, 1: 111.

[10] *C.M.I.*, 2: 445.

[11] At Sleningford a chapel was built, and in 1457-8 thirty-one suitors attended the manor court. The village was apparently destroyed a second time, but the date of this is unknown. M. W. Beresford has identified the site of the chapel ('The lost villages of Yorkshire,' *Yorks, Arch. Jour.*, 38 (1952-54): 235).

down and the pressure on land was probably less than at any time since the Conquest.

Depopulation

The Cistercians quickly acquired an unenviable reputation as depopulators. Walter Map complained (ca. 1182-92) that "they ... raze villages and churches ... and level everything before the ploughshare ... not scrupling to grow crops."[12] Similarly Guiot de Provins (poet and, for a time, monk of Clairvaux) tells us that the white monks "frightened the poor and drove them from their land" (1206).[13] Archbishop Peckham apparently had this in mind when he protested against the re-founding of Aberconway at Maenan in 1283.[14] In some cases, those who were evicted joined the ranks of lay brothers. The founder of Sibton in 1150 confirmed to the monastery the land of men who had taken this course.[15] The donor of half a carucate in Kilnsey to Fountains in 1174 became a lay brother.[16] This was much more common in the very early years of the order than later, but at all times the *conversi* were mainly local men.

The provisions of a grant may hint at depopulation. When Sallay was given seventy acres in *Akerland* the monks were obliged to promise that the men then working the land should remain until the following summer, the end of the growing season.[17] An early grant to Rievaulx in Welburn comprised villeins (*rustici*) who were to be at liberty to remain or to go

[12] Walter Map, *De nugis curialium*, trans. M. R. James, ed. E. S. Hartland, Cymmrodorion Record Series., 9 (London, 1923), pp. 49-50. See B. Griesser, 'Walther Map und die Cistercienser,' *Cistercienser-Chronik*, 36 (1924): 137-41, 164-67.

[13] *Les Oeuvres de Guiot de Provins*, ed. J. Orr (Manchester, 1915), p. 48. Cf. Nigellus Wireker, *Speculum stultorum*, in *The Anglo-Latin Satirical Poets and Epigrammatists of the Twelfth Century*, ed. T. Wright, R. S. 59 (London, 1872), 1: 84:

> Agrorum cupidi, nunquam metas sibi poni
> vicinis vellent pestis iniqua suis.

G. G. Coulton has referred to the criticism voiced by Petrarch (1304-74)—(*Five Centuries of Religion* (Cambridge, 1927), 2: 435).

[14] *Registrum Epistolarum Fratris Johannis Peckham*, ed. C. T. Martin, R. S. 77 (London, 1884), 2: 726.

[15] *Mon. Angl.*, 5: 560.

[16] *E.Y.C.*, 7: 188-89. Thame, on one occasion, was given land on condition that the donor's father was received as a monk (W. H. Turner, *Calendar of Charters and Rolls preserved in the Bodleian Library* (Oxford, 1878), p. 314.

[17] "*Scias tamen quod praedicti monachi concesserunt nobis quod homines qui modo sedent super terram illam, usque in aestatem proximam sustinebunt*" (*Mon. Angl.*, 5: 515). F. Winter refers to a similar case involving Pforta (*Die Cistercienser der nordöstlichen Deutschlands* (Gotha, 1871), 2: 178-81.

away as they wished.[18] In Willerby (1170-84) the abbot and convent could acquire "by gift or purchase" the land of the freemen as it suited their purpose; likewise the freemen of Welbury and East Heslerton were allowed to surrender their holdings, save those which the lord desired to incorporate in the demesne.[19] A charter to Kirkstall (1166-94) strikes an ominous note in confirming land and granting freedom from toll to "all men who remain on the lands which I have given to [the monks of Kirkstall]."[20] Displacement sometimes led to outright depopulation, but elsewhere a reduced community survived. So far as is known, the former only occurred close to the abbey site itself or to properties organized as granges. In the case of a grange, evictions sometimes extended over many years, but at the abbey the process was usually both swift and decisive.

There are at least three examples of the removal of inhabitants from the temporary or permanent site of a Yorkshire Cistercian house (Appendix 2 (a)). The aim was to achieve perfect seclusion and to establish a central estate or home farm. The famous edict of 1134, "*in civitatibus, castellis, villis, nulla nostra construenda sunt coenobia sed in locis a conversatione hominum semotis*," was made to apply if it did not already do so. In 1142-3 the convent at Hood was given the vill of Byland ("*totam villam Beghlandie*"), little more than one mile north-west of Rievaulx (founded 1132). Byland almost immediately became the home of the community. Not unnaturally, the senior house objected to their presence. But before moving again, in 1147, the monks reduced the vill — where, at the time of Domesday, there were seven villeins and a priest serving a wooden church — to a grange ("*eadem villa redacta est in grangiam*"). The evicted were assigned new land, and a hamlet (*villula*), now Old Byland, was built for them.[21] This is a clear case of organized re-settlement following depopulation. Kirkby's Inquest (1284-5) records eight carucates in Old Byland (*Veteri Bellaund*), all held by the abbot. The *Nomina Villarum* (1316) makes no reference to the place.

Meaux, the Domesday *Melse*, was apparently destroyed by the abbey of the same name some time during the period 1151-3/4 to make room for the neighbouring North grange. In the words of the chronicler, "*et ubi ip-*

[18] *Chart. R.*, p. 36. The whole place was held, and the grange was confirmed in 1332 (ibid., pp. 133, 286). Cf. the confirmation (1153-57) to Rievaulx of land "and meadow belonging to the rustics" in Crosby (site of a grange, 1152)—*E.Y.C.*, 2: 288.

[19] *Chart. R.*, pp. 74, 76. The estates at Willerby and East Heslerton were not apparently known as granges, but that at Welbury was probably associated with Ingram grange (ibid., p. 295). The whole of Ingram belonged to Rievaulx (1268).

[20] *Mon. Angl.*, 5: 535.

[21] Ibid., p. 350; *E.Y.C.*, 3: 445.

sum villa seu manerium de Melsa fuerat situatum, extat modo grangia nostra quae Northgrangia nuncupatur." The whole place had been granted to the monks who settled there in 1151. The "grange near the abbey" was confirmed in 1153-4. The township does not appear in Kirkby's Inquest, the Lay Subsidy of 1297 or the *Nomina Villarum*, and elsewhere *loca* stands in place of *villa*.[22] *Melse* was assessed in 1086 at less than twenty-five per cent of its value in 1066. Nevertheless, according to the chronicle, it was a fertile spot with a rich soil (*gleba fecundum*) and well planted with trees. The territory donated to the abbey comprised arable, meadow, pasture and woodland.

The monks established at Barnoldswick from 1147 moved to Kirkstall in 1152. The former abbey site was then used for a grange: "*et abbatia in grangiam redacta.*" The monastery possessed the whole of Barnoldswick. There were four parochial vills — East and West Marton, Bracewell, and Stock — and from these the inhabitants were evicted, but the people of Barnoldswick itself and of two adjacent hamlets, *Brocdene* and *Elwinsthorpe*, apparently were left undisturbed.[23] Later the church of Barnoldswick was pulled down. The extent to which the land belonging to the vills eventually formed part of the grange of Barnoldswick is uncertain. Within a few years Bracewell and Marton had churches, and one was possibly rebuilt at Barnoldswick soon after the translation to Kirkstall. In Kirkby's Inquest they are described as *villae* (Bracewell and Stock as well as the two Martons being assessed together) but Stock is not mentioned in the *Nomina Villarum*; nor is it named in the Poll Tax lists of 1378-9, when the Martons together returned forty-two persons and Bracewell twenty-six.

There were, it seems, no settlements immediately adjacent to the sites selected for Fountains, Jervaulx, Roche, and Rievaulx. But villagers were dispossessed a short distance to the south of Fountains, and it is possible that a small place near the former site of Jervaulx at Fors (1145-56) in Wensleydale was destroyed. Jervaulx was endowed with one and a half carucates there and three in neighbouring Worton and soon decided to establish a grange. Later, when the holding at Fors was confirmed, further gifts were also sanctioned. The place was completely 'waste' in 1086. Absent from the Inquest and the *Nomina Villarum*, the Lay Subsidy of 1301 refers to it as *Dalegrange*.

Sallay was founded from Newminster, Northumberland, in 1148. Now represented by a hamlet, the name is not mentioned in Domesday

[22] *Mon. Angl.*, 5: 393-94; *Chron. M.*, 1: 16.
[23] *Mon. Angl.*, 5: 530; *Mem. F.*, 1: xlviii, 90-91.

although there was probably a small settlement when the monks arrived. Sallay was part of the original endowment, and the *villa* was later confirmed. Before 1172 the property thereabouts had been organized into a grange, and the surveys of 1284-5 and 1316 again are silent.

Depopulation also occurred at Pipewell (Northamptonshire), Revesby (Lincolnshire), Rufford (Nottinghamshire), and Combe and Stoneleigh (Warwickhire). Pipewell, founded as *Sancta Maria de Divisis* in 1143, built a grange around a messuage in the settlement of the same name: "*quod ubi West grangia sita est fuit quaedam villa quae a quodam fonte nomen Pipewelle accepit.*"[24] Revesby's foundation endowment (1142-3) included "*totam terram de Revesbia et Thoresbi et Schictlesbia.*"[25] The earl of Lincoln offered the villagers the choice of fresh land or their freedom; seven *rustici* accepted the former and thirty-one the latter.[26] Thoresby grange was confirmed by Richard I.

The monks of Rufford "gave money to each of eight men [of the adjacent village] ... in return for a quitclaim of their lands."[27] M. W. Barley has shown that this house destroyed one and possibly two neighbouring settlements besides Rufford[28] and was indirectly responsible for the loss of another. Apparently a new village, Wellow, grew up in their place.

Combe was founded (1150) in the parish of Smite. The gift of the place, "*totam terram de Smite,*"[29] and the arrival of the monks were followed by the destruction of two villages or hamlets. M. W. Beresford has been able to identify their sites in the northern part of the parish.[30] In

[24] *Mon. Angl.*, 5: 432, 435. Pipewell was assessed at one and a third hides in Domesday Book; there were nine bordars and land for four ploughs.

[25] Ibid., 454-55. The sites are known (M. W. Beresford, *The Lost Villages of England* (London, 1954), p. 152). See also F. M. Stenton, ed., *Facsimilies of Early Charters from Northamptonshire Collections*, Northants. Rec. Soc. Publs., 4 (Lincoln and London, 1930), pp. 1-7.

[26] Evictions accompanied the foundation of Witham, a Carthusian house, and again personal freedom or fresh land was offered ([Adam of Eynsham], *Magna Vita S. Hugonis Episcopi Lincolniensis*, ed. J. F. Dimock, R. S. 37 (London, 1864), pp. 68-70. At Sempringham, too, a village gave way to the monastery (Rose Graham, 'Excavations on the site of Sempringham Priory,' *Jour. Brit. Arch. Assoc.*, 3rd ser., 5 (1940): 74.

[27] Stenton, *Facsimiles of Early Charters*, p. 4 n. 2. "*Totam terram de Rufford*" was a foundation gift (*Mon. Angl.*, 5: 518).

[28] Cratley and Winkerfield ('waste' in 1086); see 'Lost villages of Nottingham,' *The Listener*, 5 May 1955, pp. 795-96, and 'Cistercian land clearances in Nottinghamshire: three deserted villages and their moated successor,' *Nottingham Mediaeval Studies*, 1 (1957): 75-89. *Cratela* was in the monks' hands from the first (*Mon. Angl.*, 5: 518), and Henry III confirmed land in *Werkenfeld* (*C.Ch.R.*, AD 1226-57, p. 177).

[29] *Mon. Angl.*, 5: 584, where the "*villam de Smite*" is also mentioned.

[30] 'The deserted villages of Warwickshire,' *Trans. Birm. Arch. Soc.*, 66 (1945-46): 82-83. Cf. "Smite in Combe fields" (1202-3)—Frederick Christian Wellstood, ed., *Warwick-*

1086 Smite had forty-seven households and fourteen ploughs at work (with two more on the demesne); and since 1066 it had risen considerably in value.

The Cistercian community at Red Moor, established 1141, migrated to the district of Stoneleigh some time between 1156 and 1159. The monks first settled at the place now known as Cryfield grange, moving the inhabitants to Hurst.[31] Later the Home grange at Stoneleigh was preferred. William Dugdale in his *Antiquities of Warwickshire* wrote: "And to the end that these monks should have Stoneley intire, the said King [Henry II] gave command ... to the Sheriff ... to assigne the freeholders there, as much land in value, in other places, by way of exchange ... ."[32] Domesday indicates a place of considerable size at the close of the eleventh century. Apart from the demesne, there were sixty-eight villeins and four bordars with thirty ploughs and two mills; the woodland measured four leagues by two and supported 2000 swine. It appears that the monks were responsible for the loss of two settlements, although Cryfield was probably very small.

The remaining evidence is less conclusive. Newminster, founded in 1138, lay in the valley of the river Wansbeck about a mile from Mitford. There was formerly a vill named 'Aldworth' on the eastern limits of the parish of Mitford — it must, therefore, have stood very close to the abbey — but there is now no trace of it. A document of about the middle of the thirteenth century refers to the "*campum de Aldwood.*" From the latter half of the reign of Henry II the abbey possessed "*medietatem villae Aldworth*"[33] and the estate became known as a grange. If there were evictions, as seems probable, the time that elapsed after the foundation makes this case somewhat different from those already discussed.

Richard I confirmed Boxley in the manor of the same name, all the agreements which the monks had made with those who enjoyed rights therein, and the resulting exchanges and purchases of land. Again, the abbey of Sibton's holding in Sibton included land which had been acquired through exchange, the death of the owner, and the failure of certain persons to carry out services on the demesne.[34]

---

shire Feet of Fines, Dugdale Society Publications, 11 (London, 1932), 1 (AD 1195-1284): 25.

[31] *Mon. Angl.*, 5: 446.

[32] 2nd ed. (1730), 1: 254; *C.Cl.R.*, AD 1323-7, p. 265.

[33] *Chart. N.*, p. 41.

[34] *Mon. Angl.*, 5: 558. The following details concerning Bytham (1147/8; later Vaudey), Revesby and Swineshead are taken from a list of Lincolnshire 'lost' vills in C. W. Foster and T. Langley, eds., *The Lincolnshire Domesday and the Lindsey Survey*, Lincoln Record Society, Publs., 19 (1924): xlix, lxi, lxvii:

The incontrovertible cases of depopulation in the vicinity of a monastery date from before 1160, and possibly before 1155. With the ideal of isolation still fresh, it seems unlikely that houses founded by the middle of the twelfth century would willingly have tolerated villagers close at hand for more than a few years. The monks were, however, readily prepared to accept virgin ground as a foundation gift and evictions were by no means inevitable.

Population changes most often occurred around granges. *Grangia* in Cistercian records has two principal meanings — a largely consolidated, independently controlled estate, and the buildings from which the land was worked. Developed perhaps under Alberic, the second abbot of Cîteaux (1099-1109), granges were characteristic by the time of the earliest settlement in England. The first known reference to a particular grange in this country is dated 1145-6. The names of seventy-four belonging to the eight Yorkshire houses have been found in documents of the twelfth century, and forty-five more before 1350. Many of the latter were probably begun before 1200, although some were certainly founded in the thirteenth century.[35] T. A. M. Bishop has observed that a number of estates known as granges in the thirteenth century are not described as such in later documents. The opposite is also true. By the time of the Dissolution the term *grangia* was used of holdings bearing little resemblance to the original model.

Although some granges were almost entirely pastoral, the kind of land donated and purchased and the few remaining extents show that most were first and foremost arable estates. They varied greatly in size, from less than 100 to about 1000 acres. Moreover, if William Farrer, the editor of the Yorkshire Domesday, was correct in thinking that a carucates for geld/ploughlands ratio of between 1:1 and 2:1 indicated arable country it seems that most of the Yorkshire granges for which there are indications of depopulation lay within the territories of vills appreciably ploughed-up in 1066 if not for some time after the devastation of 1069.

Brachecourt, a "place" in the parish of Edenham was given to Bytham as a new site for the abbey; the monks renamed it Vaudey.

Medlam, "an extinct place or hamlet" in the parish of Revesby was given to the monks of Revesby; land here was confirmed in 1263 (*C.Ch.R.*, AD 1327-41, p. 95).

Stenning, "an extinct vill in the parish of Swineshead," it is named in Domesday Book and Swineshead had property there (*C.Ch.R.*, AD 1300-26, pp. 320-21, 325).

[35] For example, *Chron. M.*, 1: 365—Routh (1210-20); ibid., 2: 48-49—Croo (1235-9); ibid., 2: 59—Dalton (1235-9). None is known to have been begun in the fourteenth century.

Concerning the formation and organization of *grangiae*, Bishop concluded: "all previous distinctions in tenure or agricultural organization were obliterated in a process by which the monasteries sought to accumulate very large areas of land under their own absolute control."[36] The letter of the Cistercian Rule required that there should be no contact with lay agriculture.[37] Sometimes the monks were granted entire vills. Elsewhere they worked towards complete ownership by the purchase and exchange of land.[38] Except where charters actually describe evictions we can never be absolutely certain, but it is difficult to see how in many cases the monks could have approached their object without disturbing the lay population.

Interpretation of the available evidence must take into account the condition of the settlement before the grange was started; the clearing of fresh ground in the surrounding waste; and exchanges of land. Of the first we know very little. More than forty per cent of all known twelfth-century granges in Yorkshire lay within the territories of vills 'waste' or almost completely 'waste' in 1086.[39] But it is usually impossible to estimate the degree of recovery by the middle of the twelfth century. Baldersby and Cayton (respectively within and on the edge of the Vale of York), where the evidence of later depopulation is most explicit, were 'waste'. On the other hand, although Bramley — also 'waste' in 1086 — was granted to Fountains early in the twelfth century and transformed *en bloc* into a grange, no grants or quitclaims by inhabitants are recorded; the donation "all Bramley which is of his [the grantor's] purchase" stands alone. The case of Brimham is similar. These places had probably never been resettled. At Aldburgh, again the site of an early grange (1145-6), but not recorded in Domesday, we are expressly told that there was little arable before Fountains set to work.[40] The chartulary records few grants here and these, if measured at all, are in acres. This brings us to the second point

[36] T. A. M. Bishop, 'Monastic granges in Yorkshire,' *E.H.R.*, 51 (1936): 200.

[37] *Statuta*, 1: 429 (1214).

[38] The date of the first reference to complete ownership is given in Appendix 2. A map accompanying W. Hoppe, *Kloster Zinna* (Leipzig, 1914), shows the abbey's holdings in extensive blocks. G. Fournier has demonstrated how the village of Gergovie, Puy de Dôme, was gradually superseded by a Premonstratensian grange built up on the Cistercian pattern ('La création de la grange de Gergovie par les Prémontrés de Saint-André,' *Le Moyen Age*, 4e sér., 5/vol. 56 (1950): 319).

[39] 'Waste' does not, however, necessarily imply that they were entirely unoccupied in 1086. Most other places had dropped heavily in value since 1066.

[40] "*Non fuit ibi multum terre arabilis quando primum data est* [sc. Aldburgh] *eis set fere totum monachi postea sartaverunt* ..."; from a tithe composition quoted by Bishop, 'Monastic granges,' p. 213.

— assarting. In many parts of Yorkshire, and particularly in the Vale of York, the Cistercians cleared fresh land to extend and unify their holdings. There is a great mass of evidence for the twelfth and early thirteenth centuries, and much of it relates to granges. New land near at hand, given as waste or freshly cleared, was one answer to the problem of re-settlement.[41] A form of exchange, it would involve only a short distance transfer of families, and often even this would not be necessary. The majority of exchanges, of both open-field strips and assarts, took place within rather than between vills. But the latter are particularly interesting here, and a good example concerns Baldersby. When the monks of Fountains obtained the land of Hugh de Baldersby, which probably rounded off their estate, another tenement at Pickhill, four miles to the north, was given in exchange.

We may now turn to examples of depopulation involving Kirkstall and Fountains, and probably Meaux and Rievaulx too (Fig. 7).[42] By the last decade of the twelfth century Kirkstall had acquired the whole of Accrington (Lancashire) in exhange for a holding in Cliviger. The inhabitants were then removed to make way for a grange. The account is quite unequivocal: "*hanc villam, amotis habitationibus, redegit in grangiam usibus monasterii profuturam.*"[43] The dispossessed almost immediately destroyed the grange but it was rebuilt by the same abbot who ordered the evictions (1192-1221).

There is more evidence against Fountains than any other house. Its chartulary includes many grants of land in Baldersby and, under the same head, *Eseby* (the *Asebi* of 1086) and *Birkou*. There was the nucleus of a grange from at least the last quarter of the twelfth century, and the whole place probably belonged to Fountains before the middle of the thirteenth. We are told in Kirkby's Inquest (1284-5) that all three places were once vills but were then part of the grange of Baldersby.[44] It seems unlikely that *Eseby* and *Birkou* were ever settlements after the thirteenth century, and the latter was probably never more than a hamlet. They apparently lay close together and between Baldersby and Stainton. The Lay Subsidy of

[41] H. Muggenthaler, *Kolonisatorische und wirtschaftliche Tätigkeit eines deutschen Zisterzienserklosters im XII und XIII Jahrhundert* (Munich, 1924), p. 105.

[42] Cf. E. O. Schulze, *Die Kolonisierung und Germanisierung der Gebiete zwischen Saale und Elbe* (Leipzig, 1896), p. 140 (1267); and K. T. von Inama-Sternegg, 'Sallandstudien' in *Festgabe für Georg Hanssen zum 31 Mai 1889* (Tübingen, 1889), p. 105 (1152, 1160).

[43] *Mon. Angl.*, 5: 530; *Mem. F.*, 1: 91n.

[44] "*Abbas de Fontibus tenet Balderby, Birkou et Eseby ... quae quondam fuerunt villae et nunc est una grangia, quae vocatur Balderby ... .*"

1301 makes no reference to them, and only two men (*famuli*, presumably employed on the monks' estate) other than the abbot paid the tax in Baldersby.

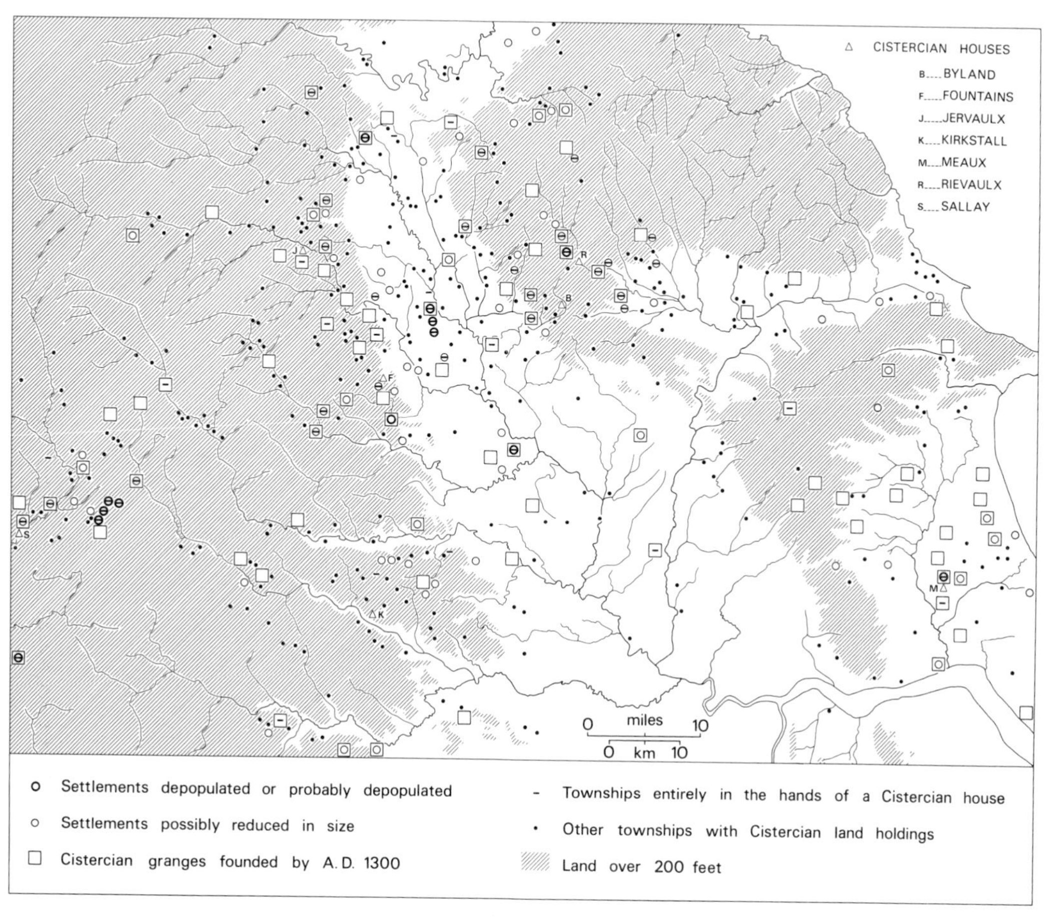

FIG. 7

Cistercian depopulation in Yorkshire (Appendix 2).

Fountains had two carucates in Cayton in 1135, and soon after we hear of it as a grange. For this the vill was 'reduced': "*et redacta est villa in grangiam.*"[45] The entire territory of Thorpe Underwood, now a hamlet in

[45] *Mem. F.*, 1: 56; *Mon. Angl.*, 5: 299. In the Poll Tax of 1378-9 ("Rotuli collectorum subsidii regi a laicis ...," *Yorks. Arch. Top. Jour.*, 7 (1882): 11) Cayton is included with South Stainley; in all there were forty-four payments. The former village site has been identified (Beresford, 'Lost villages of Yorkshire,' *Yorks. Arch. Jour.*, 38 (1952-54): 233).

the Vale of York, belonged to Fountains by 1175-99. The grange was confirmed by Richard I and later surveys ignore the place, which is hardly surprising for there had been wholesale evictions about 1175.[46] Then there is the case of Greenbury, represented today by a farm near Scorton in the northern part of the Vale. Although not in Domesday Book, later charters describe it as a vill on a number of occasions, once as late as 1273. The township included a grange which appears to have expanded at the expense of the vill. According to a charter of the late twelfth or early thirteenth century Fountains was permitted "to make a fosse to enclose all the land where were the tofts and crofts of the men formerly dwelling in *Greneberg*, towards the south. He [the grantor] has also given and quitclaimed to the monks in perpetual alms all the common of the said land within the said fosse."[47] None of the above-mentioned places appears in the *Nomina Villarum*. A reference to Kirby Wiske, where there was a grange and Fountains held four of the six carucates in 1284-5, likewise suggests evictions. The deed is undated, but after detailing exchanges of land it records the monks' right "to enclose the said land, together with the lands of the free tenants in *Kyrkebywysc*."[48]

Myton (near Hull, but of which there is now no trace) was probably depopulated by Meaux. The chapel was destroyed — "*evulsione capellae de Mytona, quae in solo nostro fuerat situata*" (1221-35);[49] and there was a grange here before the last quarter of the twelfth century.[50] There is also some indication that Rievaulx turned depopulator in Crosby on the eastern edge of the Vale of York. The grange is mentioned in 1152, and all three carucates "with the meadow of the villeins" were in the monks' hands by 1153-7.[51] Like *Myton* it was 'waste' in 1086 and was overlooked in Kirkby's Inquest and the *Nomina Villarum*. Of comparable interest are three short notices concerning the abbeys of Rufford, Basingwerk and Kingswood. The first, after receiving eight bovates and demesne land in Rotherham, was allowed (1283) to "appropriate the lands and rents of the

[46] *Mem. F.*, 1: 124; *Mon. Angl.*, 5: 305.

[47] *Chart. F.*, 1: 330. There was also a grange at Cowton less than two miles to the north-east. *Mem. F.*, 1: 86; *E.Y.C.*, 1: 75-79 (1146-6 *conf.*).

[48] *Chart. F.*, 1: 480.

[49] *Chron. M.*, 1: 425-26. Barnoldswick (*supra*, p. 41) is the only other known case of church destruction in Yorkshire. For other houses see *Rot. Parl.*, 2: 184—Thame, Oxfordshire; *Papal Letters*, 1: 155—Beaulieu, Hampshire; *V.C.H.* (*Surrey*, 1905), 2: 9—Waverley. One of Dore's estates (Herefordshire) was called *grangia de capella* (*Tax. Eccles.*, p. 172).

[50] Myton was bought by Edward I in 1294 when he founded Kingston upon Hull.

[51] *E.Y.C.*, 2: 288; *Chart. R.*, pp. 27, 174-75, 222.

free men and villeins ... without giving rise to claims from the donor."[52] Basingwerk, about the same time, had permission to buy up free tenements in Langdendale (Derbyshire).[53] In 1214 the abbot of Kingswood was summoned to explain why he had "swept away houses and uprooted trees on land over which he had but custody."[54]

There are also a number of former vills that did not give their names to granges but were almost certainly included therein. Fountains' grange of Marton le Moor included the five carucates of *Caldwell*,[55] but this place may have been entirely reclaimed by the *conversi*. Almost the final item in the chartulary of Fountains under Sleningford, the site of a twelfth-century grange, conveyed "all the vill of *Ripplyngtona*," which appears to have been levelled and incorporated. *Herleshou* is placed under Morker, described as a grange in 1156 and only one mile south-east of Fountains. Henry I confirmed 200 acres in the wood of *Erlleshou*; by this time, or soon after, the whole *villa* (three carucates) belonged to the abbey. The estate was sometimes referred to as "*grangiam de Morcher cum tota terra de Herleshou*."[56] *Thorpe juxta Brereton*[57] is perhaps another example of depopulation by Fountains. Kirkstall had holdings in *Watecroft*[58] which lay near Roundhay grange and possibly formed part of it. Similarly *Akebar* near Ruswick belonged to Jervaulx, and *Hoveton* near Skiplam grange and *Steinton* near Bilsdale grange to Rievaulx.[59] Except for *Akebar* these places were 'waste' in 1086, and none appears in Kirkby's Inquest or the *Nomina Villarum*. For the rest of the country, the list of extinct villages in Lincolnshire compiled by C. W. Foster and T. Langley includes some that were possibly replaced by granges belonging to Kirkstead[60] and Vaudey,[61]

[52] *C.Ch.R.*, AD 1257-1300, pp. 264-65. The abbot was lord of Rotherham in 1316.

[53] *C.Cl.R.*, AD 1279-88, p. 230.

[54] *C.R.R.*, 7: 75-76.

[55] *Chart. F.*, 2: 486-88 (1154-89 conf.). The abbot was the only contributor to the fifteenth (1301) in Marton.

[56] There are some earthworks, possibly of the vill (Beresford, 'Lost villages of Yorkshire,' *Yorks. Arch. Jour.*, 38 (1952-54): 236).

[57] *Chart. F.*, 1: 75.

[58] *Coucher K.*, pp. 113-15, 130-32.

[59] *Hoveton* (*Chart. R.*, pp. 81, 113 [1151]) and *Steinton* (*E.Y.C.*, 3: 481 [1145-52]; *Chart. R.*, p. 260) were fully held.

[60] *Cotes*, given to Kirkstead 1135-54. The grange here was called Linwood "and that name soon superseded Cotes" (Foster and Langley, *Lincolnshire Domesday*, p. liv).

Southorpe, in the parish of Gayton le Wold and "perhaps represented on the map by Gayton grange which formerly belonged to Kirkstead abbey" (ibid., p. lxvi). The abbey had two carucates in Gayton in the time of Henry II (*Mon. Angl.*, 5: 417) and the grange was confirmed in 1252 (*C.Ch.R.*, AD 1226-57, p. 383).

[61] *Little Lavington*, in the parish of Lavington (Foster and Langley, *Lincolnshire*

and W. G. Hoskins has cited a well-documented case involving Merevale (Warwickshire).[62] The Welsh house of Margam also is known to have destroyed villages and farmsteads, both near at hand and in the Vale of Glamorgan, during the second half of the twelfth century and early in the thirteenth.[63]

The remaining places listed in Appendix 2 (c) present no special points of interest but have the following in common — they are now very small, at the most a hamlet;[64] the Cistercian holding was large, in some cases the whole place, and lay at the centre or close to the centre of a grange; all are mentioned in 1086, but for the most part are poorly represented in surveys of the thirteenth and early fourteenth centuries. It is not suggested that all, or even most, were depopulated, but rather that many probably shrank as granges were organized. About half are noted by M.W. Beresford in his survey of lost villages.[65] A few other places are collected in Appendix 2 (d); they differ from the above only in that it has proved impossible to associate them with estates described as granges before 1300.

Probably all granges founded alongside village communities witnessed some displacement of population, and most cases of outright depopulation must be attributed to their presence. The more numerous evictions of the fifteenth century provide no exact parallel, for the earlier ones were at least as much for corn as for wool. Evictions and forced exchanges of property by the Cistercians were most common in the twelfth century, during the first fifty years of the early houses, but continued well into the thirteenth. When a grange superseded a vill, an important physical nucleus remained,

---

Domesday, pp. lix-lx). Richard I confirmed to Vaudey the grange of *Parva Lavintona* which contained four carucates (*Mon. Angl.*, 5: 490).

Sudtone, in the parish of Great Sutton; Kirkstead held all or most of it and the grange of *Stratton* is mentioned in 1252 (*C.Ch.R.*, AD 1226-57, p. 383).

[62] *Essays in Leicestershire History* (Liverpool, 1950), p. 92. Weston apparently disappeared during the last three-quarters of the thirteenth century after Merevale had acquired the whole place and established a grange. Elsewhere Hoskins notes that Garendon (Leicestershire) destroyed *Dishley* to make way for a grange (1180) (*The Making of the English Landscape* (London, 1955), p. 81).

[63] Described in some detail by F. G. Cowley, 'The Cistercian economy in Glamorgan, 1130-1349,' *Morgannwg*, 11 (1967): 13-15.

[64] Dacre (Fountains) and Rookwith (Jervaulx), a little larger than the rest, are included because not only were they granges but they were entirely owned by the monks. *Chart. F.*, 1: 203; *Mon. Angl.*, 5: 308, 576; *V.C.H. (Yorkshire, N.R.*, 1914), 1: 346.

[65] 'Lost villages of Yorkshire,' *Yorks. Arch. Jour.*, 37 (1951): 474-91; 38 (1952-54): 44-70, 215-240, 280-309. The grid references of the others are: Warsil (235660), Brimham (227633), Sandburn (665592), Birkby (357396), Barrowby (334478), Stainton (891530), Ellenthorpe (819499), Wassand (175462), Rowton (135400), Stilton (599845), Wildon (516781), *Shitlington* (parish: 270158).

and this partly accounts for the fact that few are entirely unrepresented today and some are large villages. The majority, however, are small places. By 1300 the colonizing vigour of the Middle Ages was spent and settlement was tending to contract. In the second wave of depopulation shrunken places were particularly vulnerable, and occasionally what the monks had started was completed by later landlords.[66]

THE CISTERCIAN GRANGE

The word 'grange' is here used in the sense of a directly cultivated and relatively consolidated land holding with its own nucleus of farm buildings. A. Dimier observed that "le sens de ce mot a suivi une évolution analogue à celle du mot *curtis* qui, n'étant primitivement autre chose qu'une cour entourée de bâtiments d'exploitation, en vint peu à peu à signifier l'ensemble des bâtiments, puis le domaine tout entier ... ."[67] Such estates apparently were a feature of the Cistercian economy almost from the first.[68] Furthermore, the concept of the *grangia* was adopted by several of the other new monastic orders and thus spread very widely during the twelfth and thirteenth centuries.[69]

A distinction has sometimes been drawn between the home farm and the more distant grange. The former was often comparatively large, and alone perhaps was never leased out, but there seems to have been no essential difference between them. The "*grangia juxta abbatiam*" normally comprised part of the original endowment and was sometimes named after

[66] Beresford ('Deserted villages of Warwickshire,' pp. 65-66, 82-83, 88, 100) gives some possible examples of late depopulation by Cistercian houses (Stoneleigh, Pipewell, Combe). See also I. S. Leadam, 'The Inquisition of 1517: Inclosures and evictions,' *T.R.H.S.*, 2nd ser., 7 (1893): 241 (Kirkstall); p. 252 (Meaux, Kirkstall).

[67] 'Grange,' *Dictionnaire de droit canonique* (Paris, 1953), 5: col. 987. See also K. Hofmann, 'Grangien,' *Lexikon für Theologie und Kirche* (Freiburg, 1932), vol. 4; and P. Hofmeister 'Grangien,' *Die Religion in Geschichte und Gegenwart*, 3rd. ed. (Tübingen, 1958), 2: col. 1825 ("wirtschaftszentrum"). H. Dubled has discussed the terms *grangia*, *cellarium*, *curia*, *curtis* and *locus* in 'Aspects de l'économie Cistercienne en Alsace au XIIe siècle,' *Revue d'histoire ecclésiastique*, 54 (1959): 767. Recent studies of granges belonging to several Continental houses are reviewed in *Citeaux: Commentarii Cistercienses*, 24 (1973): 79-91; 25 (1974):79-88; 26 (1975): 99-105.

[68] *Curtis* (court) is used in the *Exordium Cisterciensis Coenobii* (1119) (Migne, *PL*, 166: 1508A). The first reference to *grangiae* in the statutes of the order occurs in 1134: "*terras a saecularium hominum habitatione semotas*" (*Statuta*, 1: 14).

[69] J. Buhot thought that Savigny worked "granges" in the first half of the twelfth century, but the term *grangia* was not used until after 1147 when the house was joined to the order of Cîteaux (L'abbaye normande de Savigny, chef de l'ordre et fille de Cîteaux,' *Le Moyen Age*, 3e sér., 7/vol. 46 (1936): 110.

the abbey itself. In cases where a monastic site was evacuated, the area around about was often subsequently worked as a grange. This was also provided for where a community fell below the statutory minimum of thirteen members.[70]

The distribution of outlying granges depended upon where sufficient land was received or could be obtained by purchase or exchange. The ruling of the Chapter General that granges should be no more than a *dieta* or day's journey from the abbey[71] was very soon disregarded, if indeed it was ever observed (one of the granges of Clairvaux lay almost 100 miles away[72]). The idea of the restriction was that *conversi* and others living on a grange should be able to hear mass regularly. In 1255 Pope Alexander IV formally agreed to mass being celebrated at granges that were far from their respective abbey or a parish church;[73] but the main purpose of this seems to have been to regularize an existing state of affairs. The Chapter General also ruled that granges belonging to different houses should be at least two leagues (about eleven and a half kilometres) apart,[74] but this too was widely ignored.[75]

There are a number of early references to grants of land (*sedes*) for grange buildings, such as to Warden (ca.1139-54), Rievaulx (1150-60), Kirkstall (1152-62) and Fountains (1174-81). The actual buildings[76] at first met only the minimum requirements; but by the middle of the thirteenth century they were often both substantial and elaborate, sometimes hardly less impressive than the abbey itself. In parts of Europe, "elles ressemblaient plus à des forteresses qu'à paisibles bâtiments d'exploitation

[70] *Statuta*, 1: 111 (1189), 295 (1204), 350 (1208), 459 (1216); 2: 73 (1228).

[71] Ibid., 1: 14.

[72] R. Fossier, 'Les granges de Clairvaux et la règle cistercienne,' *Citeaux in de Nederlanden*, 6 (1955): 261 n. 13. For the economy of Clairvaux in general, see H. d'Arbois de Jubainville, *Etudes sur l'état intérieur des abbayes Cisterciennes, et principalement de Clairvaux au XIIe et au XIIIe siècle* (Paris, 1858). W. Maas noted that distant lands were sometimes granted to another house, especially a daughter house (*Les moines-défricheurs* (Moulins, 1944), p. 24). Nevertheless, Tilty (Essex) held (*ante* 1251) the grange of Thorrington, thirty miles away, "from the abbot and convent of Coggeshall" (only seventeen miles away) (*C.Ch.R.*, AD 1226-57, p. 359).

[73] For some time the order tried to prevent the erection of altars at granges (*Statuta*, 1: 87 (1180), 297-98 (1204), 307-8 (1205). Cf. ibid., 1: 436 (1215), and 2: 65 (1228).

[74] "*Grangiae autem diversarum abbatiarum distent inter se ad minus duabus leugis*"—ibid., 1: 20 (1134). The proximity of granges often gave rise to disputes—ibid., 126 (1190), 329 (1206), 341 (1207), 355 (1208); 2: 119 (1233).

[75] See Fossier, 'Les granges de Clairvaux,' pp. 260-61. The ordinance was revoked in 1278 (*Statuta*, 3: 175).

[76] Discussed in more detail and in a wider context by C. Platt, *The Monastic Grange in Medieval England: a Reassessment* (London, 1969), pp. 16-48.

Plate 3

The abbey of Beaulieu's barn at the grange of Great Coxwell, Berkshire.
The building dates from the first half of the thirteenth century.
(Copyright © 1965 by Walter Horn and Ernest Born;
reprinted by permission of the University of California Press.)

agricole."[77] As much as 500 marks was spent on Meaux's grange of Skerne between 1249 and 1269. The fully developed Cistercian grange was usually arranged around one or two courts (*curtes*) and the buildings varied according to the size and economy of the dependent estate. Some stone structures have survived to the present day, used either in farming or, more rarely, as dwellings.

Granges in England and Wales commonly included several sheep-folds and sometimes a wool shed (*lanaria*). In 1235-49 the grange of Croo consisted of a granary or general storehouse (*horreum*), a barn, a *domus principalis* for the resident staff, stables and byres.[78] By 1246 some of Louth Park's granges included a hall, a dormitory, a guest room, barns, cowsheds and sheep cotes.[79] Since most granges were predominantly arable holdings, the barn and granary must have been very prominent.[80] When the buildings at Skerne were destroyed about the middle of the thirteenth century they held some 400 quarters of grain.[81] After the Cistercians began to acquire churches, tithe barns were located on convenient properties. Many granges seem to have had a simple oratory and some, in later years, a chapel.[82] Other structures are occasionally mentioned — water mills (for grain and fulling) and an early windmill (ca. 1237),[83] dairies, forges or workshops (*fabricas*), tanneries, and 'towers' (some granges were fortified). The courts were often surrounded by a wall or ditch, and some of the enclosed area might be worked as a kitchen garden.[84]

[77] F. Goblet, *Histoire des bois et forêts de Belgique* (Paris, 1927), 1: 175, 177. See also A. Heins and V. Fris, 'Les granges monumentales des anciennes abbayes des Dunes et de Ter Doest dans la Flandre maritime,' *Bulletijn der maatschapij van Geschied en Oudheidkunde te Gent*, 13 (1905): 65, 86 ff.; M. Aubert, 'La "grange d'eau" d'Hautecombe en Savoie,' *Bulletin Monumental*, 112 (1954): 89-94; H. de Segogne et Geneviève A. Maillé, *Abbayes Cisterciennes* (Paris, 1943), p. 44. Cf. *Statuta*, 2: 62.

[78] *Chron. M.*, 2: 48. For rulings on infirmaries at granges, see *Statuta*, 2: 398 (1253), 418 (1255).

[79] *Chron. L. P.*, p. 14.

[80] See W. Horn and E. Born, *The Barns of the Abbey of Beaulieu at its Granges of Great Coxwell and Beaulieu-St Leonards* (Berkeley and Los Angeles, 1965).

[81] *Chron. M.*, 2: 109-10 (1249-69). Tharlesthorpe produced 500 quarters of grain in 1245, 300 quarters in 1246; and Salthaugh 340 quarters in 1247. S. F. Hockey (*Account B.*, p. 25) tabulates the corn production of Beaulieu's granges for 1269-70; the amounts range from 30 to 500 or more quarters.

[82] T. Gray, 'Notes on the granges of Margam Abbey,' *Jour. Brit. Arch. Assoc.*, 9 (1903): 165-66 (1239); 11 (1905): 12, 25, 96; *Coucher W.*, 2: 428; *Chart. T.*, 1: 24; *Chart. Bl.*, p. lxv. A description (1296) of the lands of the grange of Baldersby (Fountains) refers to a *cultura* "near the chapel" (*Chart. F.*, 1: 110). This may once have been the church of the village of Baldersby which the monks depopulated.

[83] *Chart. T.*, 1: 13.

[84] *Rot. Hund.*, 2: 663 (1281); *Chron.* M., 2: 93; *Account B.*, p. 37.

The majority of Cistercian granges were founded during the twelfth century.[85] Seventy-four dating from 1200 or earlier are shown in Fig. 8.[86]

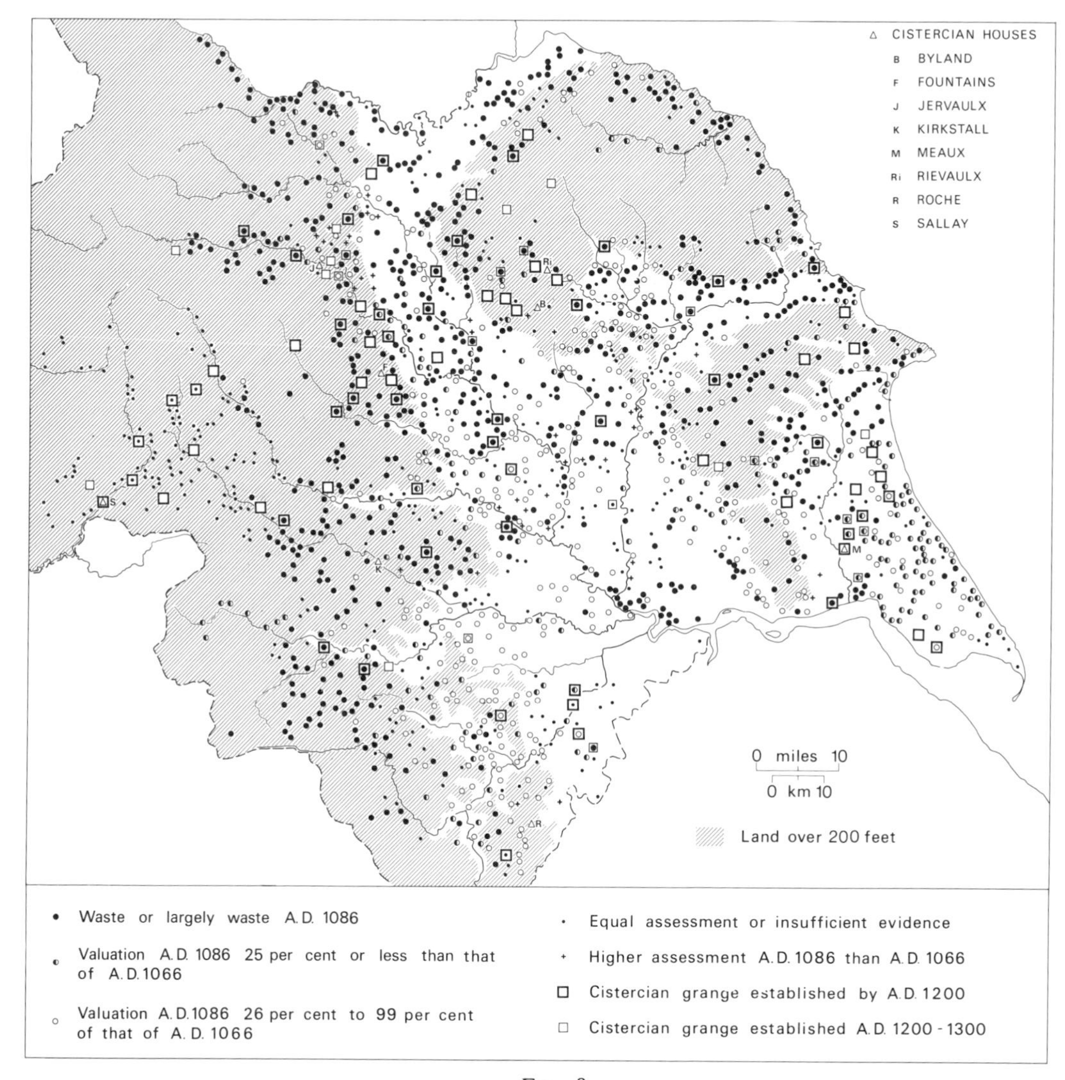

Fig. 8

'Wasted' holdings in Yorkshire (1086) and the distribution of Cistercian granges.

[85] There is a list of all known twelfth and thirteenth century granges in R. A. Donkin, 'The Cistercian grange in England in the 12th and 13th centuries,' *Studia Monastica*, 6 (1964): 124-38.

[86] In some cases the earliest reference to a grange can only be dated within a short period; where this falls on either side of 1200 the grange has been assigned to the twelfth century.

Most are named as *grangiae* for the first time in charters of the second half of the century, but it is clear that the work of developing such properties commenced almost as soon as a monastery was founded. A few belonging to Fountains and Rievaulx are mentioned in documents of the fifth and sixth decades of the twelfth century. On the other hand, granges were still being planned well into the middle of the thirteenth century and occasionally even later. Fig. 8 also shows twenty-six granges known from references dated 1200-1300. The earlier part of this period was a time of great activity on established holdings. We are told that the fourth abbot of Meaux (1197-1210) "*in grangias quoque plurima construxit aedificia.*" Six of Meaux's granges were founded 1151-60, two between 1160 and 1182, one "before 1197," one each between 1197 and 1210, and 1210 and 1220, two "before 1235," three between 1235 and 1249, and two "before 1249."[87] Altogether there were about 120 Cistercian *grangiae* in Yorkshire of which perhaps three-quarters were in existence by 1200.

Granges were more common in some parts of the country than others, and the number belonging to neighbouring houses also varied considerably. In well-settled areas the problem of assembling consolidated estates was particularly difficult. Such considerations help to explain the apparent relative scarcity of typical *grangiae* in southern England, although Beaulieu (Hampshire) and Waverley (Surrey), the first English house, each had fourteen by 1300. Elsewhere, between ten and fifteen was not unusual. Furness in Lancashire and Kirkstead in Lincolnshire each had at least sixteen, and Meaux and Fountains twenty-two and twenty-six respectively.

Although the stipulated distance (two Burgundian leagues) between granges was certainly not generally observed, it was almost unknown for any two belonging to different houses to lie within the same township. T. A. M. Bishop concluded that for a time both Fountains and Rievaulx had granges in Busby. Fountains' grange there was started early (1180-90), and eventually the monks had another at Dromonby, little more than one mile away. Rievaulx had a considerable amount of land in Busby, and at one point provisions were made in case it should absorb Fountains' holding, but its grange appears to have centred on Broughton (1180-8), a mile beyond Dromonby. Certainly, however, these properties were very close and might necessitate special agreements.[88] It was generally found

[87] J. S. Donnelly, 'Changes in the grange economy of English and Welsh Cistercian abbeys,' *Traditio*, 10 (1954): 435.

[88] *Chart. F.*, 1: 148-49. *Chart. R.* (pp. 175-76) includes an interesting general agreement between Byland and Rievaulx (*ante* 1167) and a special agreement between

convenient to leave the field clear for one house or other. Byland, for example, surrendered 150 acres in Sleningford to the monks of Fountains who had a grange there before the close of the twelfth century. Even small holdings belonging to different houses were not often long retained in the same place. Furthermore, precautions were sometimes taken against possible intrusion by members of other orders. When, some time between 1145 and 1160, the monks of Byland received half a carucate and five acres in North Cave the grantor also agreed not to favour any house of another order to Byland's disadvantage. On the other hand, Rievaulx in 1175 gave up land and the right to pasture 300 sheep in Willerby to the priory of Bridlington. The Cistercians had a holding here as early as 1152 but apparently failed to extend it, while the canons set about building up their estate (the term *grangia* was not used).[89]

The question of the relationship between areas of 'wasted' or neglected land and the distribution of Cistercian granges is particularly relevant in the case of Yorkshire. The situation arose largely as a result of deliberate devastation by the armies of William I in the autumn and winter of 1069-70. We read that the conqueror "went northward with all his force ... and completely laid waste the shire."[90] The results are to be found in Domesday Book where values are quoted for each manor for 1066 and 1086. The collective valuation of the North Riding of Yorkshire fell by eighty per cent, that of the West Riding by forty-seven per cent, and that of the East Riding by seventy-two per cent.[91] For Cheshire the comparable figure is twenty-nine per cent.[92] The Domesday evidence, plotted in Fig. 8, is based on two kinds of information: reports that certain holdings were 'waste' or 'largely waste'; and valuations for 1066 and 1086. There is reason to believe that the effects of such widespread destruction had not

---

Fountains and Rievaulx concerning certain unidentified *grangiae* in Cleveland (1170-1179). See also *Coucher F.*, 5: 475 (ca. 1220): between Furness and Sallay respecting granges at Winterburn and Stainton, about three miles apart.

[89] W. T. Lancaster, *Abstracts of the Charters and Other Documents Contained in the Chartulary of the Priory of Bridlington* (Leeds, 1912), pp. 100 ff., 114-15.

[90] *The Anglo Saxon Chronicle*, ed. B. Thorpe, R. S. 23 (London, 1861), 2: 174-75. See also *Radulphi de Coggeshall: Chronicon Anglicanum*, ed. J. Stevenson, R. S. 66 (London, 1875), pp. 1-2 (Ralph was abbot of the Cistercian house of Coggeshall from 1207 to 1218); T. A. M. Bishop, 'The Norman settlement of Yorkshire,' in *Studies in Medieval History Presented to F. M. Powicke*, ed. R. W. Hunt, et al. (Oxford, 1948), p. 2.

[91] Based on totals given in *V.C.H. (Yorkshire*, 1912), 2: 189. T. A. M. Bishop calculated that of the 1900 vills recorded in Domesday Book, about 850 were wasted, 300 partly wasted, and 400 understocked and greatly reduced in value since 1066.

[92] From data in *The Domesday Survey of Cheshire*, ed. J. Tait, Remains ..., n.s., 75 (Manchester: Chetham Society, 1916).

entirely disappeared by the time of the earliest Cistercian settlement here (Rievaulx 1132, Fountains 1132/5). Symeon of Durham (d. 1130) tells us that the district between York and Durham was so completely wasted that there was little or no cultivation for nine years: "*Interea, ita terra cultore destituta, lata ubique solitudo patebat per novem annos. Inter Eboracum et Dunelmum nusquam villa inhabitata.*"[93] Again, William of Malmesbury reported that the land for sixty miles around York was unproductive even in his own day (ca. 1130): "*humus, per sexaginta et eo amplius miliara, omnifariam inculta; nudum omnium solum usque ad hoc etiam tempus.*"[94]

These conditions formed the background to a new phase in the settlement of Yorkshire, one in which there was much assarting and much reorganization of holdings, leading in time to the full revival of farming. The Cistercian houses were well placed to play a prominent part in this work, something of which their founders and later benefactors were no doubt aware.[95] Rievaulx and Fountains each lay close to conspicuous clusters of wasted and low-value holdings, one in the western end of the Vale of Pickering, another covering the western half of the Vale of York and the neighbouring Pennine foothills from the river Nidd in the south to almost the borders of County Durham. The area around Fountains, according to the *Narratio de fundatione Fontanis*, had long been uninhabited: "*locum a cunctis retro seculis inhabitatum.*"[96] There is also evidence of loss of population along some of the dales, including lower Wensleydale and Airedale where the monks of Jervaulx (1150/56) and Kirkstall (1147/52) finally settled (it may well be that the presence of reclaimable land played some part in the decision of the original colonies at Fors and Barnoldswick to migrate).[97] Meaux lay in Holderness where

[93] *Symonis monachi opera omnia*, ed. T. Arnold, R. S. 75 (London, 1885), 2: 188.

[94] *Willelmi Malmesbiriensis de Gestis Regum Anglorum libri quinque*, ed. W. Stubbs, R. S. 90 (London, 1889), 2: 308-9.

[95] Comparable devastation occurred in Stephen's reign, particularly in the South, the south Midlands and the Fen district. William of Newburgh (*Historia rerum Anglicarum*, in *Chronicles of the Reigns of Stephen, Henry II, and Richard I*, ed. R. Howlett, R. S. 82 (London, 1884), 1: 53) observed that more religious houses were founded under Stephen than over the preceding 100 years. Forty-three Cistercian houses belong to the period 1135-54; twenty-four of these between 1143, about the time when the anarchy reached its height, and 1154. From ca. 1145 the focus of Cistercian settlement began to shift towards the south Midlands and the margins of the Fens.

[96] *Mem. F.*, 1: 32 (based on the statements of an eye witness).

[97] T. A. M. Bishop has argued that after 1069-70 the dales and poorer areas generally were drained of population (leaving deserted or partly deserted villages) in attempts to recolonize potentially more fertile areas, especially in the Vale of York ('Norman settlement of Yorkshire,' p. 6).

few holdings were described as 'waste' but many had dropped heavily in value. Byland was not far from the northern part of the Vale of York, the area specially referred to by Symeon of Durham, and most of its arable lay there rather than in Pickering.

The English Cistercians generally occupied sites within the existing pattern of rural settlement, but in Yorkshire it is necessary to make allowance for the possible effects of a widespread retreat of settlement. The degree of recovery by ca. 1135 cannot be estimated precisely, but it is very possible that certain houses stood, when first occupied, on the outer margins of settlement or even some way beyond. This is most likely in the cases of Fountains, Rievaulx and Jervaulx.

About forty-four per cent of all known twelfth-century granges lay in territories that were 'waste' or 'largely waste' or were of very low relative value in 1086. Between fifty and sixty per cent of the granges belonging to Rievaulx and Fountains were started in such areas. Some of the early buildings, like the monasteries themselves, probably stood on the very edge of settlement around the Pennines and the North Yorkshire Moors.

Even before the close of the twelfth century, granges had been developed in a wide variety of country. Those recorded for the first time after 1200 consolidate rather than extend the distribution. The northern Vale of York and the foothills to east and west, the area of most severe devastation, contained the largest number of granges. Indeed the largest concentration of Cistercian-controlled arable ca. 1300 lay in this area, that is between Fountains, Jervaulx and Byland. These houses were the most important landowners in the narrowest part of the Vale. It is an area of good loamy soil derived chiefly from lacustrine deposits and from glacial sands and gravels. Here, if anywhere, "the work of the Cistercians in Yorkshire in the thirteenth and fourteenth centuries may be said to anticipate the whole subsequent development of English agriculture."[98] Kirkstall's arable lay around the abbey itself, in the valley of the Aire and on the interfluve of gritstone and shale between the Aire and the Wharfe; the bulk was worked from several closely situated granges, part of a broad chain along the Pennine foothills. Another group, belonging to Fountains, Sallay and Kirkstall, lay in the Craven depression. The soils of the lower part of this area are almost entirely derived from heavy glacial drift, and the relatively high rainfall (40-45″ per annum) makes arable farming difficult. On the other hand, the surrounding limestone uplands provided excellent grazing. There must also have been a considerable pastoral bias in the case of granges along the middle and upper dales: Micklethwaite and *Elam* in

[98] R. A. L. Smith, *Collected Papers* (London, 1947), p. 104.

Airedale, Askwith in Wharfedale, Dacre and Bouthwaite in Nidderdale, Snilesworth in upper Ryedale, and Rievaulx's grange in Bilsdale (North Yorkshire Moors). Bouthwaite (confirmed 1189-99), Snilesworth (early thirteenth century) and Bilsdale (1280) even stood beyond the limits of settlement in 1066 as recorded in Domesday Book. Although the typical grange was a predominantly arable estate there were clearly marked exceptions to this, and not only in the uplands. Some of Meaux's granges in Holderness appear to have been largely pastoral.[99] Rievaulx's holdings in the Vale of Pickering were suited to mixed farming. Henry II gave the monks a stretch of waste, presumably natural, within the forest of Pickering ("*totum vastum ... et totam pasturam*"), adding the right to cultivate.[100] The result is probably to be found in the Hundred Rolls of 1275-6 where it is recorded that the grange of Marishes included 300 acres of arable and the same amount of pasture.[101]

Until ca. 1250 most Cistercian houses were constantly receiving grants of land of all kinds: open-field strips, cultures held in severalty, patches of waste, meadow and woodland, scattered in perhaps dozens of villages.[102] Some of this property was both considerable in extent and conveniently situated. But the pattern as a whole left much to be desired, and while the monks worked their estates directly they strived by assarting and by purchase and exchange to produce a more rational and efficient arrangement. The general aim was to concentrate holdings to form consolidated estates. This was not an entirely novel procedure; the benefits of consolidation had long been obvious to laymen and ecclesiastics alike, although the difficulties were usually considerable. The new monastic orders, and above all the

[99] Ca. 1400 one was entirely and another partly laid down to meadow and pasture (Bishop, 'Monastic granges,' p. 193 n. 2).

[100] R. B. Turton, *The Honor and Forest of Pickering*, North Riding Rec. Soc., Publs., n.s., 2 (1895): 91 (1158).

[101] *Rot. Hund.*, 1: 107. In 1206 the dean and chapter of York claimed the sum of "*XXti solidos bonorum et legalium sterlingorum*" in tithes from the grange of *Kekemarays* (parish of Pickering) (*Chart. R.*, p. 255). Part of the seven carucates in the parish of Thornton and the three in the parish of Kirby Misperton (both adjoining Pickering), cultivated by Rievaulx in 1308-9, may have centred on Marishes (W. Brown and A. H. Thompson, eds., *The Register of William Greenfield, Lord Archbishop of York, 1306-1315*, Publications of the Surtees Society, 153 (London, 1938), 5: 239.

[102] After the middle of the century, the number of grants declined sharply; then, in 1279, the Statute of Mortmain forbade the alienation of property to monasteries without special permission. See L. A. Desmond, 'The Statute *De Viris Religiosis* and the English monks of the Cistercian affiliation,' *Citeaux: Commentarii Cistercienses*, 25 (1974): 137-55. Combe (Warwickshire, not Wiltshire) was the first house to obtain permission (August 1280), and there were seventeen others between 1282 and 1292.

Cistercians, were remarkable in that their ideal was not to make the best of communal husbandry, to build up substantial and fairly compact demesnes, but to cultivate independently large, clearly defined *blocs* of land which in some cases cut across township boundaries. The statutes of the Cistercian order prescribed isolation from peasant farming, and for some time tenanted property formed no essential part of the scheme; holdings were to be worked by *conversi* and hired workmen[103] under the supervision of a *magister grangiae*. Nevertheless the completely consolidated estate seems to have been the exception rather than the rule, and some of the later granges in particular remained quite fragmented. Tenants, from whom labour services could, if necessary, be claimed, were rarely entirely absent, and some contact with peasant agriculture was inevitable. The work of consolidation was indeed far from complete when adverse market conditions and the mounting difficulty of recruiting *conversi* made direct exploitation far less attractive. We have, however, got ample evidence of the monks' aims and methods over the period ca.1150-1250.

It was unusual for a grange to be carved entirely out of primeval waste. As we have seen, Rievaulx transformed a tract in the Vale of Pickering into a grange of perhaps a thousand acres of improved land. Salthaugh in Holderness was begun in 1150-53 on a stretch of pasture ("*totae pasturae de Saltehache*") and Blanch, also belonging to Meaux, on about a hundred acres "throughout which no one had ever enjoyed rights of common." Almost certainly, too, some of the Pennine granges with their extensive sheep walks were largely consolidated from the first. The lowland granges as a whole present a more diverse picture. Some corresponded to entire village territories which, when granted, had probably recovered little if at all from the devastations of the late eleventh century. Here the monks faced the prospect of extensive reclearing. This is almost certainly what happened at Bramley, Brimham and Aldburgh, all belonging to Fountains, and probably other places too. Where peasant farmers remained or had

[103] *Statuta*, 1: 14 (1134): "*per conversos ... et mercenarios.*" There is a reference in the *Dialogus inter Cluniacensem et Cisterciensem Monachum* (second half of the twelfth century) to "*mercenarii nostri*" (E. Martène and U. Durand, *Thesaurus novus anecdotorum* (Paris, 1717), 5: 1623-24. An account of expenses at Kingswood, 1241, includes "In pay of mercenaries to the Feast of St. Michael ... £24.16.7," and the wage bill for 1255, mostly relating to granges, mentions ploughmen, carters, harvesters, horsemen, ox drivers, and swine-herds (*Docs. K.*, pp. 200, 209-13). In 1231 special provision was made for monks to live and to reap corn at Cwmhir's granges of *Cubalva* and *Caernaf* (*C.Cl.R.*, AD 1227-31, p. 547). Platt (*Monastic Grange*, pp. 76-93) discusses the staffing of the grange. See also the important analysis of Beaulieu's labour force (1269-70), including 67 or 68 *conversi*, in *Account B.*, pp. 20-23, 315 (*tabula mercenariorum*), 317 (*tabula stipendiorum*).

returned by the time a vill fell into the hands of the Cistercians they might be expelled in a single operation if the land was granted *en bloc*, more gradually if it was acquired piecemeal. Or, alternatively, they might be kept to provide an additional work-force.

Consolidation also proceeded through the exchange of strips and of land held in severalty. Land received in exchange served to extend properties that were already granges or that later became granges. Only one or two dated references to exchanges are later than 1300; they belong almost entirely to the period of grange formation. The earliest discovered fall between 1150 and 1160 (Meaux). The evidence from the second half of the thirteenth century mostly concerns granges that were started relatively late, for example Arnold (1197-1210), Routh (1210-20) and Cranswick (1235-49). Exchanges, of course, only implied the reorganization of holdings; a monastery's total arable acreage was not necessarily increased. It might even be reduced if the monks were willing to accept less than they gave. Thus Rievaulx gave ten acres in Wombleton for five in Skiplam where it maintained a grange; and Meaux released eight acres of arable and meadow "*in diversis locis de Suttona*" (1235-49) in exchange for four acres elsewhere in the same place. In such cases the monks were effectively buying land, just as many so-called grants were really purchases.[104]

The majority of exchange agreements convey the minimum of information; it may only be apparent that one or two *culturae* are named more often than others. Some notices are, however, very explicit. In the chartulary of Fountains under Malham, the site of a grange confirmed 1189-99, we read, "He [the grantor] has exchanged with them [the monks] a certain part of his land and the land of his men living in Malham, namely an acre for an acre, so that their [the monks'] cultures shall be together in the same field, separate from the grantor's." And under Liversedge, following a grant to Fountains of a bovate: "if the monks should wish to have the land of the said bovate together (*insimul*) he will make it up to them to the amount of so much land in four cultures." Another agreement shows the same house consolidating its estate in Kettlewell in upper Wharfedale: "confirmation by William de Arches to the monks of the exchange which they made with him and his men of the land of those six bovates which they have of his fee in Kettlewell, so that the monks may have acre for acre together beside (*juxta*) that land which Walter de Faukenberg ex-

[104] In 1190 the Chapter General tried to curb the buying of land ("*omni emptione terrarum*"), the order having, by this time, acquired a reputation for cupidity (*Statuta*, 1: 117; see also p. 428 (1214), relaxed p. 449 (1216)). *Chart. Bl.* includes many examples of "grants" for which money was given or debts settled.

changed with them."[105] The nucleus of what eventually became the grange of Bolton, belonging to Rievaulx, comprised four and a half acres of arable and twenty-one acres of uncultivated and wooded land (1173). Five tenants who had holdings (*singulas portiones*) within the twenty-five and a half acres were persuaded to relinquish them, receiving from the monastery's benefactor other land in the fields of Bolton;[106] furthermore, the monks were permitted to surround the whole area with a dyke and to assart the uncultivated portion. By the terms of another exchange, Rievaulx obtained half an acre lying "*inter culturas eorum*" in the grange of Bolton. Likewise land that Meaux received by exchange in Dunnington (1221-35), within or close to Moor grange, lay between property that it already owned.[107] Most explicit of all perhaps is a passage in the *Chronica de Melsa* in which we are told that by means of a certain exchange (1286-1310) cultures in the grange of Arnold were consolidated (*integriores*) and thus held more conveniently (*ad commodum*).[108]

The advantages of consolidation applied as much to meadow as to arable. An agreement concluded between Fountains and Sallay in 1251 contained the clause: "If they [the monks of Sallay] are able so to arrange with their free men of Litton that they [the monks] have their own portion separate in one place in that meadow, the monks of Fountains will be well content."[109]

Cistercian houses received many parcels of land measured in acres and often recently asserted and held in severalty. It is sometimes clearly stated that the land was in one piece, such as a certain sixty acres granted to Fountains near the grange of Sleningford.[110] But even where this was not so, the problem of consolidation was not likely to be as great as in the case of bundles of open-field strips.[111] Moreover the monks were assarting on

[105] *Chart. F.*, 1: 380 (the nearest *grangia* was Kilnsey, about three miles downstream; confirmed 1156). Early in the thirteenth century William of Kirby confirmed all the exchanges that had taken place between the monks of Fountains and the men of Kirby Wiske (*Chart. F.*, 1: 306).

[106] *Chart. R.*, p. 86.

[107] *Chron. M.*, 1: 424. See also *Chart. W.*, p. 40 (1200-20); *C.A.D.*, 4: 3 (Cleeve); *Chart. T.*, 1: 63 (1190-1200), 11-12 (1210-30).

[108] *Chron. M.*, 2: 217.

[109] *Chart. F.*, 1: 321. Cf. *Docs. R.*, pp. 41 (134), 42 (136), 50 (161), 54 (169), 56 (175, 176).

[110] *Chart. F.*, 2: 662, 787-88. Thame was confirmed, 1154-89, in thirty-six acres near Ot Moor "without intermixture of any other lands" (*Mon. Angl.*, 5: 403-4). See also *Chart. W.*, p. 123 (ca. 1180-1200).

[111] Almost all the grants to Newminster were measured in acres. Bishop ('Monastic granges,' p. 211) refers to the township of North Cowton which included a grange belonging to Fountains from a very early date (confirmed 1145-6). The holding was built up

their own account, and new land was taken in around the margins of and between existing arable, both to extend and to consolidate such estates. There are also many references to the purchase of land alongside property already owned, and a high proportion of these notices concern granges. The aim throughout was the same: to accumulate land in certain selected areas, to form compact estates, and to farm these directly and, so far as possible, independently.

Granges varied in size as much as in degree of consolidation. Just when a particular property came to be described as a *grangia* probably depended on a variety of circumstances, but principally on its size and degree of consolidation relative to the monastery's estates as a whole and possibly to other, neighbouring tenements. An extensive sheep run might never be described as a *grangia*, and cattle stations were generally called *vaccariae*. On the other hand, comparatively large arable or mixed farms were almost invariably *grangiae*. So far as a comparison with neighbouring holdings is concerned, the Yorkshire Lay Subsidy of 1301[112] is instructive. The Cistercian contribution in a particular township was usually well above that demanded of anyone else. The amount *pro grangia* averaged over £2, but there was a considerable range above and below this. The granges of Baldersby, Marton and Aldburgh, corresponding to entire townships, were assessed at £6.16.0, £6.6.9 and £4.3.6 respectively, Dromonby at only 18s.1d. out of a total of £1.12.4, involving five contributors.

T. A. M. Bishop calculated that the average Cistercian grange amounted to between three and four hundred (arable) acres. This was about the size of Crosby (belonging to Rievaulx); Aldburgh and Kirby Wiske (Fountains); Osgodby and Murton (Byland); Ellington, Hutton Hang and Diddersley (Jervaulx). Fourteen of Meaux's granges contained altogether 6500 acres,[113] an average of 460 acres. Two of its later granges, Routh (1210-20) and Sutton (1249-69), had, however, only about a hundred acres of arable apiece. Within a decade of being founded Meaux possessed approximately thirteen hundred acres; by 1400 the total stood at 19,600,[114] although much of this was then leased out.

---

from numerous small grants of land (*Chart. F.*, 1: 173-203) located in more than forty cultures but principally in three. Although the monks demised land here before 1301 they almost invariably retained what they had accumulated in these three cultures.

[112] W. Brown, ed., *Yorkshire Lay Subsidy... Collected 30 Edward I (1301)*, Yorks. Arch. Soc., Rec. Ser., 21 (Leeds, 1896)—(a fifteenth). The extant portion covers little more than the North Riding. All temporal goods, whether belonging to ecclesiastics or laymen, were taxed.

[113] Bishop, 'Monastic granges,' p. 209.

[114] *Chron. M.*, 1: xxiii. 3: lxiii.

The full acreage of a grange with 400 acres of arable might well approach a thousand acres. At Tharlesthorpe, which was started on "500 acres of demesne" (1188), we are told that 321 acres of arable, 100 acres of meadow, and 152 acres of pasture were destroyed by the waters of the Humber ca. 1318. Fountains' grange of Bradley amounted in 1497 (having been leased out in 1487) to "1000 acres of arable, 2000 acres of pasture, 100 acres of meadow, 300 acres of wood, and 1000 acres of moor."[115] Wharram, which belonged to Meaux, eventually (1396) included approximately 1100 acres of arable and 200 acres of meadow. Skerne (1210-20) comprised 998 acres; 409 of these were valued at 20d. per acre, 422 at 12d., and 167 at 6d. The entire territory of Old Byland belonged (1142-3) to the monks of Byland; according to Kirkby's Inquest (1284-5) this contained eight carucates, and it had been worked as a grange since 1146. Fountains' estate in Wheldrake amounted (after much assarting by the monks) to ten carucates and Jervaulx's home grange to six.[116] Baldersby's 800 acres of improved land (1296) may have been "the largest or most productive single tenement in the North Riding."[117] A survey of this grange in 1296 refers to several cultures that are earlier named in grants, suggesting that the layout of the former village lands had been at least in part retained. Three 'fields' are also mentioned but, judging by the distribution of crops, they probably did not form the basis of a rotation.

There seems to have been an unusually large number of very substantial arable granges in Yorkshire, more particularly in the Vale of York and the lower dales. The *Ledger Book* of Vale Royal (Cheshire) describes six granges under the year 1336. One was entirely, and another partly, leased out; the rest had either two or three carucates and also some pasture or meadow. In eleven granges belonging to Furness in Lancashire ca. 1292 there were only ten and a half carucates, but then the estates of this house were largely pastoral and the monks relied on Ireland as a source of grain. In 1325, Sibton in Suffolk had two large home granges (785 and 855 acres of arable, 818 and 963 acres in all) ; one of moderate size (375/562 acres); two that were rather small (210/256 acres, and 192/205 acres); and one that was very small (74/78 acres).[118] Elsewhere, there were cer-

[115] C. T. Clay, 'Bradley, a grange of Fountains,' *Yorks. Arch. Jour.*, 29 (1929): 102, 105.

[116] *Mon. Angl.*, 5: 571: "*Jorevallem, ubi nunc est bona grangia cum sex carucis quae vocatur vallis grangia...*" (twelfth century).

[117] Bishop, 'Monastic granges,' p. 209.

[118] *Docs. S.*, p. 148.

tainly a few granges equal to or not far short of any in Yorkshire. Vaudey's South grange contained "*sexies centum acras terrae arabilis*" in 1189; by 1275 it amounted to eight carucates and 500 acres of woodland and pasture.[119] The *Taxatio Ecclesiastica* ca. 1291 names several granges with over five carucates, and a few with more than ten. Some of these were home farms. The Cistercians did not recognise an upper limit of size for the mixed or arable *grangia*, but in fact a thousand acres of tillage was about the maximum. Even for the wealthiest and best organized house, a single farm much larger than this might have proved unmanageable, if only on account of the amount of labour required. In any case, the period of development of the grange lasted at most only about one hundred and fifty years.[120]

There is comparatively little direct evidence of improvements in arable farming by Cistercian houses. For most of the twelfth and thirteenth centuries, the monks commanded an adequate labour force and may be assumed to have directed it intelligently. The *Account Book* of Beaulieu (1269-70) reveals an extraordinarily systematic approach to estate management. Monastic communities could afford to adopt the long view in working their estates and presumably were in a better position than most to take advantage of such agricultural treatises as Walter of Henley's *Husbandry* and Robert Grosseteste's *Rules* (both written about the middle of the thirteenth century). In travelling between houses[121] the monks had an opportunity to observe improved methods and to obtain new varieties of crops.[122] Unfortunately, one cannot expect land charters to shed much light on such matters. Grants of pasture for sheep or cattle sometimes include directions for the disposal of manure and it is clear that its importance was fully appreciated. By the standards of the time Cistercian estates must have had a favourable ratio of stock to land, and when sheep

[119] *Rot. Hund.*, 1: 260.

[120] On the question of size, cf. C. Higounet, 'Les types d'exploitation cisterciennes et prémontrées du XIIIe siècle et leur rôle dans la formation de l'habitat et des paysages ruraux,' *Géographie et Histoire Agraires* (*Annales de l'Est*, mémoire no. 21; Nancy, 1959), p. 261: grange of Vaulerent, 380-90 hectares (950-75 acres); also Heins and Fris, 'Granges monumentales,' p. 76: examples of 420-780 *mensuris* (462-858 acres).

[121] Abbots were supposed to visit daughter houses once each year and, in most cases, to attend the annual Chapter General at Cîteaux. Neither duty was invariably executed. On the other hand, ordinary monks are from time to time reported travelling on the internal business of a house.

[122] G. G. Coulton maintained that "the Warden pear came from Burgundy and was popularized in England by the monks of Warden" (*The Medieval Village* (Cambridge, 1925), p. 217).

and cattle stations lay far from any considerable stretch of arable, manure was probably carted away. The earliest reference to marling is in a confirmation of Tintern's foundation charter (1131). A grant to Dore in 1272 included marl, shingle and gravel. About the same time, the monks of Stanlaw were allowed to marl their assarts in a particular stretch of woodland.[123] The records of Beaulieu and Fountains also contain several references to marling.[124] Moreover, behind all such improvements lay the superior organization of the grange.

The advantages of consolidation, ownership in severalty and enclosure are briefly summarized in a charter to Warden. When, between 1190 and 1207, this house received twelve acres in Sandy the grantor agreed that they could be enclosed "so as to be better managed."[125] Where tied to a system of communal husbandry the monks could achieve little, and they enclosed whenever and wherever they could. The greatest opportunity existed where the grange simply replaced an entire township. More commonly, enclosure followed piecemeal consolidation. In 1325 two of Sibton's granges were more than half enclosed (311 acres enclosed: 218 unenclosed; and 144: 97), two slightly less than half (67: 83, and 41: 56), and one remained largely unenclosed (131: 641).[126] Direct evidence of enclosure belongs largely to the twelfth and thirteenth centuries. The chronicle of Meaux provides examples from the first to the final quarter of the thirteenth century. In places, however, the Cistercians were still enclosing long after this. Thus Byland in 1380 was allowed "to enclose 100 acres of land and pasture adjacent to the monastery,"[127] and some years earlier Fountains obtained permission to enclose land in Thorpe Underwood for "up to 100 years."[128] The bulk of surviving notices refer simply to "land," but non-arable generally appears to have been singled out (pasture, wood, waste, moor and meadow). The area involved was mostly a few acres, sometimes only recently cleared. Enclosure of considerable

[123] *Coucher W.*, 2: 405. Marl is a calcareous clay and might be applied on fresh ground to reduce acidity. One of Robertsbridge's rents (fixed 1536-7) included "four waggonloads of chalk" (R. H. d'Elboux, ed., *Surveys of the Manors of Robertsbridge, Sussex*, Sussex Record Society, Publs., 47 (Lewes, 1944), p. 183).

[124] *Account B.*, p. 104 (1269-70). In an expense account of Fountains (1456-7) forty-nine loads of marl are mentioned. Marl also appears in a list of carriage charges for the following year; the tenants of the abbey at Dishforth in the Vale of York led sixty-nine loads to land still farmed by the monks (*Mem. F.*, 3: 14, 58).

[125] *Chart. W.*, p. 181: "*fossare et ad se includere et sicut voluerint melius custodire.*"

[126] *Docs. S.*, p. 14.

[127] *C.P.R.*, AD 1377-81, p. 433.

[128] *Chart. F.*, 2: 724 (1361).

areas of arable was probably largely confined to granges[129] where it could easily escape being mentioned. Boundaries were marked by a ditch and bank (*fossatum*), or by a hedge (*sepes*), or wall. When Bradley grange was leased out by Fountains it was stipulated that the fences, ditches and stone walls were to be maintained. Since consolidation was rarely achieved in a single operation and properties were extended by assarting, boundaries were probably often readjusted.

The *grangia* was the most important single contribution of the new monastic orders, and particularly of the Cistercians, to the landscape and economy of the twelfth and thirteenth centuries. Throughout Europe it formed the basis of their agrarian operations. The emphasis upon the consolidation of holdings, some of the means employed to achieve this, and the importance of the grange in a system of agriculture, had no contemporary parallel. And the activities for which the Cistercians are perhaps best known, land reclamation and sheep-farming, were closely connected with the formation and management of such estates.

[129] The monks of Fountains had a fosse around all they owned (at least one and a half carucates before 1216) in *Kirbyusburne* (Kirby Hall) ca. 1260 (*Chart. F.*, 1: 414); and Byland was once accused of enclosing a large area in Kilburn: "*magnam partem de solo quod pertinebat ad villam suam de Kilburne*" (*Mon. Angl.*, 5: 352). These places were close to the granges of Thorpe Underwood and Osgodby respectively.

3

Animal Husbandry

Cattle and Hides

In 1237 the monks and *conversi* of English Cistercian houses were forbidden to trade in wool and hides.[1] There is, however, little direct evidence of their marketing hides at this time. One possible shred to come to light is of much later date: a note among the records of the borough of Nottingham under the year 1397 showing that, in an action for debt, the abbot of Rufford had been "attached by a cart with tanned leather to answer."[2] On the other hand it is quite clear from surveys of stock, references to tanneries and vaccaries, and grants of pasture and rights of way that cattle commonly occupied an important place in the Cistercian economy, notwithstanding the well-known interest of the order as a whole and of certain houses in particular in the great wool trade. Sheep were not everywhere and at all times second to none among the monks' farm animals and perhaps only stood well to the fore during the middle period of Cistercian activity from ca. 1175 to ca. 1325.

Vaccaries and Tanneries

Some Yorkshire houses had established *vaccariae* (dairy farms or cattle-breeding stations) by the middle of the twelfth century (Appendix 3). The first known reference, to *Cambe* belonging to Byland, is dated 1140.

[1] *C.Cl.R.*, AD 1234-37, p. 532.

[2] [Nottingham], *Records of the Borough of Nottingham* (London, 1882), 1: 353. In 1427 Fountains sold to Robert de Burton of York 45 *dickers* (450 skins) of tanned leather (John Stanley Purvis, ed., *Monastic Chancery Proceedings: Yorkshire*, Yorkshire Archaeological Association, Record Series 88 (Huddersfield, 1934), p. 41.

Meaux had at least one in 1151 and others by the end of the century. Kirkstall, Jervaulx, Sallay, and Swineshead in Lincolnshire also are known to have possessed vaccaries before 1200. Considerably more evidence has survived from the thirteenth century: for Woburn, Biddlesden, Thame and Beaulieu; Sawtry, Louth Park, Revesby and Kirkstead; Furness, Holm Cultram and Fountains; Conway (Aberconway), Valle Crucis and Strata Marcella. Houses around the Fenland, within the northern uplands and in North Wales are well represented (Fig. 9). Marshland grazing was particularly suitable for cattle, and store beasts thrived better and were more welcome than sheep in the private forests or chases of Cumbria and the Pennines. Furthermore, the easterly houses were well placed to buy and sell in some of the major urban centres, and those of North Wales stood reasonably close to the English garrison towns. The Yorkshire houses and Holm Cultram (Cumberland) were also advantageously situated in relation to Newcastle, the leading hide-exporting port at the close of the thirteenth century.[3]

No evidence of a Cistercian house working a tannery during the twelfth century has been found (Appendix 4). Sallay had rights in one ca. 1226. Between 1235 and 1249 Meaux employed a "master of the tannery" and transferred the pelterers' buildings from the North grange to Wawne and to the abbey itself; at the same time twenty ox or cow hides were reserved for making and repairing the shoes of the poor. The *Taxatio Ecclesiastica*, ca. 1291, refers to other tanneries: at Margam, Tintern, Dore (*grangia de capella*), Hulton (Abbey grange) and Quarr. Furness and Whalley also had one each by about 1300. Fountains' *monachus tannariae* makes an appearance around the middle of the fifteenth century, and there are several references to tanneries in the Dissolution surveys. A site close to the conventual buildings appears to have been normal. When leather formed such an important raw material on the farm and in the household most houses probably did some tanning, but larger operations no doubt depended on the quantity of hides regularly available and upon the level of external demand. Houses close to the sheep country of the Cotswolds and the western Downs and known to have been marketing a considerable wool clip towards the end of the thirteenth century are notably absent from Fig. 9.

[3] R. A. Pelham, 'Medieval foreign trade: eastern ports,' in *An Historical Geography of England before A.D. 1800*, ed. H. C. Darby (Cambridge, 1936), p. 315.

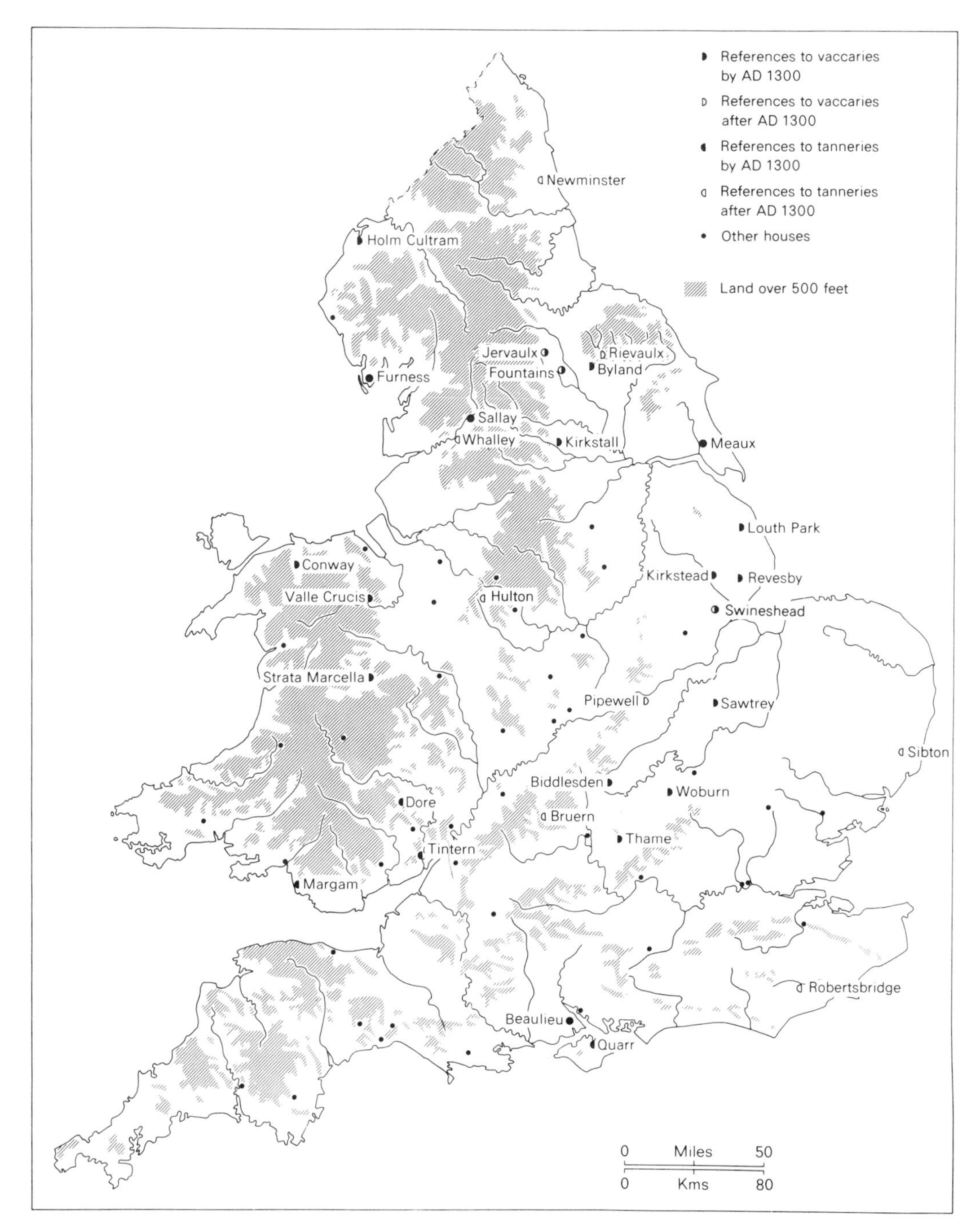

FIG. 9

Cistercian houses with vaccaries and/or tanneries (Appendices 3 and 4).

Surveys of Stock and Grants of Pasture

We are poorly supplied with figures of Cistercian live-stock, particularly for the period of direct exploitation, that is before ca. 1325. The series of statements in the *Chronica monasterii de Melsa* for the period 1270/80-1399 (Table 2) is exceptional.

TABLE 2: MEAUX (YORKSHIRE): LIVESTOCK

Date*	Sheep	Cattle	Cows	%	*Chron. Melsa*
1270/80	11,000	1,000	—	9	2: 156
1286	1,320	477	—	35	2: 176
1310	5,406	606	—	11	2: 238
1353	2,638	515	—	18	3: 87
1356	1,689	206	—	12	3: 110
1367	1,471	338	—	23	3: 152
1372	2,540	349	—	13	3: 167
1396	2,361	330	—	14	3: 234
1399	2,397	271	116	16	3: 276

* The terminal dates of abbacies between 1280 and 1399. There is no information for 1339 and 1349. 1270/80 refers to "*uno anno tempore hujus abbatis Roberti.*" In the fifth column, the number of cattle (and cows) is expressed as a percentage of the number of sheep.

The figures for sheep are fairly straightforward, and apart from that for 1270/80 they do not appear to be merely round numbers. Cattle, however, are subsumed under *grossa animalia* until 1310 and under *averia* in 1367, 1372 and 1396. In 1353, cows, oxen and cattle are explicitly grouped together, and the first are not mentioned at all in 1356. Horses (between 80 and 120) are listed separately after 1286, but only for 1399 do we have a reasonably complete break-down into live-stock classes; for the first time the number of *vaccas* is given. If the figures for 1286 are disregarded (477 probably includes horses), it appears that the number of horned cattle varied between nine per cent and twenty-three per cent of the number of sheep. The latter were the more liable to illness and this may partly account for some marked fluctuations in number. The grazing requirements of sheep and cattle probably stood in the ratio of 4 or 5:1,[4]

[4] 4:1 on the Holderness estates of Meaux, 1286-1310: "*loco, cujuslibet grossi animalis 4 bidentes in pasturis praedictis*" (*Chron. M.*, 2: 221). Similarly, when Fountains leased out half of the grange of Aldburgh the lessee was to keep for the monastery "*cc hogges sive matrices oves, vel quinquaginta averia*" (*Mem. F.*, 1: 327n.). 5:1 at Sutton

suggesting that over the period in question something less than half to about as much feed (but not necessarily area) was required for cattle as for sheep.

There are also some isolated statements relating to other northern houses. In 1320 Whalley reported 805 head of horned cattle, including 199 cows, and only 837 sheep. Forty-six years later the numbers had dropped considerably, to 172 and 555 respectively,[5] but since the monks are known to have leased out a good deal of land over this period the change in the proportion of sheep to cattle may reflect the kind of land lost as much as a deliberate change of policy. *Compoti* drawn up in 1478 and 1521 do not refer to sheep at all; woollen cloth was being purchased, while the combined profits from hides and the tannery amounted to £9.19.8 and £7.16.8 in respective years. Sallay, a neighbouring house in Yorkshire, still made 18s. 8d. from wool-fells and £16 from clipped wool, including that from tithes, in 1481. During the same year, however, the monks disbursed £38.11.3 on the purchase of bullocks and their tannery brought in £7.[6] Kirkstall's fortunes were at a low ebb in 1284 and its estates carried only eighty-four cows and thirty-two other large beasts. By 1301 the monks grazed 4000 sheep and 618 head of cattle, a ratio of 6 or 7: 1, comparable to those of Meaux. At this time the Cistercians, and particularly such well-placed houses as Kirkstall, were riding the crest of the export trade in wool. Even Meaux — probably more interested in cattle than most houses — surrendered pasture for cows in 1249-69 and was anxious to use such grazing for sheep in 1286-1310.[7]

Within and to the west of the Pennines, cattle seem to have gained appreciably on sheep by the end of the fourteenth century. If the data for Meaux are representative the trend was not strongly evident to the east, but it became so between then and the Dissolution. Fountains probably had an annual wool surplus of about seventy-five sacks in the final quarter of the thirteenth century; in 1457-8 it sold only seven and in the following year a little over four. When valued in 1536-8 the monastery had

---

belonging to Meaux, 1280-6: "*et ubi grossa animalia non habentur in loco cujuslibet animalis quinque oves possunt haberi*" (*Chron. M.*, 2: 171). A considerably higher ratio, 8:1, applied at Wawne, 1221-35 (ibid., 1: 413-14).

[5] T. D. Whitaker, *An History of the Original Parish of Whalley*, 2nd ed. (London, 1806), pp. 56-57 (a visitation account), 61-62.

[6] T. D. Whitaker, *The History and Antiquities of the Deanery of Craven*, 3rd ed. (London, 1878), p. 63. For the date (1481, not 1381 as given by Whitaker) see *Chart. S.*, 2: 197.

[7] *Chron. M.*, 2: 85, 221.

1326 sheep, 536 oxen, 738 cows and more than 1000 head of other horned cattle.

The evidence of pastoral grants described in terms of cattle, oxen or cows is also of some value.[8] The numbers involved were, of course, generally smaller than in the case of sheep, rarely more than fifty and normally less than thirty. Oxen were the principal ploughing beasts and an important means of traction. Pasture was sometimes given for so many 'teams' (*carrucatas*), and on one occasion at least, in a charter to Rievaulx, it is clear that these were of eight beasts.[9] Some relatively large numbers were associated with *grangiae*. Byland received a grant for seventy-seven oxen at Wildon[10] where there was a grange in the twelfth century. Caistron grange (Newminster) had pasture for at least eighty-two oxen.[11] The chartulary of Fountains includes a grant for fifty oxen at Busby where the monastic estate was probably organised as a grange in the last quarter of the twelfth century. These are the known instances of grazing rights for oxen amounting to fifty head or more. The granges in question do not, however, appear to have been particularly extensive and it may well be that beasts kept at these places (assuming that rights were, in fact, exercised) were also used elsewhere.[12]

Important grants of pasture for cows and 'cattle' (200 was the known maximum[13]) were not usually associated with granges. The few exceptions relate to lowland areas favourable to a mixed economy, for example Meaux's estate at Sutton in Holderness. The *Chronica* records gifts of arable amounting in all to about eight bovates and 160 acres, the latter mainly in small parcels. These formed the nucleus of a grange by at least the second half of the thirteenth century. Earlier (1150/60; 1210/20) the monks received two separate grants of pasture for forty cows, and there

[8] Listed in R. A. Donkin, 'Cattle on the estates of medieval Cistercian monasteries in England and Wales,' *Ec. H. R.*, 2nd ser. 15 (1962-63): 48-53, and 'The Cistercian settlement and the English royal forests,' *Citeaux: Commentarii Cistercienses*, 11 (1960): 131-32.

[9] *Chart. R.*, p. 65: "*quatuor carrucatas boum, unamquamque de VIII bobus.*" See also ibid., pp. 73, 115, 282.

[10] *Mon. Angl.*, 5: 350. In 1223-4 the monks claimed pasture in Kilburn for ninety-five oxen and thirty cows from the granges of Stocking and Wildon (W. P. Baildon, *Notes on the Religious and Secular Houses of Yorkshire*, Yorks. Arch. Assoc., Rec. Ser., 17 (London, 1895), 1: 28.

[11] *Chart. N.*, pp. 123, 125, 143 (1296).

[12] For the oxen (and other cattle) on granges belonging to Beaulieu, Hampshire, see *Account B.*, p. 30 (1269-70); two estates had more than 100 draught animals.

[13] However between 1155 and 1166 Kirkstall received two carcucates in Brampton with pasture for 1000 sheep, and cows "*sine numero*" (*E.Y.C.*, 2: 156).

was a vaccary "*super Hullo cum adjacente marisco de Sutton*" (1194-1216). This low-lying, marshy area provided much good grazing, as did parts of the Fenland (for Swineshead, Vaudey, Kirkstead), the Medway marshes (Boxley), and the shores of the Solway (Holm Cultram).

The first known grants of pasture for particular animals belong to the sixth decade of the twelfth century. Those for cattle were then at least as numerous as for sheep, but the position of the latter strengthened as the century wore on.[14] Near its close (1182-97) we find Meaux converting cattle sheds into sheep folds: "*Sed tamen cum ibidem vaccariae deficere incepissent vaccariae in bercharias sunt conversae.*" This, and the early evidence of vaccaries already discussed, suggests that for a few decades cattle may have been on at least a parity with sheep in the North and West.

The Movement of Cattle

Most grants of pasture were located merely in terms of some township which was often both extensive and physically diverse. Consequently it is hardly surprising that no specific references to seasonal grazing have been found. On the other hand, it is sometimes stated that cattle were or could be kept "throughout the year," for example in Wharfedale (1278) and in Nidderdale (1308) by Fountains. When necessary, they were brought down into the neighbourhood of the *logias* which, by this time, were not only summer shielings.[15] At Kirkhammerton in the Vale of York Fountains was allowed woodland pasture (and consequently shelter) for fifteen head of cattle throughout the year (1268). The rights claimed by Meaux in the fens around Arnold in Holderness have some interest here too. Around the turn of the thirteenth century (1286-1310) an attempt was made to prevent the house commoning sheep in 260 acres "*morae et pasturae*" from the middle of March to Michaelmas and from using six acres of marsh (*marisci*) for cattle throughout the year; from which it would appear

[14] The first endowments to Cîteaux itself were of land and cattle (A. M. Cooke, 'A study in twelfth-century revival and reform,' *Bull. John Rylands Library*, 9 (1925): 149). On the estates of Glastonbury cattle were fairly important early in the twelfth century but declined in number towards the end (M. M. Postan, 'Glastonbury estates in the twelfth century,' *Ec.H.R.*, 2nd ser., 5 (1953): 363).

[15] T. B. Franklin (*A History of Scottish Farming* (London, 1952), p. 65) states that cattle belonging to Coupar Angus, a Scottish Cistercian house, wintered out of doors in sheltered glens. It has also been shown for Scotland how, much later, shielings became permanent crofts (V. Gaffney, 'Summer Shealings,' *Scottish Hist. Rev.*, 38 (1959): 10-19).

that cattle normally weathered the winter in such areas whereas sheep were withdrawn in the autumn.

Although there are references to the movement of cattle, its precise purpose is not always fully apparent. Thus Fountains in 1312 was granted 'free passage' for beasts in Craven. Cattle were moved between widely separated estates; an undated charter records the gift of eight acres of land in Allerdale (Cumberland) "to construct a shed for cattle going and returning from *Alredale* to [Fountains] abbey." Furness (1280) enjoyed a right of way "through all the lands of Adam of Derwentwater" with halting places and 'baitage' for up to a day and a night.

The monks were sometimes permitted to pasture animals based on granges in areas around about, the distances in such cases being only a mile or two. Occasionally a form of transhumance is almost certainly indicated. Fountains (1190-1210) had rights in Ripley for cattle passing between Cayton, a grange as early as 1145-53, and Brimham.[16] Although only five miles apart these places are physically very different, Cayton on the edge of the Vale of York, and Brimham at 600 feet overlooking the Nidd. One can probably assume that this right was exercised in the late spring or early summer. (Winter undoubtedly reduced operations but, so far as we know, witnessed no outright evacuation of Brimham or any other substantial settlement). In the same way Rievaulx's plough oxen at the grange of Griff in the valley of the Rye were allowed 'common of pasture' at Newton on the northwestern flanks of the Hambleton Hills. This movement of stock over both long and short distances was one aspect of the centralized administration of a great abbey.

Yorkshire

Perhaps the most striking feature of Cistercian cattle-farming in Yorkshire was its long association with private forests or chases. The larger part of these, comprising scrub and bog, stands of high timber and rough grazing, stretched from an uneven base in the lower Pennines deep into several of the dales. Here the monks had extensive privileges, particularly pasture for cattle. R. Trow-Smith observed that in the twelfth century "the cow appears to be mainly associated with forest and upland ranges, where it is found recorded as being kept in large numbers."[17] This was still true at the end of the thirteenth and the beginning of the four-

[16] *E.Y.C.*, 1: 404.
[17] *A History of British Livestock Husbandry to 1700* (London, 1957), pp. 93-94.

teenth centuries when the activities of the Yorkshire Cistercians can be matched, further to the west, by developments on the Lancaster estates.[18]

Jervaulx had pasture in the forests of Wensleydale and Richmond (on the Swale) before ca. 1170. The monks were permitted to establish vaccaries, and there were at least three in Wensleydale and thirteen in the forest of Richmond in the second half of the thirteenth century. Fountains obtained rights for seventy beasts (forty cows and thirty oxen) in the forest of Marsden between 1177 and 1193. Similar grants of pasture are also recorded for the forests of Kirkby Malzeard and Brimham, in the latter case in a confirmation of privileges issued by Richard I. Before 1200 Rievaulx could use the forest of Westerdale on the crest of the North Yorkshire Moors for 120 head of cattle.[19] Others belonging to the same house grazed in the forests of Swaledale (1251), Teesdale (1161-67) and Helmsley (twelfth century). Before 1203 Sallay had the right to put forty cows in the forest of Gisburn. Newminster in Northumberland used the afforested foothills of the Cheviot range in much the same way as the Yorkshire houses used the Pennines. Its rights of pasture "*in Chiuiet mores*" date from at least 1181.[20] Cattle could survive on the coarse herbage of scrub and open woodland. Fountains' animals browsed in the woods of Bradley grange in the valley of the Calder; similarly Jervaulx, about the close of the twelfth century, had pasture in woodland around Masham.

Some valleys were given over almost entirely to cattle breeding. Nidderdale (Fig. 10), where both Byland and Fountains owned land and exercised grazing privileges, is a case in point.[21] Much of the area was under local forest law. Fountains took estovers in the forest of Nidderdale; an area on the left bank known as the forest of *Warsall*, opposite the grange of Dacre, was in the hands of the monks from 1135-40, and in 1175 they

[18] D. Oschinsky, 'Notes on the Lancaster estates in the 13th and 14th centuries,' *Trans. Hist. Soc. Lancs. and Chesh.*, 100 (1949): 26: vaccaries in Wyresdale based on twelve 'booths' under the supervision of a head stock-keeper. There were twenty-eight vaccaries in the forests of Blackburnshire, 1295-6 (C.H. Tupling, *The Economic History of Rossendale* (Manchester, 1927), p. 19). The Templars in Yorkshire appear to have concentrated on grain and cattle, in Lincolnshire on wool-growing (E. J. Martin, 'The Templars in Yorkshire and a list of Templar lands in Yorkshire, 1185-1308,' *Yorks. Arch. Jour.*, 29 (1929): 366).

[19] *Chart. R.*, p. 68; *E.Y.C.*, 1: 440.

[20] *Chart. N.*, pp. 41-44, 73-74, 76. The house also had rights in 'forests' around Rothbury (ibid., p. 11).

[21] See T.S. Gowland, 'The honour of Kirkby Malzeard and the chase of Nidderdale,' *Yorks. Arch. Jour.*, 33 (1938): 388.

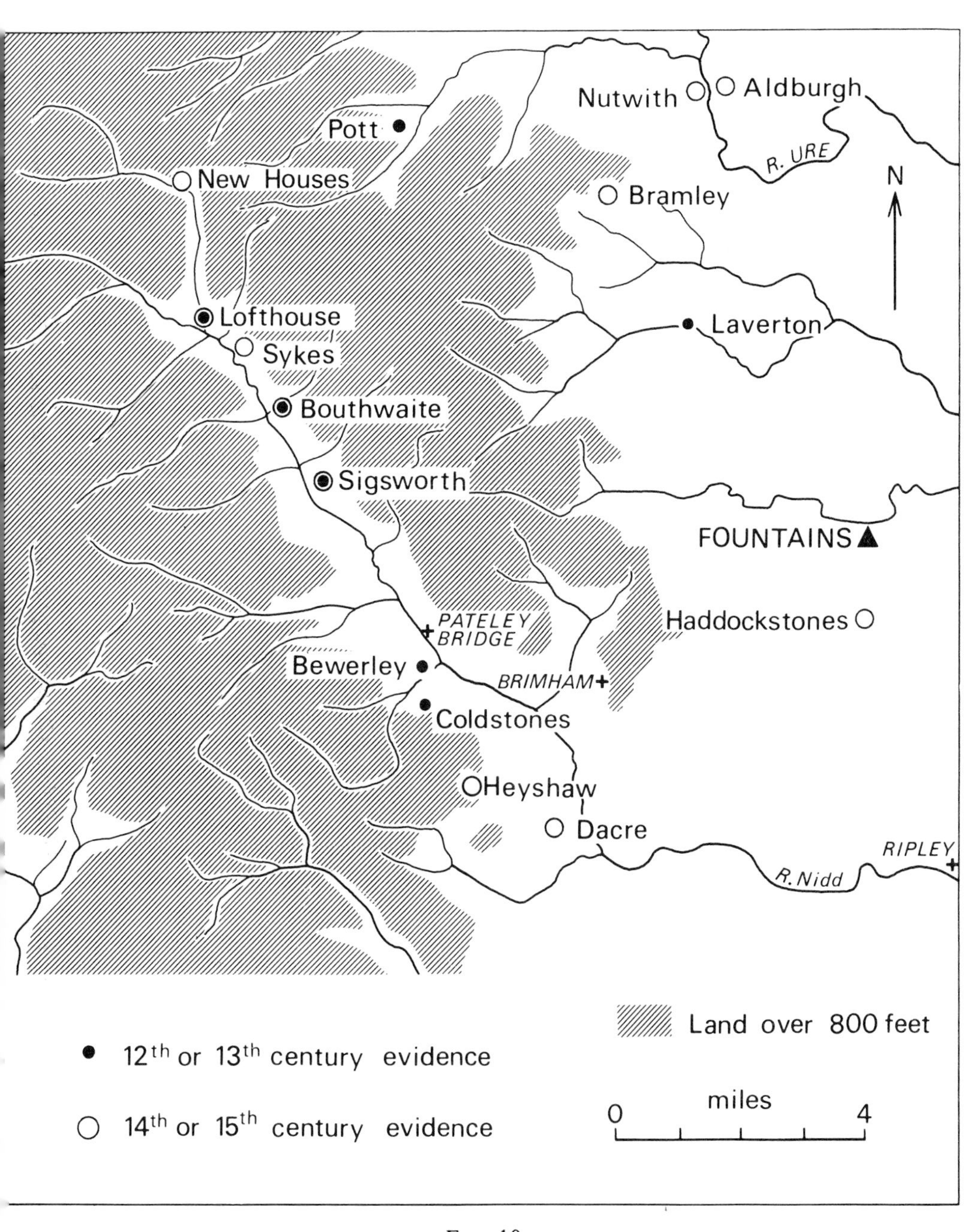

FIG. 10

Cattle farms (*vaccaria, logia*) belonging to Fountains abbey.

received all that lay to the north-east of the Nidd.[22] Notices have survived of at least five grants of pasture for cattle in Nidderdale. Use of the forest of Brimham by Fountains (before 1200) has already been mentioned. The monks had cattle around Ripley ca. 1270, and in 1308 they concluded an agreement with John de Mowbray whereby there should be no resident farmers in certain parts of Nidderdale "other than [the abbey's] own servants to take care of their cattle in winter."[23] Much earlier, however, in a charter of confirmation issued by Richard I, both *grangiae* and *logias* are mentioned. Bouthwaite ranked as a grange and there were 'lodges' at Bewerley (four), Lofthouse, Sigsworth, and Coldstones.[24] A *logia* apparently consisted of a group of byres and simple living accommodation. Jervaulx (1228) was permitted to make "*logias ad vaccarias suas in marginibus forestae*" of Wensleydale. Rievaulx had *logias* in the forests of Swaledale and Teesdale; another in upper Eskdale measured only fifteen feet in each direction, but it was then (before 1180) perhaps only a summer shieling.[25]

Before the close of the twelfth century, Fountains' influence had penetrated almost to the head of Nidderdale. If present-day settlements of the same name occupy the sites of former *logias* the most characteristic position was just at the meeting of the flood-plain and the sharply inclined valley walls, a sheltered base for operations and close to richer pasture and invaluable water meadow. Domesday Book makes no reference to any settlements above Pateley Bridge; if present, they were either very small or largely 'wasted' like many townships further downstream. Almost certainly, we have here an example of pastoral colonization, the opening up of a remote valley by Cistercian *conversi*, very nearly the final phase of a movement which commenced with the earliest Anglian settlers more than 700 years before.

In the latter half of the fifteenth century the estates in Nidderdale were managed by 'keepers' under the general supervision of the abbey's herdmaster. Each keeper looked after a number of cows — usually twenty or a multiple of twenty, up to sixty — their calves and other horned cattle. Fixed amounts of butter and cheese, or their monetary equivalent, had to be delivered to the abbey. Young animals were regularly branded and the

[22] *Chart. F.*, 1: 204-6. The whole township of Fountains Earth belonged to Fountains before 1200.

[23] Ibid., p. 213.

[24] Pott, in a tributary valley of the river Burn to the north-east of Nidderdale, was described as a *logia* in the thirteenth century (*Chart. F.*, 2: 867). New Houses, almost at the head of Nidderdale, is called a *logia* in the *Valor Ecclesiasticus*.

[25] *Chart. R.*, p. 158.

old replaced. Walls and buildings had to be properly maintained, although major repairs seem to have been the responsiblity of the monks themselves. Such vaccaries were not confined to the dales proper but included at least three of Fountains' former granges on the flanks of the Pennines: Bramley, Aldburgh, and Dacre. Contracts were still being drawn up as late as 1537, and by the Dissolution, as we have seen, the ratio of cattle to sheep stood at nearly 2:1.

Wales

The *Taxatio Ecclesiastica* is sufficiently detailed in the case of Wales and the diocese of Hereford to get some idea of the importance of cattle-farming on Cistercian estates ca. 1291.[26] The data are tabulated below (p. 81) and their distribution shown in Fig. 11.[27]

A major contrast existed between the houses of South and Central Wales, both in terms of total live-stock profits and in the proportion derived from cattle-farming. The annual (rentable) values of all temporal property followed approximately the former, except that Whitland stood considerably higher when ranked according to the pastoral assessment alone. In the relatively accessible South sheep assumed considerable importance, even by English standards. Their value exceeded sixty-five per cent of the pastoral assessment on the estates of Margam, Neath, Flaxley, Dore (in Hereford, a county famous for its high quality wool), Whitland and Tintern. The *Taxatio* generally supports the evidence of Pegolotti's wool list. At the same time it is clear that cattle also brought in a considerable income at Margam, the house most interested in animal husbandry generally, and the monks of Grace Dieu and Llantarnam appear to have been at least as interested in cattle as sheep. The latter houses were rather small and poor communities like those of Central Wales where cattle decisively overhauled sheep. Vaccaries are mentioned at Strata Marcella (1282), Valle Crucis (ca. 1291) and also Conway (ca. 1291). In the North, sheep again were important, particularly on the estates of Basingwerk.

[26] For a critical discussion of the *Taxatio*, see R. Graham, *English Ecclesiastical Studies* (London, 1929), pp. 271-301.

[27] The reputation of Wales as a centre of cattle-rearing during the Middle Ages is well known. See Trow-Smith, *British Livestock Husbandry*, pp. 56-57, 94; W. Rees, *South Wales and the March, 1284-1415* (London, 1924), p. 232; H. P. R. Finberg, 'An early reference to the Welsh cattle trade,' *Ag.H.R.*, 2 (1954): 12-14.

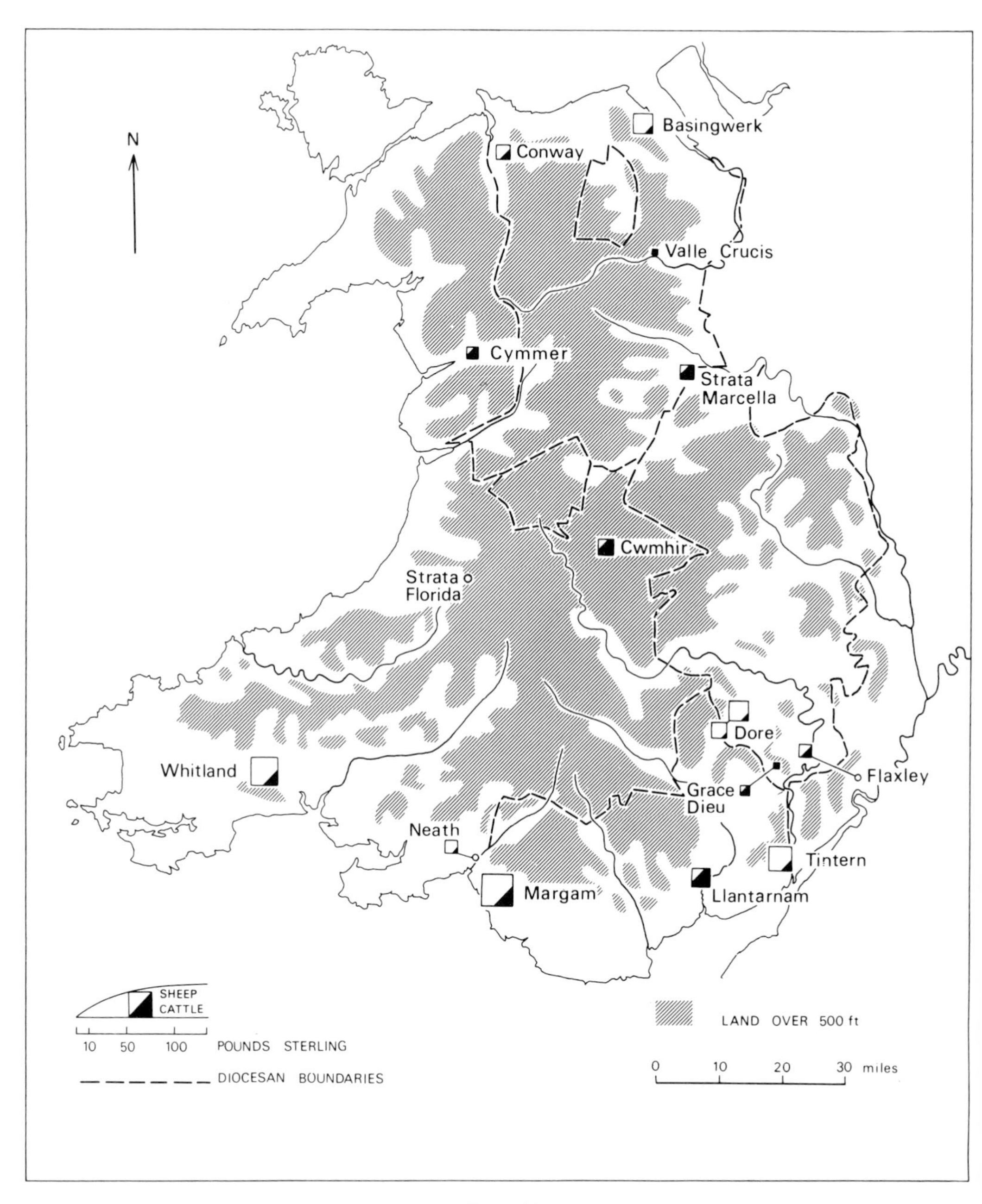

FIG. 11

Valuation of stock on Cistercian estates within the Welsh dioceses and that of Hereford ca. 1291 (*Taxatio Ecclesiastica*).

TABLE 3: *TAXATIO ECCLESIASTICA*: LIVESTOCK

		Sheep						Cattle (*vaccas*)						
Monastery	Diocese	Nos.	Value £	Value s.	Value d.	Per cent value	Per capita value	Nos.	Value £	Value s.	Value d.	Per cent value	Per capita value	Sacks of wool
Basingwerk	St Asph	2000	30	0	0	91	4d.	53	2	13	0	9	12d.	10
Conway	St Asph	560	8	5	0	56	4d.	106	6	6	0	44	13d.	20
Cymmer	Bangor	25		6	3	9	3d.	60	3	0	0	91	12d.	8
Cwmhir	St Davids	300	4	10	0	37	4d.	128	7	8	0	63	14d.	
S. Marcella	St Asph	110	1	12	6	21	3d.	100	6	0	0	79	14d.	12
V. Crucis	St Asph							30	1	10	0	100	12d.	
Llantarnam	Llandaff	588	12	5	0	48	5d.		13	0	0	52		18
Dore	Hereford	1760	35	13	4	93	5d.	40	3	0	0	7	18d.	16
	Llandaff	980	18	16	8	94	5d.	14	1	1	0	6	18d.	
Flaxley	Hereford	240	5	3	4	66	5d.	35	2	12	6	33	18d.	6
Grace Dieu	Llandaff	22		10	0	38	5d.	11		16	6	62	18d.	5
	Hereford									4	6	100	18d.	
Margam	Llandaff	5285	102	12	4	79	5d.	425	31	17	6	21	18d.	25
Neath	St Davids	693	10	1	0	90	4d.	20	1	0	0	10	12d.	10
Tintern	Llandaff	3264	62	14	8	89	5d.	100	7	10	0	11	18d.	15
Whitland	St Davids	1100	16	10	0	78	4d.	88	4	8	0	22	12d.	15

Numbers and valuation (*verus valor*) of stock on Cistercian estates within the Welsh dioceses and that of Hereford, ca. 1291, according to thhe *Taxatio Ecclesiastica*. Per capita value to the nearest penny. The wool (final column) was that normally available for export ca. 1300 (after F. B. Pegolotti).

From about 1300 Cistercian holdings began to be regularly leased out. The process gathered momentum around the middle of the fourteenth century and was virtually complete by the time of the Dissolution. All that then generally remained in the hands of the monks were a few parcels of land, mostly close to the abbey buildings, although, as we have seen, arrangements were sometimes made for others to keep live-stock on behalf of the monastery. Stoneleigh was buying cattle just before the Dissolution.[28] The stock belonging to Vale Royal in 1509 still amounted to eighteen draught oxen, thirty plough oxen and sixteen cows ("the stock of the house"), and twenty oxen, two "animals of three years," five cows and fourteen calves ("the stock of Darnhall").[29] Sibton, according to a *compotus* of 1363-4, had three small dairies, one at the gate of the monastery and another on property organized as a grange before the Black Death.[30] Two other granges returned ewes' milk. "Substantial purchases of cows" were made in 1371, and it has been claimed that "the Suffolk cow was being improved [at Sibton] by the importation of a northern breed as early as the end of the fifteenth century."[31] The dairy at the North grange (apparently incorporating that earlier established at the gate of the monastery) occupies an important place in a *compotus* of 1508-9 when there were sixty-three cows. The number stood at 128 in 1510 and then climbed steadily to 140 by 1513. About half the natural increase was retained. Care of the herd and some pigs and poultry did not, however, fully occupy the dairy servants for they were also employed in fulling and the weaving of wool and flax.

Sheep and Wool

The bias towards sheep or cattle on Cistercian estates at different periods conformed to no simple pattern. The wide distribution of houses alone would lead one to expect this. Holdings varied considerably in size and even a common approach to organization could not possibly produce the same result in areas of very different physical and human character. The monks were everywhere obliged to pursue their economic policies within an existing regional framework and what general trends can be detected are subject to differences of emphasis and even important exceptions.

[28] *Mon. Angl.*, 5: 449.
[29] *Ledger V.R.*, p. 191. Darnhall was the former site of the abbey.
[30] *Docs. S.*, p. 116.
[31] Ibid., pp. 37-38.

During the very early years, subsistence was the primary, even the sole economic objective, and the differences between houses were least marked. There is some evidence that most of those founded before the middle of the twelfth century passed through a short phase when cattle were quite as important as sheep. Meat was then scarcely ever eaten, but there was great need of dairy produce, some means of transport, assistance in ploughing and threshing, and materials for clothing and building. In these circumstances cattle were generally the more useful. Houses hardly had the means to work up wool into cloth, whereas hides could be readily employed in a great variety of ways. At the same time, cattle were more suited to scrubland and stretches of coarse, wet herbage. Such conditions prevailed for some time over large parts of early holdings, even those immediately around the monasteries themselves, especially in the North and West and Wales.

Before the close of the twelfth century a strong interest in wool-growing spread among the Cistercian houses of most of England. Extending into North and South Wales, it never dominated the centre, and probably also failed to develop fully in south-west England. Sheep numbers generally increased but, so far as one can tell, only occasionally at the expense of cattle. Indeed, the latter increased too, although at a rate generally commensurate with the more modest expansion in the number of monks and of arable acres rather than of overseas trade.

Wool was undoubtedly the principal cash crop over the period when the order directly worked the bulk of its holdings, that is until about the middle of the fourteenth century. The market was so assured and the scale of operations so considerable that in most cases there can have been neither the urge nor the opportunity to seriously develop any other. Although the available hides (like grain) were probably often in excess of household needs there is no reason to suppose that, commercially, they were ever more important than wool, except perhaps in Central Wales. The houses of north-east England each had several cattle stations in the Pennines or in the North Yorkshire Moors, but they were also leading producers of wool. Furthermore, throughout the whole country tanning, like fulling, seems to have been chiefly related to internal needs.

Cistercian wool never fed the home cloth industry which expanded considerably during the second half of the fourteenth century to anything like the extent that it had earlier served the Continental market. The increasing amount of land leased out would in itself have made this impossible, at any rate under the old system of production. Sheep numbers fell, enhancing the position of cattle, and in some cases existing ranches were further developed and even new ones started. After about two hundred years (and in very different circumstances) pastoral activities were again primarily arranged so as to meet the immediate needs of the monastery, and, to simplify matters, tenants were sometimes obliged to act as keepers of monastic stock, delivering dairy produce, wool and hides according to fixed agreements.

Statutes and Guarantees of Protection

The statutes of the Cistercian order include several references to wool-growing and to stock generally. The restrictions that were imposed can hardly ever have been fully effective, and undoubtedly became less so as time went on. An early edict (1134) stipulated that flocks and herds should be brought at nightfall to the monks' own estates,[32] although exception was made of animals belonging to Alpine houses where transhumance was practised. Houses were also instructed not to associate with laymen in the feeding of stock (1214-5). Yet we know that rights in common grazing were accepted within a very few years of the introduction of the order into England in 1128, and these continued to be widely used.

On the other hand, privileges conferred by church and state were fully exploited and keenly defended; some applied to the whole or large parts of the order, others to particular houses only. The payment of tithes was a never-ending source of dispute,[33] not least in respect of pastoral products. The papal correspondence of 1221 contains a "letter to the abbots of the Cistercian order in England who are free from payment of tithes of fodder (*nutrimentis animalium*) inhibiting rectors of parishes in which Cistercian sheep are pastured to exact tithe wool, milk or lambs."[34] Similar protection for houses in the provinces of Canterbury and York was accorded in 1244, and three years earlier to Stanley and Fountains, houses which, by the end of the century at least, were very considerable wool producers. Other monasteries enjoyed the special protection of the king or some great lord. Thus Henry III in 1227 ordered that "no one on pain of forfeiting ten pounds is to kill, impound (*imparcare*) or trouble [the sheep of Vaudey]."[35] More often the monks were simply promised that, in the

[32] *Statuta*, 1: 26.

[33] For the history of Cistercian 'exemption' from tithes, see J. S. Donnelly, 'Changes in the grange economy of English and Welsh Cistercian abbeys, 1300-1540,' *Traditio*, 10 (1954): 424-5; G. Constable, *Monastic Tithes from their Origins to the Twelfth Century* (Cambridge, 1964), pp. 220-26; J. Gilchrist, *The Church and Economic Activity in the Middle Ages* (London, 1969), pp. 42-44.

[34] *Papal Letters*, 1: 78.

[35] *C.Ch.R.*, AD 1226-57, p. 2.

event of debt, their sheep would not be distrained so long as they possessed other goods. Examples include Fountains (1199), Meaux (1204), Forde (1205), Rievaulx (1208), Vaudey (1228), Bruern (1233), Pipewell (1235), Byland (1247), Bordesley (1250), Warden (1252), Combermere (1253), Hulton (1256), Revesby (1263), Garendon (1268), and Kingswood (undated). Wool production rose steadily during the thirteenth century and many houses got themselves into serious financial difficulties, mainly through selling wool up to ten or more years in advance.[36]

Only two references to similar protection for Cistercian 'cattle' have come to light. Roger de Lascy, constable of Chester, ordered (1208-11) that the beasts (*averiis eorum*) at Penistone, Yorkshire, belonging to Kirkstead were not to be distrained, and the concession to Garendon in 1268 mentioned both cows and sheep. However Revesby was not to be distrained by its sheep while it possessed other animals, and a certain Robert de Rochefort affirmed that Kingswood could be 'compelled' by its cattle but never by its sheep.

Management of Sheep and the Preparation of Wool

The list of wool-producing monasteries preserved by Francesco Balducci Pegolotti, a member of the merchant house of Bardi, contains a larger proportion of Cistercian houses (about eighty-five per cent) than of any other religious order.[37] Prices per sack are quoted for almost every house, but these must be used with care. They are not directly comparable with those fixed on a county basis for the wool grant of 1337.[38] The Pegolotti figures are the earlier, possibly by as much as forty years;[39] they

[36] The Chapter General at first attempted to prevent this; then in 1181 houses were allowed to sell one year in advance: "*lanam unius anni licet prae vendere, si necesse fuerit; ultra annum non fiat*" (*Statuta*, 1: 89). However, violations continued, and regulations were almost totally relaxed in 1279.

[37] Printed in *Francisco Balducci Pegolotti: La Pratica della Mercatura*, ed. A. Evans (Cambridge, Mass.: Mediaeval Academy of America, 1936), pp. 258-69. There is a similar but inferior list in G. Espinas, *La vie urbaine de Douai au moyen âge* (Paris, 1913), 3: 232-34.

[38] *C.P.R.*, AD 1334-38, pp. 480-83.

[39] This emerges if one considers the Cistercian houses included in the list. The critical entries appear to be: (a) Vale Royal (*Vareale in Gualesi*), Cheshire, a community established — from an earlier site, Darnhall — in 1281; no house founded after Vale Royal, the last clearly identifiable item in the list, is included; (b) Stanlaw (*Stalleo in Zestri*) is listed although the monks were moved to Whalley, Lancashire, in 1296. Nevertheless, T. H. Lloyd (*The Movement of Wool Prices in Medieval England*, Economic History Review, Supplement, 6 (Cambridge, 1973), p. 10) thinks that the "list may have

include the cost of carriage from England to Flanders and the profit due to the merchant; and they are usually given for three grades, of which the 'middle' wool probably corresponded to the average county product. Nevertheless, if we subtract four marks from the prices of 'best' wool and two from those of 'middle' wool — amounts suggested by a study of prices actually obtained on various occasions by Cistercian houses — there is still every indication that the monks were getting more for their wool than most other producers. How much more would of course depend upon the proportion which 'best' wool bore to the total, and this we have no means of knowing. There is, however, some evidence to support the view that the Cistercians occasionally marketed an intrinsically better product and very often prepared their clip more carefully.

Here we are directly concerned only with the management of sheep and the preparation of wool, but it should also be noted that the monasteries supplied wool in bulk, thus, no doubt, saving the buyer miles of tedious travel; that they were in a position to make long-term contracts; and that they were prepared, if necessary, to carry their wool-sacks to some convenient rendezvous, possessing as they did numerous toll exemptions, suitable carts and waggons, and unsalaried lay brothers.

The improvements in sheep-breeding during the eighteenth century probably effaced any remaining traces of improvements made five hundred years previously. In any case, these traces were doubtless slight. Certain writers appear convinced, however, that early improvements did take place. "Kirkstead ... cultivated the originals of the Lincoln breed," we are told,[40] and "to the Cistercians this country is indebted for its finer wool."[41] J. S. Fletcher, in his study of the Cistercians in Yorkshire, states that "the order, because of its intercourse with foreign countries, brought about great and important improvements in the breeding of sheep."[42] But little or no documentary evidence is produced in support of these assertions; and as far as better stock was concerned there was no need for growers in the poorer districts to look beyond England.

To illustrate, first, the reputation of the Cistercians as flock-masters, we may cite a letter written to the bishop of Chichester (1222-38) by his

been compiled during the time (1318-21) which [Balducci Pegolotti] spent in England." Espinas suggests a date about the middle of the thirteenth century for the document he published, but it is doubtful whether this view takes into account the inclusion of Darnhall (*Dorenhalline*), 1274-81.

[40] H. E. Wroot, 'Yorkshire abbeys and the wool trade,' in *Miscellanea*, Thoresby Society Publications, 33 (Leeds, 1935 [first printed, 1930]), p. 11.

[41] *Giraldi Cambrensis Opera*, ed. J.S. Brewer, R.S., 21 (London, 1873), 4: xxiii.

[42] *The Cistercians in Yorkshire* (London, 1919), p. 152.

steward, Simon de Senliz. "Moreover, my lord, please to think about procuring sheep at the abbey of Vaudey or elsewhere." Later, Simon wrote, "I retain in Sussex the *frater* of Vaudey ... as I have proposed to keep sheep in our lands, in your manors, and therefore I keep back the *frater* in order that the sheep may be more advisedly and usefully provided for through him." On yet another occasion he reported, "Know, moreover, my lord, that on the Saturday next after the Exaltation of the Holy Cross (September 14th) there came to me a certain monk from *Bordele* [Bordesley, Worcestershire] telling me that forty lambs and two sheep had been sent to you from the abbot of *Bordele* and were at a certain grange of the house of Waverley; in consequence of which I asked the said monk to lend you his shepherd until I could procure another suitable."[43] Both Vaudey and Bordesley marketed wool of high quality according to Pegolotti, above the average of the order, but a clip of superior grade was the rule rather than the exception in Lincolnshire and Worcestershire.[44] The native wool of Sussex was generally of a much lower standard.[45] If the Cistercians had graded up their flocks as a whole by the mid-thirteenth century, it would presumably have been unnecessary for men such as Simon de Senliz to look to houses as much as a hundred and fifty miles away. Yet it may be that for some reason their flocks had acquired an exceptional reputation or were thought particularly suitable; sheep from Vaudey, accustomed to the Fens, would probably have prospered on the Plain of Selsey around Chichester and behind the Solent.

Kingswood, at the foot of the Cotswold scarp, was also an important wool house, having apparently an annual surplus of some twenty-five sacks of high quality ca. 1300. It was selling sheep in 1241, 1262 ("old sheep" to the abbot of Malmesbury and others), 1289 (twenty-four sheep), and 1314 (forty-three sheep). On the other hand, the house bought some Lincolnshire (Lindsey) rams in 1241 — clearly most valuable evidence — and twenty sheep and thirty-one ewes in 1288.[46] The New Year's gifts to Vale Royal in 1330 included sheep, among them

[43] W. H. Blaauw, 'Letters of Ralph de Nevill, bishop of Chichester,' *Sussex Arch. Coll.*, 3 (1850): 52, 54, 70. The letters are undated.

[44] In 1337, 10 marks and 9.5 marks per sack. Herefordshire and Shropshire were the only other counties to exceed 9.5 marks. In another list (*Rot. Parl.*, 2: 138), dated 1343, the wool of south-east Lincolnshire (*Holand et le marrois*), an area including Vaudey, was priced at 11 marks while the rest of the county obtained 14 marks. Similarly the marsh wools (*le marrois*) of Kent, Essex, Sussex and Middlesex were ranked in 1343 below those grown elsewhere.

[45] Quoted at 6 marks in 1337.

[46] *Docs. K.*, pp. 200, 234.

twelve from the abbot of Dieulacres and twelve from the abbot of Basingwerk.[47]

A complicated agreement drawn up in 1290 between Pipewell (Northamptonshire) and some merchants of Cahors contained clauses covering the care and management of the flocks. Thus "it is ... ordained that 900 of the common two-tooth sheep (*bidentibus*) of the abbey shall be separated, half of which shall be ewes and the other half males, by the view of the merchants before mid-Lent next, which sheep the monks shall hold of the merchants and they shall be signed with the mark of both parties, and then shall remain in divers places with the two-tooth sheep of the monks in as good pasture and custody of the abbey as the monks' own two-tooth sheep."[48]

The remaining evidence belongs to the fifteenth century, but there is every reason to suppose that the activities described were usual in earlier times too. In 1457-8 the expenses of the sheep-master at Fountains included "*pro uno cado bituminis: viis-id.*" The accounts for the preceding and succeeding years mention the washing and clipping of sheep (*lociones et tonciones*). Much tar was bought, usually by the barrel (*cadus*);[49] mixed with grease it formed the sheep salve then in general use. Cistercian records sometimes mention disease among animals ('murrain', 'scab', 'rot'); yet we may assume that the monks, being able to isolate flocks on different estates, were more likely to escape disaster than smaller men. Perhaps woolmen had this in mind too when they set out to buy and to place orders.

The last of the monks' responsibilities was usually that of preparing, grading, and packing the wool. Buyers not only knew in most cases exactly what they were purchasing but could expect well cleansed fleeces. The monks more than most others had the wherewithal to do this, and no doubt expected appropriate recompense. In 1290 arbitrators decided that Pipewell should vouch that their wool "left the sheep-fold well washed, dry, and cleaned." Darnhall, when selling twelve sacks of wool to John Wermond of Cambrai (1275), agreed that it should be washed before delivery. While washing, it seems, was normally the responsibility of the

[47] *Ledger V.R.*, pp. 179-80. When Beaulieu (Faringdon) was founded by King John, 584 sheep (? ewes) and 100 *multones* were purchased in Lincolnshire (*The Great Roll of the Pipe for the Fifth Year of King John, Michaelmas 1203—Pipe Roll 49*, ed. Doris M. Stenton, P.R.S. Publs., n. s. 16 (London, 1938), pp. xx, 105).

[48] *C.Cl.R.*, AD 1288-96, p. 193.

[49] *Mem. F.*, 3: 10, 44, 88, 112.

abbey alone, the merchant or his agent sometimes played a part in the further stages of preparation. Fountains in 1276 was under contract to supply to certain Florentine merchants "*sexaginta duos saccos lanae* ... *sine clack*' (sheep's mark) *et lok*' (short clippings), *god et card* (clotted and coarse wool), *nigra, grissa* (black and grisled wool), *et sine pelliciis* (pelt wool)."[50] Furthermore, the house was obliged to "prepare" and weigh the wool. In 1280 Rievaulx owed three and a half sacks of good wool to Hugelino de Vithio and Lotherio Bonaguide of Florence, and this had to be prepared and weighed (*praeparatae et ponderatae*) before it was dispatched.[51] The following statement from the Pipewell contract of 1290 suggests that the buyer sometimes nominated the 'dresser': "It is ordained that the merchants' preparer shall be at the costs and expenses of the abbey ... and he shall prepare the wool well and faithfully without hindrance from the monks and that the merchants shall have free entry and issue to the preparer while he is occupied. After the preparation of the wool ... neither party shall have power to reject or refuse any part of the wool against his deed, or challenge his proceedings in any way." The earlier Darnhall agreement also stipulated that the wool should be "as good as the better crop of Dore" and be 'dressed' in Hereford by an employee of the merchants. Dore, within an area renowned for its fine wool, marketed a clip of exceptionally high quality. Cheshire wool, while good, was not generally comparable. For it to have been possible for Darnhall to supply wool equal to that of Dore suggests that the best wool of these houses did not differ as much as the standard county products. Finally, to turn again to the Pipewell provisions, the wool sometimes has to be "faithfully packed (*impaccatas*) ... according to the ancient and due custom of the abbey ... in the sarplers of the monks, at the expense of the monks."[52]

First-class wool always commanded a substantially higher price than the standard clip. In 1429 the finest selected wool was sometimes twice the value of the unsorted fleece, and in 1454 three times.[53] Fifty-six of the sixty-five English and Welsh Cistercian houses and all seven of the Scottish houses in Pegolotti's wool list are shown as supplying wool in at least two of the usual three grades (Fig. 12).[54] Three-quarters of the Gilbertine houses apparently did so too, but in all there were only twenty. The

[50] *Mem. F.*, 1: 177; *C.Cl.R.*, AD 1272-79, p. 387.

[51] *Chart. R.*, p. 409.

[52] Kingswood bought 'canvas' and 'cloth for sacks' in 1240 (*Docs. K.*, pp. 193-99).

[53] *Rot. Parl.*, 4: 360; 5: 277.

[54] In 1269-70 Beaulieu sold wool in six grades, the prices per sack ranging from £10.6.8 ("good") to £1.17.6. ("*gardus*") (*Account B.*, p. 33).

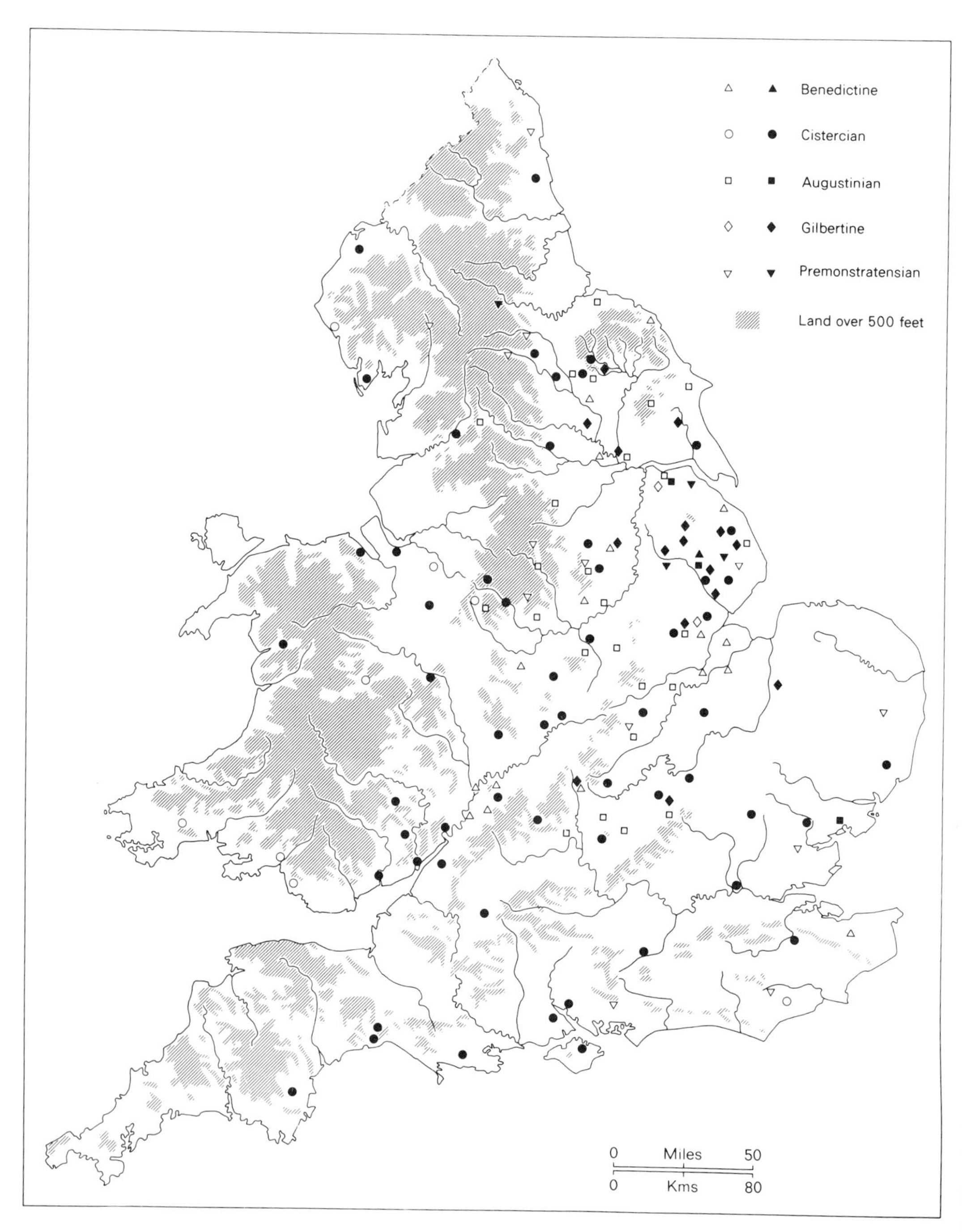

FIG. 12

Religious houses with wool for sale according to F. B. Pegolotti (ca. 1300). The solid symbols represent houses marketing wool in the usual three grades and with quotations for at least two.

proportion was small in the case of the remaining orders — at most twenty-three per cent. Even among the Cistercians it is unlikely that any house invariably supplied separated wool. In 1292 Kirkstall agreed to supply some merchants of the Society of Betti of Lucca with all the wool of the house for the following decade. Only after three years was the wool to be graded (*bona*, *mediana*, *locca*); at first it was to be delivered unsorted at an almost strictly average price.[55] While the Cistercian distribution in Fig. 12 is notably widespread, altogether there appears to have been a concentration of more specialized producers in eastern and central England, in particular around Boston, the focus of the export trade with Flanders.

Evidence of a superior Cistercian product, justifying a higher price, increases as we pass from a consideration of enlightened breeding, through the care and management of sheep and the cleansing and sorting of wool to its grading and bulk delivery. There may be some doubt whether the monks were, to any significant extent, forerunners of the eighteenth-century flockmasters, but there can be none that they were pre-eminent in the preparation of wool for sale.

Supplementary Sources of Wool

The bulk of the wool marketed by the Cistercians doubtless came from their own flocks. There were, however, at least two other sources of supply: tithes, and wool produced elsewhere in the neighbourhood. Tithe wool has to be seriously reckoned with from about the beginning of the fourteenth century as more churches were appropriated and the main source of supply diminished. The *Exordium Coenobii et Ordinis Cisterciensis*, approved in 1119, stated that churches and advowsons were not to be accepted, but in time this was widely disregarded. Meaux, sometime between 1310 and 1339, brought an action against the parishioners of Skipsea for possession of the tithes of wool and lambs, and tithe wool was an item in the income of the same house just before the Dissolution. The parson of Louth delivered three sacks of wool to Louth Park in 1338.[56] In a *compotus* relating to Sallay dated 1481 tithe wool is valued with the rest ("*lana communi et decimali*"); the church of Gargrave alone was respon-

[55] *Coucher K.*, pp. 226-27. H. E. Wroot, 'The Pennines in history,' *The Naturalist*, February-March 1930, p. 109: "They [the Benedictine monks and Augustinian canons] sold their wool in the entire fleece and sale by the unbroken fleece would seem to have been the custom of the secular market." For further examples of separation into three grades, see *Docs.K.*, p. 120; and H. Hall, ed., *Select Cases Concerning the Law Merchant*, Selden Society Publications, 46 (London, 1930), pp. 63-64.

[56] *C.M.I.*, AD 1307-49, no. 1628.

sible for forty stones. Combermere in 1519-20 farmed out tithes of lambs and wool in the parish of Nantwich,[57] and Dieulacres too seems to have settled for money payments by the time of the Dissolution. On the other hand, wool and other tithes might at all times go, not to the monastery, but to the vicar placed in charge of the church.

A much more important source of wool, especially over the period when the monks were most concerned to increase their output, was that purchased by *conversi* or by the abbey's servants and marketed with the monastic clip. The Cistercians enjoyed many advantages in the marketing of wool, but houses often found themselves struggling to fulfil long-term contracts. Flocks, as we have seen, fluctuated greatly in size, chiefly on account of their liability to disease. Even the chroniclers of Waverley (1277) and Louth Park (1275), mostly concerned with great events, found room to comment when 'murrain' was rampant.[58] On Beaulieu's estates in 1269-70, *morina* reduced the number of lambs by almost fifty per cent and of adult sheep by sixteen per cent (1677 animals in all).[59] Flaxley (1281) and Rievaulx (1288) also suffered severely during the second half of the thirteenth century.[60] Complaints recur throughout the fourteenth and fifteenth centuries,[61] and even as late as 1530 Vaudey lost a thousand sheep through 'rot'. Probably in many cases the buying-up of wool (notwithstanding stiff opposition from towns that were deprived of revenue) was to make good such occasional losses and in general to compensate for too optimistic estimates of future production. We know that between 1285 and 1288 Kirkstead was allowed to purchase wool throughout Lincolnshire to make up for mortality among its sheep.[62] In 1268 the monastery's practice of buying wool had been upheld:

> Whereas the king has taken under his protection the abbot and convent of Kirkstead ... and certain men of the county of Lincoln prevent the said abbot and their brethren and their servants who buy, sell, collect and make profit of wool and hides to the use of the abbot and convent from trading and making profit thereof as they have been used to do: the king commands

[57] *Book Comb.*, p. 37.

[58] *Ann. Wav.*, pp. 388-89; *Chron. L. P.*, p. 18: sheep attacked by 'scab.' 'Scab' was apparently introduced from Spain.

[59] *Account B.*, p. 31. See also C. H. Talbot, 'The Account Book of Beaulieu Abbey,' *Citeaux in de Nederlanden*, 9 (1958): 197.

[60] *C.P.R.*, AD 1281-92, pp. 2, 294.

[61] On the effects of both sheep and cattle murrain in the early fourteenth century, see I. Kershaw, 'The great famine and agrarian crisis in England, 1315-22,' *Past and Present*, no. 59 (1973): 14, 20, 22, 24, 26-28.

[62] *C.P.R.*, AD 1281-92, p. 160.

all bailiffs not to interfere with them or permit them to be molested, for three years.[63]

The Chapter General of the order prohibited such ventures as early as 1157.[64] In 1214 Fountains and Whitland were ordered to investigate reports of trading in wool by the English *conversi.*[65] Although mentioned again in 1237,[66] the practice may have been largely confined to certain districts, particularly Yorkshire and Lincolnshire, counties which included most of the great wool houses. The citizens of Lincoln protested to Henry III that *conversi* of the order were buying up wool, with the following result:

> To the abbots of the Cistercian order and other religious men in the county of Lincoln [1262]. The king is informed that they have caused wool and other things to be bought in parcels (*particulatim*) by their lay brethren in divers places of the said county, and afterwards caused these to be sold to merchants of beyond seas and others together with their own wool, in this way carrying on business contrary to the debt of honesty (*debitum honestatis*) of their order and to the impoverishment of the city of Lincoln, and other of the king's market towns in that county, whereby the farms and customs due to him are fraudulently withdrawn; wherefore the king commands them to desist from this kind of business, or the king will lay the hand of correction upon them not lightly.[67]

The general charge was repeated in 1342[68] but never, so far as is known, after the Black Death. The Hundred Rolls of 1275 specifically mention Revesby, Kirkstead, Louth Park and Vaudey, all in Lincolnshire. A brother of Vaudey had apparently collected wool to the amount of fifty sacks in the wapentake of *Belteslawe* and was taking it to Boston. About the same time (1276) Fountains was selling to Dunelmo Joute and Bernardo Thechaldi, Florentine merchants, sixty-two sacks "*de collecta monasterii nostri.*" This amount, which had to be delivered over a period of four years, was only fourteen sacks short of what Pegolotti indicated was available each year from Fountains. Robert of Skyrne, abbot of Meaux 1270-80, sold six score sacks of his *collecta* to merchants of Boston and

[63] *C.P.R.*, AD 1266-72, p. 237. Beaulieu purchased 5 1/2 sacks and 10 1/2 stones of wool in 1269-70 (*Account B.*, p. 32). "Thomas de Haneworth, monk of Tintern" appears in a list of wool merchants of 1272 (*C.P.R.*, AD 1266-72, p. 703).

[64] *Statuta*, 1: 61.

[65] Ibid., p. 426.

[66] *C.Cl.R.*, AD 1234-37, p. 532.

[67] *C.P.R.*, AD 1258-66, p. 203; *Rot. Parl.*, 1: 156-57.

[68] *C.P.R.*, AD 1340-43, p. 441; *Foedera*, 2: 1186.

another quantity to the Ricardi of Lucca. In 1287 a successor agreed to deliver eleven sacks from his own sheep (*de propriis bidentibus*) while already under contract to sell to the Cerchi of Florence 108 sacks of wool from estates immediately adjacent to the monastery. These provisions were no doubt inserted to prevent the inclusion of inferior *collecta*.

Finally, there is the question of rents in wool. They seem to have been a late feature of the Cistercian economy, perhaps first appearing after the Black Death. Strata Florida, Whitland (both Welsh houses) and Furness received rents in wool about the time of the Dissolution.

Common of Pasture and Contacts with the Neighbouring Population

The foundation endowments of Cistercian houses often included large amounts of pasture. Much of this was of low quality and the grantor consequently surrendered very little. From about the middle of the twelfth century, the monks' growing reputation as graziers attracted further grants. Two descriptions were used: simply 'pasture', and 'common of pasture' (*communa pasturae*). The latter implied the right to use common grazing. On the other hand, 'pasture' was not always held in severalty; the wording of certain charters makes this clear. Fountains, for example, received between 1170 and 1185 'pasture' for thirty sheep at Kirkheaton "*per totum ubi alia averia de Heton vadunt.*" Again Rievaulx in 1152 was granted "*pasturam ad trecentas oves per omnem pasturam de Willardby*," which appears to refer to the common land of the vill of Willerby. Common grazing probably played a more important part in the Cistercian economy than the charters would necessarily indicate.

In any case, nearly half the grants made before ca. 1350 were of 'common of pasture', and from the middle of the twelfth century at least there does not seem to have been any reluctance on the part of the monks to accept these. The first to specify the actual number of sheep belong, so far as is known, to the sixth decade of the twelfth century.[69] F. A. Mullin thought that some grants were of a temporary nature,[70] but only one clear example of this has been discovered; in 1154 Fountains obtained 'common of pasture' in Well and Snape for a period of ten years.[71]

Grazing rights attached to open-field arable are sometimes referred to in general terms; thus Kirkstall (1170-82) received twelve bovates in

[69] *E.Y.C.*, 2: 156 (1155-6): 1000 sheep; ibid., 4: 46 (1158): 200 sheep.

[70] *A History of the Work of the Cistercians in Yorkshire (1131-1300)* (Washington, 1932), p. 10.

[71] *E.Y.C.*, 5: 314.

Bessacar "*et quicquid ad illas pertinet in pasturis.*" When animals are mentioned, numbers varied greatly per unit of arable, even between villages in broadly similar physical settings. Meaux had rights in Sutton and Arnold, both within the plain of Holderness. In the former, 100 sheep and twenty larger animals were allowed per bovate in 1269-70, but at Arnold (1286-1310) only twenty sheep and eight larger animals, which corresponded to the position in another neighbouring township, Wawne, in 1221-35. Rievaulx (1162-75) obtained grazing for 1000 sheep in respect of half a carucate, or four bovates, in Folkton, whereas at Allerston on the opposite side of the Vale of Pickering a whole carucate carried with it in 1160 the right to pasture only 500 sheep. Naturally enough there was a generous allowance in places within the Pennines: 200 per bovate at West Morton (ca. 1200) and Malham (1259) and 150 at Preston. On the other hand, the number was only twenty-five at Aldwark in the predominantly arable Vale of York.

The use of common pasture necessarily involved contact with the neighbouring population. There were also sometimes special arrangements concerning the folding of animals, an important matter in itself and one which concerned the disposal of animal manure. Kirkstead (1185-93) received pasture for 700 sheep in Seacroft. The grantor, exercising the manorial *jus faldae*, stipulated that 400 of these had to be kept in his cote; if, however, there happened to be any murrain about, the sheep could, by mutual consent, be folded elsewhere between Michaelmas and Whitsuntide — but 400 had to be in the said cote by the latter date.[72] Between 1190 and 1200 Hugh de Beauchamp gave Warden pasture for 480 sheep in Sandy. These were to be folded upon the grantor's land from mid-April until Martinmas when the weather allowed; any manure was to go to the abbey only when the sheep were under cover.[73] About a hundred years later (ca. 1291) a descendant of Hugh remitted the right to have 600 of the monks' sheep folded on his land at Sandy over the same period. In return for this concession, some 'common of pasture' and confirmation of all land held within his fee, Warden gave the very considerable sum of £20. Rievaulx was granted pasture for 500 sheep in Allerston in 1160, but was entitled to only half their droppings. The monks of Fountains on one occasion could "do what they wished with the manure" from 300 sheep, while on another, involving grazing for 200, the grantor claimed all of it.[74] Such petty bargaining occurred in every branch of the Cistercian economy.

[72] Ibid., 3: 308-9.
[73] *Chart. W.*, p. 246.
[74] *Chart. F.*, 1: 132; 2: 619.

Complete withdrawal from the affairs of the neighbouring population was hardly possible at any time, and after a decade or two does not seem to have been seriously attempted in England and Wales.

Seasonal Grazing and the Movement of Sheep

Much of our detailed knowledge of Cistercian sheep-farming comes from charters conveying rights of pasture. The information given is usually inadequate in at least two respects. In the first place, the grant may only be located with reference to some township. Evidence of seasonal grazing is often quite incidental and cannot be regarded as an adequate reflection of its importance. Secondly, we do not usually know for certain that these grants, however defined, were actually exercised, that sheep were grazed at all in the areas in question. Sometimes the grant included a bercary or sheep-fold, or one was later built by the monks, which may be taken as proof. But perhaps the most cogent reason for assuming that grants were regularly exploited lies in the widespread evidence of pressure upon grazing land during the twelfth and thirteenth centuries, and of houses being only too ready to overstep their rights if given the slightest opportunity. Contemporary statements illustrate different aspects of this situation. Between 1188 and 1205 Roche received two bovates in Bramley accompanied by 'common of pasture' for 100 sheep "and no more." Kirkstall's grazing in Riddlesden and Morton, sufficient for 200 sheep, was carefully limited by "the highway extending from the house of Robert of Mohaut to the vill of Bingley." Louth Park had common for a maximum of 1313 sheep (the odd number is perhaps significant) in Binbrook, and a certain William of Gaunt claimed the right to see that the monks did not exceed their entitlement. We are told that Kirkstead kept the maximum number of animals at Blankney in 1185. Rievaulx was not to pasture more than 400 sheep ("*plures quam CCCC oves*") in and around Raventhorpe. When in 1214 Dieulacres received some grazing "*ad omnia averia*" an assurance was obtained that the grantor would not enclose any part of this without leave of the abbot. Jervaulx's sheep in Wensleydale south of the Ure had to be counted thrice yearly and for every animal in excess of 1800 the abbey was fined a halfpenny. There were also many cases of grazing rights being retained when the holdings to which they belonged were demised.[75]

[75] For examples of litigation over rights of pasture, see *Fines*, 1: 55 (1205): Warden; *Rot. Orig.*, 1: 182 (1307-27): Sallay; *Pedes Finium*, P.R.S., 17 (1894), p. 71, no. 87 (1195): Revesby; *Pipe Roll 1198-9*, P.R.S., new ser., 9 (1932), p. 252: Vaudey.

To fully exploit available pasture, stock had to be moved about, particularly in early and late summer, to and from high ground and also low ground subject to flooding. This, incidently, further complicated the problem of tithes. As stated in the *Constitution* of Alexander, bishop of Coventry and Lichfield (1224-38), "if sheep are fed in one place in winter and another place in summer the tithes [of wool] shall be divided."[76]

Sallay could keep 480 sheep in Marton in summer and 720 in winter (1213-23); lying in the valley of the Aire, Marton was well suited to accommodate flocks from the surrounding hills in winter. Fountains (1268) had pasture for 500 sheep in Kettlewell on the upper Wharfe, "in winter only from *Calcuecotes* as far as *Wytebec.*" The same house also kept sheep in winter (Michaelmas to May 3rd) along the valleys of the Ure and the Nidd — 400 at Aldburgh and 200 at both Bewerley and Heyshaw grange. Rievaulx (1162-75) grazed up to 1000 sheep around Folkton in the Vale of Pickering, using either the open fields or adjacent marshland. Another 300 could be kept in 300 acres of 'waste' (*mora*) at Beadlam. This was probably marshland on the edge of the Vale, and it is interesting to find that the monks also enjoyed a right of way from Beadlam to a sheep cote at Skiplam grange towards the North Yorkshire Moors.

Cistercian houses received many rights of way during the twelfth and thirteenth centuries. As we have seen, Fountains wintered sheep at Kettlewell in Wharfedale. These were brought down the dale for shearing and then returned to the uplands; one grant allowed free transit for men and sheep going to and returning from shearing,[77] and another referred to the monks' right of way for cattle and 460 sheep in certain parts of Kettlewell. The convergence upon some place of large numbers of sheep at shearing time might mean arranging for extra pasture. Thus Warden could regularly graze 200 sheep in West Warden and (from 1205) another 400 during the eight days spent in shearing between Easter and midsummer. The need to dip sheep also might involve crossing other people's land. Dieulacres was granted a right of way and a special fold for this purpose in 1252; similarly Buildwas (1292) had "access to the Severn for washing sheep." The movement of animals is again implied in grants of pasture for sheep that were folded some distance away. Kirkstall received 'common of pasture' for 600 sheep around Harewood in 1209; 200 were to be drawn from the bercary at Wike and the remainder from Bardsey, each about two

[76] *Ledger V.R.*, p. 158.

[77] *Chart. F.*, 1: 350. See also R.H.C. Davis, ed. *The Kalendar of Abbot Samson of Bury St. Edmunds*, Camden Society Publications, 3rd ser., 84 (London, 1954), p. 134: to Sibton (ca. 1181-1211), free transit for up to 1500 sheep and lambs during four days of shearing.

miles distant. Three hundred sheep grazed at Bramhope were folded at Cookridge; and others from the grange of Micklethwaite were sometimes stationed at Clifford, ten miles to the east.

Flocks moved between high and low pastures according to the season, but there is no evidence of transhumance involving the temporary occupation of isolated huts or shielings. The distance between permanently occupied buildings along the valley floor and the most far-ranging sheep was never very great, and milking and the making of butter and cheese, which probably made shielings necessary in the case of dairy cattle, were not usually associated with Cistercian sheep-farming.

Sheep Fold and Wool Shed

Charters to Cistercian houses occasionally throw some light on the form of the medieval *bercaria* (bercary or sheep-fold) and *lanaria* (wool shed). The area of the bercary, including perhaps an adjacent close, is sometimes mentioned. This amounted to half an acre at Willerby (1152) where Rievaulx owned land, and again at *Le Cotes* (1291) belonging to Combermere. The sheep-folds at Fountains' grange at Kirby Wiske occupied a full acre (ca. 1174-84). As much as three acres were set aside at the large, predominantly arable grange of Baldersby in the Vale of York and again at Allerston near the northern margin of the Vale of Pickering. These places with large cotes probably accommodated flocks which spent the summer months on the high moors or in the upper dales. Furthermore, the value of animal manure on or close to extensive ploughlands was certainly not overlooked by the monks.

Towards the close of the fourteenth century there was a "new bercary," 160 feet in length, at Wharram grange (Meaux). Another at Greenbury (Fountains) measured 260 feet in each direction. The larger areal and linear measurements probably refer to the site of the bercary rather than to the ground actually within the fold or folds. In 1173-4 Rievaulx received the site (*sedem*) of a bercary at Bolton grange. The surrounding area would doubtless be used for marshalling or sorting the sheep. Closes, courts (*curtis, curia*) and enclosures were often associated with bercaries. In 1285 Fountains was granted "three roods of meadow within the enclosure (*clausturam*) of the *bercarie* of the abbot [in East Morton]." Combermere's sheep-fold, already mentioned, had four acres attached to it. Occasionally, *bercaria* may simply mean 'pasture' or 'sheepwalk',[78] but as

[78] *C.A.D.*, 1: 228, B. 123, (1256); see also *Account B.*, p. 164. Crofts were sometimes granted for use as bercaries (*Chart. F.*, 1: 43; *Chart. D.*, p. 338).

a rule we should visualize a corner of land, possibly hedged or dyked, mainly but not entirely occupied by cotes.

Meaux had pasture for 2000 sheep at Sutton grange ca. 1280-6 and there were eight bercaries — an average of 250 sheep to each fold. Byland's bercary at West Bretton (ca. 1190-1220) could take 200. Grants of sites for sheep-folds at Austhorpe and West Morton to Kirkstall (ca. 1170-90) and Fountains (ca. 1200) respectively were followed in each case by pasture for 200 sheep. The corresponding number was 260 in a grant to Kirkstall at Morley, 1190-1210, and 500 to Rievaulx at Allerston in 1160. In 1253 Warden was given a fold (*unam faldam*) and 'common of pasture' for 400 sheep. Louth Park (ca. 1275) had a bercary at Fulstow (Lincolnshire) with grazing for 900 sheep.

The walls of many bercaries appear to have resembled the brushwood 'hedges' placed around growing meadows. *Caula* could mean either a sheep-fold or a hurdle. Tilty used "alder wood, thorns and dead wood" (1251) for folds. Fountains made use of boughs (*virgas*) as well as stone. More often we are simply told that wood was granted for the purpose of erecting bercaries. Between 1185 and 1193 Kirkstall was provided with wood in Seacroft for making and repairing "hedges, sheep-folds and folds" (*bercharias et faldas*). The destruction of woodland around Pipewell was explained as partly due to the construction of bercaries.[79] Fountains was allowed to cut ferns (*feugeriam*) for roofing cotes. There are many references to sheep "under cover" or "in houses."

Most monasteries would possess only one, central wool house and references to the *lanaria* are disappointingly meagre. That at Wawne grange near Meaux was built of stone and roofed with lead (1235-49).[80] Wool from Beaulieu's estates was brought to a central depot (*bergerie*), about three miles south of the abbey. *Conversi* ran Fountains' *lanaria* in 1279. Byland had a wool shed at Thorpe, about three miles south-east of the abbey; the prioress of Arden, in an agreement with merchants of the Frescobaldi of Florence, was obliged to take her convent's wool "*ad lanaria de Bella Landa.*"[81] A stone building was probably preferred because of the value of the wool clip. For the same reason it is unlikely that wool was ever stored in isolated depots, although the above examples show that the place might lie outside the immediate vicinity of the abbey. A neighbouring grange would be very convenient, while preserving peace

[79] *Mon. Angl.*, 5: 435; cf. *Chart. Bl.*, p. xxxiv.

[80] *Chron. M.*, 2: 64: "*lanaria lapidea apud Waghnam constructa est et plumbo cooperta.*"

[81] Hall, *Select Cases*, p. 69.

within the abbey precincts, for wool was not only stored, cleansed, sorted, graded and packed at the wool shed but inspected there by merchants or their agents. In the agreement between Pipewell and some merchants of Cahors (already quoted), one of the clauses ran:

> It is ordained that the wool-shed (*lanar'*) in which the wool shall be and has been wont to be prepared shall be got ready with boards firmly attached that the wool shall reach from the land or pavement of the wool-shed to the height of half a foot, and in the same way the said wool-shed shall be got ready with boards firmly attached along (*per*) the walls about the wool during the term aforesaid ... .

Wool and Wealth

It is possible broadly to compare the 'wealth' of Cistercian houses and their respective wool surpluses. The wool list bequeathed by F. B. Pegolotti probably belongs to the period 1281-96. This spans the date (ca. 1291) of the valuation of temporal property in the *Taxatio Ecclesiastica* which provides details of the seventy-five Cistercian houses of England and Wales. Twenty-nine exceeded the average valuation of members of the order, and of these nineteen also marketed more than the average quantity of wool (18.8 sacks).[82] The remaining ten had a respectable average of thirteen sacks. Moreover, all houses with over twenty-five sacks for sale were assessed at relatively high sums in the *Taxatio*.

The Coucher Book of Furness abbey lists the contributions of fifty-nine Cistercian houses to an exaction of £12,000,[83] and these sums also can be compared with wool output. Vale Royal (*Vallis Regalis*), which the assessment includes, was not founded until 1281 and no house founded after this is given. The document appears to belong to the close of the thirteenth century. In comparing the monetary contributions of these fifty-nine houses with their marketable wool (Fig. 13), a distinction may be drawn between communities to the north-west and to the south-east of a line running diagonally across England and roughly following the Oolitic scarp. Among the former, a disproportionate interest in wool growing appears to have been the rule rather than the exception, whereas the opposite was the case in the South East. The latter was relatively closely settled and included most of the long-established Benedictine houses. Consequently, grants of pasture were for the most part less generous. The zone wherein

[82] The amounts in the various grades are not given; consequently we cannot calculate the value of the wool available, either collectively or for individual houses.

[83] *Coucher F.*, 3: 639.

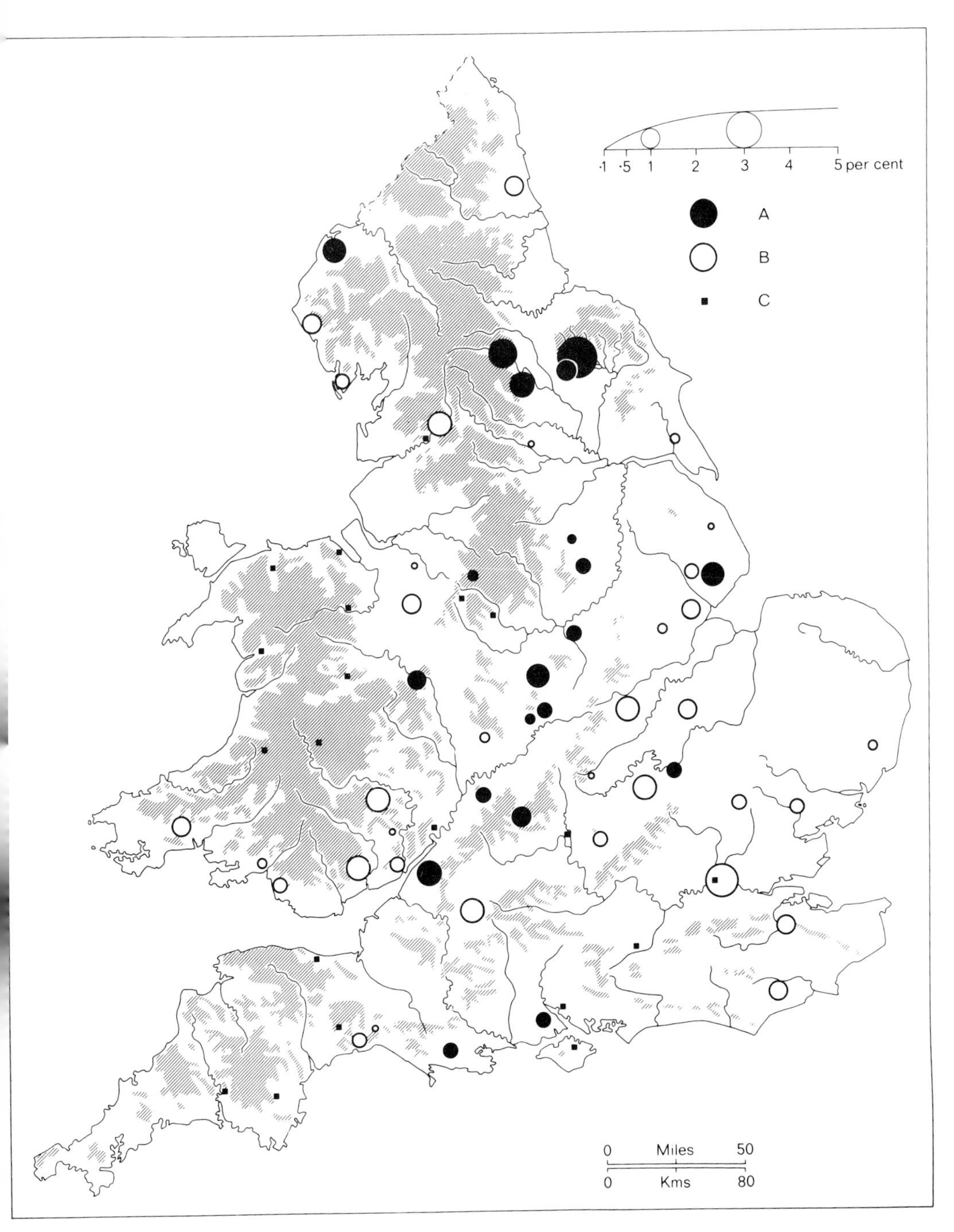

Fig. 13

A comparison of the wool surplus and 'wealth' of Cistercian houses ca. 1300. The amount by which their percentage contribution to the combined Cistercian wool clip (after Pegolotti) exceeded [A] or fell short [B] of their percentage contribution to an exaction of £12,000.
C: houses founded after 1300 or for which there is insufficient information.

wool was of overriding importance broadly extended from North Yorkshire through the Midlands to the Cotswold scarp. The Lincolnshire houses rivalled those of Yorkshire in terms of production alone, but, with the exception of Revesby, they were probably not disproportionately interested in wool. The houses of South Wales also were wealthier than their wool surpluses (above average only in the case of Margam) might suggest.

4

New Land and Natural Products

Clearing and Draining

The Setting

It is generally assumed that Cistercian houses were sited in remote and desolate places, conforming in practice to the statute of 1134.[1] The monks usually chose unoccupied ground that was more or less secluded; but, as we have seen, over one-third of the English and Welsh communities migrated at least once, usually to live under less adverse physical conditions. Furthermore, a study of the early English houses shows that few, if any, were particularly remote. They lay rather around the margins of a substantially complete pattern of settlement. By the twelfth century there were no very extensive areas waiting to be colonized, and from the first the monks and *conversi* worked in fairly close proximity to peasant cultivators who were extending village arable.

To describe and to compare settlement conditions in widely scattered districts around the middle of the twelfth century clearly is difficult. However something may be learned from the place names within a limited radius — say five miles — of each of the thirty-three English houses founded between 1128 and 1152 (excluding houses of Savignac derivation united to Cîteaux in 1147). All names appearing on the Ordnance Survey one-inch to one-mile (1: 63360) sheets may usefully be considered; most field names, on the other hand, are not recorded before the period for which we have abundant evidence of Cistercian activity. Even in respect of settlement names there are many problems. The interpretation of some quite common suffixes is not generally agreed, and

[1] *Statuta*, 1: 13.

one has to allow for a considerable margin of error in deciding when a name was first applied as distinct from when it was first recorded. If, for some reason, a place is not given in Domesday Book (1086), then it is quite probable that the first reference to it will post-date the founding of the neighbouring Cistercian house. Yet it certainly cannot be concluded from this that it is a later settlement; the opposite is at least as likely to be true for, apart from what we know of the chronology of peasant colonization, very few settlements seem to have been started near existing Cistercian communities.

All but one of the thirty-three areas include place names recorded before the date of foundation of the local monastery (the exception is Newminster in Northumberland which was omitted from the Domesday survey). There are only a few such names around Holm Cultram (Cumberland), Rievaulx and Sallay (Yorkshire), but some other northern houses — Fountains, Kirkstall and Meaux — are quite thickly surrounded, and the same is generally true of those in the Midlands and the South where several areas contain more than ten.

Scrub and low vegetation: Place-name elements indicative of scrubland are found in combination with *-lēah, -feld* and other 'clearing' suffixes. Examples include brier (*brerehagh*) in the vicinity of Kirkstall; bent-grass (*beonet-*) near Merevale, Bordesley and Waverley; broom (*brom-*) near Kirkstall, Roche and Boxley; and furze (*fyrs-*) near Kirkstead. Others are not combined with 'clearing' suffixes:

thorn (*thorne*)	Fountains, Rievaulx, Holm Cultram, Sallay, Garendon, Meaux, Kirkstead, Sibton, Woburn, Flexley, Forde, Dore.
lichen (*lav*)	Rievaulx.
hips (*hēope*)	Fountains.
heather-heath (*hāēth*)	Bordesley, Kingswood, Stoneleigh, Woburn.
bracken (*brachen*)	Louth Park.
thicket (*wrāēst*)	Warden.
fern (*fearn*)	Waverley.
gorse (*ceart*)	Waverley.

Scrub occurred very widely, under various geological and geographical conditions (there has perhaps been a tendency to overwork the phrase 'woodland clearing'). Cistercian documents abound in references to grants of 'waste' (*terra vasta*) and to heathland or brushwood (*brueria*, *brusua*, *brucosa*), broom (*geneteum*, *genectum*) and thorn-covered ground (*spina*). The monks of Kirkstall when they moved into the valley of the Aire ca. 1152 were confronted with "*spineta condensa.*" Combe, around the beginning of the thirteenth century, received "*C acris terre in brueria de*

Wlueia" (Wolvey). Such awards were often followed by assarting to improve grazing or for the purpose of cultivation.

Marshland: The tradition of marshland siting was as old as the order itself; the name *Cistercium* was derived from *cisternae* or *cistels* meaning wet, reed-covered ground.[2] Contemporary descriptions of marshy tracts around Louth Park, Kirkstead, Revesby, Sawtry (all close by the Fens), Meaux in Holderness, Holm Cultram on the Solway Firth, and Stanlaw on the Mersey estuary are discussed below. Place and locality names reinforce these statements (although only at Stanlaw did conditions result in any significant re-siting), and marshland elements also occur along valleys near Flaxley, Biddlesden, Bordesley, Dore, Roche, Merevale, Waverley and Sallay. 'Alder' and 'willow' are incorporated in place names around Kirkstall, Rufford, Waverley, Combe, Stoneleigh and Dore. These species are generally associated with wet conditions, as an early description of the site of Swineshead illustrates — "*locus infra salices in marisco de Swynesheved, in quo abbatia fundata est*" (1154-89).

Woodland: Wooded districts, affording both solitude and the most essential building material, were favoured by most religious orders. Orderic Vital, writing about the beginning of the Cistercian era, quoted a contemporary view that supplies of wood and water were essential prerequisites for the foundation of a monastery.[3] Several of the early houses of the new orders, including the founder members, lay in or alongside extensive tracts of woodland.[4] Cîteaux and Clairvaux gave their names to *forêts domaniales*,[5] while other names of monasteries were directly inspired by the presence of woodland.[6] One-third of the English houses founded by 1250, including six of the eight royal foundations, lay in or very near royal forests. Some of these 'forests,' especially in the Midlands, contained considerable stands of timber, but elsewhere scrub and rough pasture were more prominent.

[2] C. Du Cange, *Glossarium mediae et infimae Latinitatis* (Paris, 1842), vol. 2: "*loco humili et paludoso*"; alternatively *citeals* or *cisteauls* (*Catholic Encyclopedia*, 3: 792). See also W. A. Mason, 'The Beginnings of the Cistercian Order,' *T.R.H.S.*, 2nd ser., 19 (1905): 169-70; and A. Dimier, 'Cîteaux et les emplacements malsains,' *Cîteaux in de Nederlanden*, 6 (1955): 89-97.

[3] *The Ecclesiastical History of Orderic Vitalis*, ed. and trans. M. Chibnall (Oxford, 1969), 2: 14-15 — "*Certum est quod absque istis duobus elementis, monachi esse non possunt.*"

[4] P. Deffontaines, *L'Homme et la forêt* (Paris, 1933), p. 22; J. Buhot, 'L'abbaye normande de Savigny, chef d'ordre et fille de Cîteaux,' *Le Moyen Age*, 3e ser., 7/vol. 46 (1936): 1-2, 5; G. Roupnel, *Histoire de la campagne française* (Paris, 1932), p. 88.

[5] M. Cateland, 'La forêt domaniale de Cîteaux,' *Revue du bois*, 10, no. 2 (1955): 10.

[6] G. Plaisance, 'Les Cisterciens et la forêt,' *Revue du bois*, 10, no. 7/8 (1955): 4.

The sites of houses along the eastern Pennines and in the north-east Midlands, between Fountains and Rufford, are surrounded by place-name elements suggesting clearing, the great majority documented before the middle of the twelfth century. Those combined with descriptions of low vegetation have already been mentioned. Others suggest the removal of high woodland. Fourteen are clustered along the river Aire to the east and west of Kirkstall, an area that we know was still wooded ("*locum nemorosum*") when the monks moved from Barnoldswick. The pattern around Fountains is more diffuse but the site of the monastery was still flanked by woods some time before 1189.[7] Notable groups also occur near Newminster (mostly of late documentation), Meaux, Vaudey, Combe, and Merevale.

Names that refer to woodland generally (*hyrst, wudu*) or to particular species (without a suffix in *-lēah* or *-feld*, but implying clearing) are absent around Rievaulx and not at all prominent along the Pennine slopes in the vicinity of Cistercian houses. The opposite, however, is true of the Midlands. Fifteen lie around Stoneleigh, "*in bruillo de Eacheles.*"[8] Near Bordesley there are ten such names, and rather fewer around Combe, Pipewell (ash, oak, birch), Rufford (maple, oak), Garendon, and Merevale (no more than an 'outwood' of Grendon in 1086).[9] Further south, the area around Thame provides evidence of oak and hazel, Woburn of aspen and oak, Warden of maple, Kingswood of yew and birch, and Waverley of ash, alder and yew.

Folk and settlement names: Finally, there are the suffixes associated with the basic framework of Anglo-Saxon settlement: *-ingas* (ing), *-ingahām* (ingham), *-hām* (ham), *-ingatūn* (ington) and *-tūn* (ton), the first two at least being generally regarded as early. The rest remained in use until later, in certain areas in the case of *-tūn* until after the Norman conquest. Nevertheless, the great majority undoubtedly belong to the main period of settlement. It is therefore significant that they are to be found in fairly close proximity to all Cistercian sites. By the beginning of the

[7] *Mem. F.*, 1: 95.

[8] *Mon. Angl.*, 5: 447; *Ledger S.*, pp. xii-xvi, 15. In Domesday Book "the vast wood of Stoneleigh is entered as capable of feeding 2000 pigs" (*V.C.H.* (*Warwickshire*, 1908), 2: 288; 6 (1957): 229.

[9] W. Dugdale, *The Antiquities of Warwickshire Illustrated*, 2nd ed. (London, 1730), 2: 1086. Dugdale described the site as within "this mountainous and woody desert." Vale Royal (Darnhall, 1274) in Cheshire was also sited within woodland (1281) (*Mon. Angl.*, 5: 703). The place was earlier called *Munechenwro* (*wro*, woodland) (*Ledger V.R.*, p. 7). In 1360 the bishop of St. Davids described Vale Royal as "situated in a poor district in the woodland" (ibid., p. 190).

second quarter of the twelfth century the tide of colonization had passed beyond these areas or at least stood level with them. At the same time, much undeveloped country remained within the pattern of villages and hamlets and this provided the chief opportunity for Cistercian land clearing and other secondary colonization.

Only to the south-east of the Chilterns did each house lie adjacent to settlements with names incorporating *-ingas* or *ingahām* or *-hām*. *Ingas* is sometimes found as far as the Oolitic escarpment, the last two elements on rare occasions beyond it. In the north-western half of the country only *-ingatūn* or *-tūn* appear in all areas. These differences correspond with the general advance of settlement from the south and east towards the north-west.

Assarts and Assarting

Strictly speaking, assarting was the process of clearing and stubbing up vegetation, to be followed, in the normal course of events, by cultivation. Permission *excolere* was a stage beyond that *assartare*. Henry II confirmed to Warden the wood of *Ravenshoe* which the monks assarted and made arable ("*fecerunt sartari et in terram arabilem redigi*"). A grant to Dieulacres in Pulford included the right "*ad assartanda et seminanda et aranda*," and the phrase "*assartare et in agriculturam terram redigere*" occurs in a description of woodland clearing around Pipewell. Whatever might be of use, such as constructional timber, firewood and bedding for animals, was first removed; then the ground could be finally cleared by burning.[10] Although assarts sometimes formed part of an 'outfield', cultivated for a few years and then left fallow for a much longer period,[11] this was certainly not always so. Assarts were managed in as wide a variety of ways as any other land and some were used as permanent pasture or as meadow.[12]

The available evidence comes largely from charters of the twelfth and thirteenth centuries. These sometimes convey assarts, or give permission

[10] G. Plaisance glosses *le sartage* as *brûlage de couverture* ('Les caractères originaux de l'exploitation ancienne des forêts,' *Rev. de Géog. de Lyon*, 28 (1953): 19).

[11] L. Champier, 'Cîteaux, ultime étape dans l'aménagement agraire de l'Occident,' in *Mélanges Saint Bernard. 24e Congrès de l'Association bourguignonne des sociétés savantes* (Dijon, 1953), p. 260.

[12] *E.Y.C.*, 3: 483 (1185-1215) — Kirkstall; *Chart. F.*, 1: 44, 51; 2: 534; *C.Ch.R.*, AD 1300-26, p. 251 (1314, *conf.*) — Louth Park; W. Maas, *Les moines-défricheurs* (Moulins, 1944), pp. 33, 43-45, 51.

to assart, or indicate that land had been or was being assarted.[13] The important distinction between gifts and clearing by the monks themselves is generally lost in later documents. Nevertheless, an exhaustive examination of the activities of a particular house would necessarily involve consideration of the many 'riddings', 'stubbings', 'intakes', 'cultures', and 'closes' in surveys of Cistercian property from the late fourteenth century onwards.[14]

There are many more references to grants of assarts than to clearings made by the monks themselves.[15] At the same time, the monasteries often enjoyed considerable freedom of action. We read of grants of land "*ad sartandam et arandam vel quicquid eis inde placuerit faciendam.*"[16] The phrase "do whatever they wish" is found in many Cistercian charters, sometimes in a context that does not specifically mention assarting. Yet it could obviously be interpreted as permission to clear and to cultivate, especially when combined with a licence to enclose. Furthermore, we rarely have any information about what happened to a great many gifts of uncultivated land, most of them without any special conditions or rights attached. Conversely, Cistercian houses were at times responsible for clearing land which was only later conveyed to them; in other words, some 'gifts' followed preliminary work by or on behalf of the monks. Thus Rievaulx in the period 1150-7 was given ten acres of land in Pilley "*quas ipsi sartaverunt.*" Similarly Fountains received land in South Stainley (1165-75), and Warden in Paxton (1157-65) and Diddington (1154-63), in each case after they had cleared and possibly cultivated the ground.

A large number of assarts were acquired as appurtenances to open-field holdings. T. A. M. Bishop concluded that "not merely does the assart occur as appurtenant to open-field holdings [in Yorkshire]; we are justified ... in suspecting that it was a normal appurtenance."[17] Bishop

[13] Tabulated for houses in Yorkshire and Northumberland in R. A. Donkin, 'The English Cistercians and assarting, c. 1128-1350,' *A.S.O.C.*, 20 (1964): 86-72 (Appendix 1).

[14] 'Assart' and 'ridding' were virtually synonymous. Tintern's *grangia de Assarto* (*Tax. Eccles.*, p. 282) elsewhere is called Rudding grange. In a Vale Royal rental of 1334 there is "an assart which is called *Badecok rudinges*" (*Ledger V. R.*, p. 96). For other examples see *Coucher W.*, 3: 923 (*Greneruydyng*); *Chart. R.*, p. 292 (*Swinesridding*); and *Chart. F.*, 2: 825 (*Helewiseridding*).

[15] Similarly W. Maas, *Les moines-défricheurs*, p. 52: "De notre région non plus, nous ne possedons pas beaucoup de documents où l'ont dit, expressis verbis, que les moines ont défriché."

[16] *Documents Illustrative of the Social and Economic History of the Danelaw, from Various Collections*. Records of the Social and Economic History of England and Wales, 5 (London, 1920), p. 88.

[17] 'Assarting and the growth of the open fields,' *Ec. Hist. Rev.*, 6 (1935-36): 26.

quotes a few examples involving Cistercian houses and there are many others that support his argument. Although perhaps particularly common in Yorkshire, where much despoiled land was cleared during the twelfth century, it is a feature that has been widely reported. The evidence is sometimes quite specific ("*totam terram cum assartis eidem terrae conjunctis*"); but it is more usual to find assarts listed in a very formal way along with 'moor', 'marsh' and 'pasture'.

The extent to which the Cistercians developed arable and pasture at the expense of 'waste' and woodland varied from region to region and even between neighbouring houses. While many studies stress their contribution,[18] others have produced conclusions that are less in accord with the general reputation of the order.[19]

An assart was usually held in severalty; it could be enclosed and worked as its owner wished. For example, when Warden was permitted to assart the wood of *Pirie* (East Perry, Huntingdonshire), enclosing the ground with a ditch and fence, it was also conceded "*quod nullus communicet cum illis in essarto illo.*" On the other hand, clearings made to extend the open fields usually lost their separate identity in becoming subject to communal husbandry. This only concerned the monks in so far as they might share in the increment in proportion to their existing open-field holdings — and every Cistercian house had many scattered strips in addition to relatively consolidated estates. The assarts conveyed by charter, and those for which the monks were directly responsible were, almost by definition, individually owned and could be retained as units of cultivation or combined with similar property, whichever was the more convenient.

Another important inducement to assart lay in the fact that members of the order did not have to pay tithes on freshly cultivated ground. From 1132 to the meeting of the Fourth Lateran Council in 1215 the Cister-

[18] For example, F. Goblet, *Histoire des bois et forêts de Belgique* (Paris, 1927): 'Les Cisterciens défricheurs,' 1: 159-84; B. Lyon, 'Mediaeval real estate developments and freedom,' *Amer. Hist. Rev.*, 63 (1957-58): 51 (Flanders); P. Buffault, 'Les forêts de l'Europe pendant le moyen âge,' *Revue des eaux et forêts*, 74 (1937): 148 (Germany); H. Dubled, 'Aspects de l'économie cistercienne en Alsace au XIIe siècle,' *Revue d'histoire ecclésiastique*, 54 (1959): 766, 776-77; Th. Sclafert, 'A propos du déboisement des Alpes du Sud,' *Annales de Géographie*, 42 (1933): 274.

[19] E. Krausen, 'Les particularités de l'Ordre cistercien en Bavière et en Franconie dans l'organisation agricole et l'art de ces pays,' in *Mélanges Saint Bernard. 24e Congrès de l'Association bourguignonne des sociétés savantes* (Dijon, 1953), p. 297; O Grandmottet, 'Aspects du temporel de l'abbaye d'Auberive des origines à la fin du XIIIe siècle,' *Les Cahiers Haut-Marnais*, 52 (1958): 1, 13; J. Krasoń, *Uposażenie Klasztoru Cystersów w Wiekach Srednich* (Poznań, 1950), p. 173: "Ainsi l'opinion, selon laquelle les Cisterciens auraient été convoqués ici afin de cultiver les déserts et les friches et afin de peupler les forêts et les lieux écartés ne trouve pas de confirmation dans l'histoire de l'abbaye d'Obra."

cians could claim exemption on all land cultivated by themselves.[20] Thereafter, the privilege was held to apply only to land newly brought into cultivation (*novalia*), whether acquired before or after the Council, and to land acquired before the Council and still cultivated by the monks. Exemption in any form was naturally opposed by those to whom tithes were due, and houses sometimes found it expedient to conclude special agreements, even in respect of their own assarts for which the strongest case could be made out. Newnham priory agreed (1199) that Warden's assarts should not be tithed; and in 1314 Stanley obtained a "release of the claims to tithes from [its] newly tilled land (*novalibus*) ... at *le Mershe* in the parish of Chippenham."[21] After about the middle of the fourteenth century — earlier in some areas — the situation was largely reversed; while houses of the order acquired an increasing number of churches, and thus rights to tithes, they leased out much of their landed property on which payment had earlier been excused.

The founders of the Cistercian order laid great emphasis on the value of *labor manuum*,[22] and, for some time at least, the first generation of monks on any particular site could expect to take part in clearing operations. The bulk of such work, however, eventually became the responsibility of the *conversi*.[23] The latter were numerous enough during the twelfth century, but their number had fallen considerably by the end of the thirteenth century and had reached vanishing point by the time of the Black Death. Moreover, long before this, *conversi* engaged in agricultural work were mainly employed as overseers of granges rather than actual labourers. These trends, like the leasing out of land which turned the monks into *rentiers*, were apparent throughout much of Europe. On the other hand, the relationship between Cistercian monks and the peasantry in matters of clearing and colonization during the order's active phase (lasting about 200 years in the case of houses founded before 1150) varied a good deal. East of the Elbe, in the Spanish march, and on more local scale elsewhere, they co-operated in schemes of land settlement.[24] There was little or no

[20] *Statuta*, 1: 9, 449. Adrian IV's (1154-9) decision to limit the right to newly broken land was reversed in 1160 and had little, if any, effect.

[21] *C.A.D.*, 4: A 9366. According to J. S. Donnelly, special exemption was granted by bishops as early as 1118 (*Decline of the Medieval Cistercian Laybrotherhood* (New York: Fordham University Press, 1949), p. 44). See *Chart. Bl.*, pp. 33 (1206-9), 34 (after July, 1213) for examples of the agreed division of tithes on cultivated land.

[22] *Statuta*, 1: 14.

[23] Deffontaines, *L'Homme et la forêt*, p. 22, writes of "*frères sartaires* chargés uniquement d'ouvrir de nouvelles clairières."

[24] See C. Higounet, 'Cisterciens et Bastides,' *Le Moyen Age*, 4e sér., 5/vol. 56 (1950): 69-84; and J. Flach, 'Les villages créés dans les forêts et sur les terres désertes,' in *Les*

opportunity for this in England, but even at the level of piecemeal clearing the monks did not always work apart from the local population. As estates expanded, contact between the two inevitably increased, and as recruitment to the ranks of the *conversi* slackened, wage and tenurial labour became increasingly essential.

A charter to Fountains refers to the "assart which the said monks with their partners (*participibus*) have caused to be asserted." This was at Long Marston, the site of a grange before the close of the twelfth century. A subsequent agreement gave the free tenants there equal rights with the abbot and convent in the event of certain woods being cleared. Their 'partners' too are more likely to have been freemen than *conversi* or paid labourers.[25] Another example of a working association concerns Fountains' grange at Wheldrake, which, like Long Marston, was the scene of much assarting by the monks and their neighbours. The prior of Warter, an Augustinian house, gave to Fountains seventy acres of land in Wheldrake and, we are told, "Fountains and William Darell propose to assart in the same place." The two religious houses also agreed that there should be no assarting in Elvington "unless the abbot of Fountains and his men assarted in Wheldrake." Earlier (1175-6) Fountains received a carucate in Hawswick with the right that "if Mildred [de Hawswick] or Adam [son of Gospatrick] wished to till the land on the south side of the Skirfare the monks could till one-third part of the same." Furness, on several occasions, gave permission to others to 'approve' — probably to assart and enclose. Stoneleigh (1326) could dispose of "wastes which are or hereafter shall be brought into cultivation in the manor of Stoneleigh ... to tenants willing to receive them for life." In clearing operations frequent contact between the monks and lay folk could hardly be avoided and may often have been much closer, to the point of direct co-operation, than we can now show.

Clearing land for agricultural purposes normally commenced soon after a monastery was founded. We are told that the monks of Byland "*inceperunt assartare viriliter in occidentali parte citra et dejuxta Middleburgam et aedificare subtus moram in dicto territorio de Cukewolde.*"[26]

origines de l'ancienne France (Paris, 1893), 2: 153 — "Dans les forêts seigneuriales les moines servaient d'intermédiaires intéressés entre la population rurale et les seigneurs. Ils faisaient vraiment office d'entrepreneurs de défrichement."

[25] Wage labour is indicated in an expense account (1262-3) of Kingswood, one item of which reads, "to the assarters, 13s-8" (*Docs. K.*, p. 219).

[26] *Mon. Angl.*, 5: 351; also p. 353 — "*viriliter extirpare coeperunt de nemore*" (ca. 1177).

There is also clear evidence of assarting or the prospect of assarting from the first at Kirkstall, Combermere, Tintern, and Stoneleigh.[27] At the same time, recent assarts (with or without some old arable) were often included in a foundation grant, again illustrating that the Cistercians worked within rather than beyond the pioneer fringe. Warden was first known as Sancta Maria de Essartis, recalling the fact that it was endowed with "*totam assartam de Wardona.*"[28] Evidence of assarting by the monks themselves, supported by charters of confirmation, begins to accumulate about the middle of the twelfth century. It is most impressive for the period ca. 1150-ca. 1275, when efforts were mainly directed towards estates managed as granges, and it becomes very meagre after the opening decades of the fourteenth century.

The majority of references to assarts contain no exact information about their size. T. A. M. Bishop, writing of Yorkshire generally, thought that by *unum* or *quoddam assartum* we should probably understand a plot of about three or four acres cultivated by a single tenant. Cistercian assarts varied considerably in size, and some were much larger than four acres. When the monks acquired assarting rights over a substantial area, or were given an entirely free hand,[29] they generally had the resources to develop the land as a whole, although the work of clearing might extend over more than one season. References to the "*magnum sartum monachorum*" may be found in the records of Roche, Rievaulx, and Fountains. The largest known area (outside the royal forests) was 100 acres; Sallay (1189-93) and Fountains each received permission to clear this amount of woodland.[30] Plots of over ten acres are mentioned fairly often, but it is possible that some of these were not in one piece; on one occasion it was specially remarked that a clearing of thirty-six acres lay "all together." At the other end of the scale, there were many very small assarts. While the monks sometimes had the opportunity and generally the means to clear large areas in one operation, it was often just as important to them to reclaim an odd quarter of an acre so as to round off a holding or to connect two or more isolated plots.

[27] *Ledger S.*, p. 25: "*De bruillo de Echelus in quo abbacia est fundata per abbates et conuentus de Stonle redacti sunt in culturam apud le Homgrange campi.*"

[28] *Mon. Angl.*, 5: 372. G. Plaisance, "Les Cisterciens et la forêt,' p. 5, has given two other examples of similar nomenclature: *Sartum Beatae Mariae* (Rothem) and *Novale Sanctae Mariae* (Marienrode).

[29] For example, "*quantum de predictis boscis et pasturis eis placuerit assartare et excoli facere*" (*Coucher K.*, p. 25).

[30] *Chart. F.*, 2: 833; *Chart. S.*, 1: 126.

The Cistercian houses of Yorkshire made and acquired assarts over a wide area, but principally (a) along the north-western rim of the Vale of Pickering and the slopes of the Hambleton Hills; (b) in the Vale of York, north of the city of York; (c) in the Pennine dales, from the Calder to the Ure. Concerning the first of these areas, we know that Byland cleared woodland around Coxwold before 1177, and Rievaulx was permitted to "clear and cultivate" in Skiplam after receiving a stretch of 'waste'. The estate at Skiplam probably ranked as a grange and apparently lay beyond the general limits of Domesday settlement. In the Vale of York, Fountains in particular made a notable contribution to the revival of farming after the systematic destruction wrought by the armies of William I. Its granges of Wheldrake and Long Marston appear to have been very largely made up of recently assarted land. Both Fountains and Byland extended cultivation around holdings in the narrowest part of the Vale, scene of the most severe devastation in 1069. At Moulton (ca. 1150) Fountains reclaimed at least sixty acres of 'moor' (*mora*). The monks of Kirkstall were more interested in areas further south; between 1183 and 1200, for example, they were allowed to clear woodland for tillage near the grange of Bessacar — "*ut liceat eis totas illas terras colere, arare et inbladare.*"

Large numbers of assarts were acquired immediately around Fountains and Kirkstall, in the lower dales and on the interfluvial uplands. One of the many assarts granted to Kirkstall in Bramley (one mile to the south) was described as lying "next to the moor," and the same house made and received woodland clearings along the river Aire and its tributaries. Fountains, according to two undated charters, was allowed to assart woodland around the early granges of Brimham and Bradley. In 1193-1200 the monks received assarts in Kirkheaton, about two miles south of Bradley; at least one of these had displaced woodland and we are further informed that it was still bounded on one side by woodland and on the rest by assarts.[31]

There was also some assarting further up the dales, again not infrequently at the expense of woodland. At Bolton in Wensleydale, Rievaulx (1173-4) was given twenty-one acres of woodland and uncultivated ground wherein to assart; the estate here was managed as a grange before the end of the twelfth century. As late as 1330, Jervaulx was permitted to assart "as much woodland as it wished" at Askrigg, also in Wensleydale. Fountains made clearings around Kettlewell in Wharfedale and had the right to "approve and enclose" in Littondale. Kirkstall, before

[31] *E.Y.C.*, 3: 340.

1190, converted woodland in Riddlesden, eleven miles upstream of the house and between the granges of Micklethwaite and Elam. Fountains and Sallay too were active in upper Airedale. The first monks of Sallay were allowed to clear thirty acres of brushwood (*dumos*) around their house; this, like Byland's work at Coxwold and Kirkstall's in the valley of the Aire, shows the Cistercians commencing the task of improving their chosen sites.

Woodland soils normally promised to make good arable.[32] For this reason and also because of the value of cut timber, the removal of woodland is most frequently mentioned in connection with assarting. Apart from cases involving the Yorkshire houses and the royal forests, there is good evidence for Tintern (1131), Combermere (ca. 1133), Revesby (twelfth century), Basingwerk (1278-85), Stanlaw (before 1296), Garendon, Strata Florida,[33] Warden[34] and Pipewell.[35] At the same time, the value attached to growing timber sometimes effectively limited assarting.[36]

In 1246 Kirkstall was permitted to assart "woodland and pasture" in Scarcroft. On one occasion Combermere disposed of fifteen acres of pasture "which they had licence from the king to cultivate." Warden (1206-21) received a quitclaim to pasture with permission to bring it into cultivation (*infringere seminare*), and in 1210 the monks of Thame were allowed to till "or do whatever they wished" with pasture in Stoke Talmage where they had a grange. But, as in the case of woodland, steps were sometimes taken to prevent encroachment on grazing land. Fountains was given some clearings in Crosthwaite in 1256 and simultaneously warned not to assart in the common of the vill. Roche (1176-89) agreed that a piece of land should remain common pasture of the grange of *Banclif* and the township of North Anston; neither the monks nor the men of

[32] J. W. Thompson observed: "instead of the former haphazard way of making clearings without reference to the value of the soil underneath [Cistercian houses] studied both the timber and the soil ... where hardwoods grew, there good soil was to be found. They never wholly denuded the forest but left patches of standing timber" ('The Cistercian Order and colonization in mediaeval Germany,' *Amer. Jour. Theol.*, 24 (1920): 80).

[33] Strata Florida was rebuilt in 1300 (after being destroyed by fire in 1295) on condition that the surrounding woods were cut down.

[34] *Chart. W.*, pp. 79 (1200-10), 244 (before 1187 — an assart called *maneswude*), 81 (1200-20 — an assart bounded on at least one side by woodland).

[35] *Mon. Angl.*, 5: 432 (1154-89 — *kingmanneswode* assart; 1247 — rights in *yngwode* assart). At the time of the Dissolution, Pipewell had a wood of twelve acres called *le sart*.

[36] In 1279 Fountains and Sallay agreed not to assart a wood in Littondale (it probably served as shelter for stock) (*Chart. F.*, 1: 322). Sometime after 1251 Fountains was allowed to assart in Marston "outside the wood" (ibid., 2: 544).

the vill were to make improvements therein. Furness was party to a similar agreement in 1327, and when the monks received grazing for 500 sheep in Halton (1226-7) the grantor undertook not to make any purpresture there.

The description 'open land' (*planum*) was occasionally employed; it probably covered rough pasture, 'waste', 'moor' and 'heath'. Several examples have already been given of the clearing of 'waste'. The right of Garendon to assart in the 'heath' of Swannington was confirmed in 1340. Louth Park had assarts in the 'heath' of Kelstern (the site of a grange) in 1314. Grants of 'waste', 'heath' and 'moor' were numerous and assarting may often have followed, but this was by no means inevitable. Such land was also widely used as grazing and as a source of turbary, rough thatch and other building materials.

Charters occasionally show the assart as part of an advancing frontier of reclamation. This is implied in references to 'new' and 'old' assarts. For example, Kirkstall was given one and a half acres "*de novis assartis*" in Horsforth, and likewise Fountains half an acre "lying in *Waytebrec* of the old assart" and another half acre "at the head of *Waytebrec* of the new assart." *Waytebrec* lay in Marston where in 1258 Fountains received fourteen acres "in the new assart" and also one and a half acres on the edge of cultivation, "in *Phwaytebrec* ... partly of cultivated land, partly of land previously uncultivated" (*-brec* may be interpreted either as a copse or thicket, or *brǣc*, ground newly broken up for cultivation). An undated deed refers to Byland's encroachments (*purprestura*) "towards the moor of Bagby, that is at the head of their culture lying between the said moor and their grange of Balk."

Grants of land adjoining assarts are of similar interest. Kirkstall was given an assart next to another in Bramley, Roche in *Ligulf* (before 1189), and Fountains on different occasions in Kirkheaton (1192-1200), Markenfield and Wheldrake. A further grant of twelve acres in Kirkheaton was described as "next to the assart which the monks have in the wood of Hetton," and thirteen acres added to the grange of Aldburgh lay adjacent to another of the monks' assarts. Whalley's estate in Rochdale was from time to time increased by the grant of an assart next to another, an assart between two others (one belonging to the monks), and a further eight acres, part of which lay "*inter assartum Suani et assartum Leysingi a capite assarte Leysingi usque in Calder*." Hardly less informative are the many grants of land lying next to 'moor' or 'marsh'. Even when not described as 'assarts', they must often have been only recently cleared and quite evidently lay near the limits of improved land.

Marshland

Several Cistercian houses stood in close proximity to extensive tracts of marsh. The example of Swineshead, the only community fully within the great Fenland, has already been mentioned. The foundation charters of Kirkstead, Revesby and Sawtry make clear that they overlooked the Fens. A document confirming the lands of Louth Park (1314) refers to "the island where the said monks dwell and the marsh as the outer dike surrounds it";[37] and even at the time of the Dissolution there were 116 acres in the vicinity of the abbey that were reportedly thorn-covered and flooded in winter. The site of Meaux in Holderness was described as dry and fertile, but all around stretched mere and fen — "*aquis et paludibus cinctum.*" Holm Cultram, by the shores of the Solway, occupied an 'island' between two great marshes, and flood-water occasionally extended to the very gates of Stanlaw on the Mersey estuary (the monks eventually moved to Whalley).

Unreclaimed fen is mentioned among the earliest gifts to Kirkstead, Revesby, Swineshead, Sawtry, Vaudey (also on the edge of the Fens), Meaux, Combermere, Stratford Langthorn, Stanlaw and Holm Cultram. In 1189 Boxley was confirmed in parts of Romney Marsh, and Robertsbridge too had a stretch of salt marsh (*salsa mora*) near Rye before 1199. Probably most houses had access to some marshland within a few decades.

The Fenland houses took turbary and in summer grazed extensive areas of marsh — Kirkstead throughout 40,000 acres of Wildmore; Sawtry in all the fen of Walton and Connington. Meaux had at least 260 acres of "*mora et pastura*" in Arnold where it worked a grange. But grants of marsh more often consisted of quite small areas adjoining the improved land of a grange or other estate; thus two acres in Routh, and twenty acres (in three lots) in Keyingham to Meaux; about eleven acres in Normanby, near the estuary of the river Tees, to Rievaulx; three acres in Aisenby, one acre in Newsham, and half an acre in Acaster Malbis, all within the Vale of York, to Fountains.

One of the earliest references (ca. 1177) to the improvement of marshland is that concerning Byland in Coxwold and between this place and the final site of the abbey. The chronicler relates that the monks cleared woodland and organised a system of drainage — "*et per fossas longas et latas magnas aquas de paludibus extrahere*" — eventually making the

[37] *C.Ch.R.*, AD 1300-26, p. 267.

ground firm (*solida terra*).[38] Fountains had large holdings along the low-lying axis of the Vale of York. A charter of ca. 1200 sets out provisions for draining a marsh in Newsham (probably worked from the grange of Kirby Wiske); others permitted the monastery "to make a fosse for draining the marsh of *Traneker*," to "make a watercourse to the grange of Kirby Wiske," and (1340) to "drain the marsh to make dry land or turbary and to approve as desired."[39] Similarly in Dishforth the monks were "given leave to make a fosse to carry away the water from *Hwiteker* as far as *Thimeker* ... [and] from their land."

The abbey of Meaux was virtually surrounded by marshes, and the *Chronica de Melsa* refers to many dikes and ditches. One, leading from marshes near the grange of Arnold, brought water to drive a mill; like many other watercourses this flowed into the river Hull and the abbey was obliged to construct gates (*clusas*) to prevent flooding.[40] About the same time (1235-49) Meaux was permitted to make ditches (*duo fossata*) to protect the road from Routh grange to the abbey. A main drainage channel might be twenty feet broad; the *Forthdyke* (1221-35) was sixteen feet across and six feet deep, and that which served the grange at Skerne could take small boats. As for the tributary leads, the chronicle refers to "*unam contrafossatam v. vel vi. pedum in latitudine, juxta ipsam magnam fossatam*" (in Riston) and, on another occasion, to a ten-foot ditch. Much timber was used in the construction of supporting banks and flood-gates.

Between 1249 and 1269, Meaux received land that was partly marsh in *Holyholm* (six miles north of the abbey) wherein to enclose and improve: "*ad includendum fossato defensabile xii pedum — ac meliorandum prout voluerimus ad opus nostrum.*" It had similar rights in the west marsh of Sutton. In both cases there can be little doubt that draining was necessary. From the middle of the thirteenth century Meaux lost considerable ground in southern Holderness, especially along the north bank of the Humber. In 1253 farmland was inundated throughout eastern England.[41] The Humber rose and parts of Cottingham, five miles away, were under water. Land at Salthaugh, *Myton*, Sutton and *Tharlesthorpe* (all granges) was swept away, and erosion continued even after the water had subsided. *Tharlesthorpe* was again devastated in 1353-6 when the monks constructed a flood-gate "*inter villam de Tharlesthorpia et grangiam nostram.*" Some years later, the 'sea' wall and flood-gates at Salthaugh had to be repaired after being

[38] *Mon. Angl.*, 5: 353.
[39] *Chart. F.*, 2: 772-80.
[40] *Chron. M.*, 1: 354-55 (1210-20); 2: 84 (1249-69). Cf. *Coucher W.*, 2: 421, 535.
[41] Britton, *Meteorological Chronology*, p. 103.

breached in two places near the grange. Further embankments were erected at *Tharlesthorpe* but only four of its eleven bovates were saved.[42] As the monks themselves gradually ceased to farm on a large scale they took their obligations less seriously. This led to much litigation and suits sometimes dragged on for many years.

Much of the remaining evidence of draining concerns houses closely associated with the Fenland.[43] In 1314 Louth Park was confirmed in forty perches of moor and marsh in *Inkelmore* near the village of Swinefleet "and in all that may be opened in new moors or marshes given to them, with power to make gutters, sewers and openings to drain the said moors and marshes with liberty to open, till and dyke, cut turf and carry it [away]."[44] A few years later, the monks were permitted to enclose "thirty acres of the marsh of Farlesthorpe out of their own pasture and marsh." The abbey precincts were moated,[45] and a *compotus*, probably of the fifteenth century, records the expenditure of twenty-two shillings on the repair of a section of sea wall.[46] Swineshead had "common from the sea to the end of the marsh in Drayton hundred in Holland ... as much as belongs to half a bovate of land ... provided that if any enclosure be made on the sea side or in the marsh then the monks shall take their share thereof."[47] Kirkstead in 1375 was responsible for "a bank in Wildmoor on the east side of Witham stream ... to keep the waters of the said stream out of Wildmoor and the West Fen."[48] Negligence on the part of the abbot and convent had apparently resulted in £2000 worth of damage in the East and West Fen. An agreement between Sawtry and the neighbouring Benedictine house of Ramsey shows that the former had made water-courses (*ladae*); the Cistercian monks were, however, debarred from making further ditches (*trencheiae*) or planting trees ("*nec arbores plantabunt*").[49]

[42] *Chron. M.*, 3: 182-83. Tharlesthorpe lay near the present Sunk Island. See J. R. Boyle, *The Lost Towns of the Humber* (Hull, 1889). There are surveys of inundated land in *Chron. M.*, 3: 283-86, 293-94.

[43] G. G. Coulton (*The Mediaeval Village* (Cambridge, 1925), pp. 219, 512-513) has referred to the work of Revesby.

[44] *C. Ch. R.*, AD 1300-26, p. 254. See also C. T. Flower, *Public Works in Mediaeval Law*, Selden Society Publs., 32 (London, 1915), 1: 218.

[45] *Chron. L. P.*, p. xlii.

[46] Ibid., p. 74. For notices of flooding around Louth Park and in eastern England generally, see ibid., pp. 16 (1253), 24 (1315), 42 (1382).

[47] *C.Ch.R.*, AD 1300-26, p. 321 (*conf.* 1316).

[48] Flower, *Public Works*, pp. xxvii, 257-60.

[49] *Mon. Angl.*, 5: 525. The tenants of Coupar Angus abbey (Cistercian, Perthshire) planted broom, ash and osiers to 'recover' marsh (*Rental C.*, 1: xxviii, xxxi, 142-43 (1468)).

Stratford Langthorn had rights and responsibilities in the marshes along the Thames at West Ham.[50] In 1292 the monks complained that certain people were "not contributing to the upkeep of the walls and dikes (*fossata*) in *Westhamme.*" A grant "beyond the river Lea" provided that "if the land increase in size through the draining off of water ("*per attractum aque*") such increment shall belong to the abbot and convent." Stanlaw was allowed to "draw water" from a mere or marsh (*mara*) by the Mersey and near the grange of Stanney. In 1292 Holm Cultram obtained permission to reclaim land along the Solway.

A papal *indultum* of 1257 sheds light on the work of the monks and *conversi* of Robertsbridge (Sussex) who "in consideration of the sterility caused by the influx of the sea shall not be bound to pay tithes on land brought into cultivation by themselves at great expense and labour except for that portion for which they paid when sterile."[51] Later (1309) the same house was allowed to "acquire lands and rents to the yearly value of £100 as compensation for its losses through the inundation by the sea of the marshes of Winchelsea, Rye and Broomhill."[52] More than a century before this (ca. 1200) Robertsbridge helped to build defence walls;[53] and by an agreement of 1234 the monks could approve "as much of the marsh of Leigh as they reasonably can in the coming summer and over the next ten years." Furthermore, "after enclosure one third of the arable [was] to fall to Homo's share (Sir Homo de Crevequer, the other signatory) and the remainder [was] to be the monks' property in frankalmoign, the monks to maintain the wall and waterways at their own cost."[54] Such piecemeal operations around inland fen or sea marsh were doubtless undertaken by the great majority of Cistercian monasteries, but especially those in eastern England with rights or property in the Vale of York, Holderness and the Fenland.

The Robertsbridge agreement of 1234 provides the only clear example of the cultivation of former marshland.[55] To improve grazing was a less

[50] Marshland is mentioned in the original grant of *Hamme* to the abbey (*Mon. Angl.*, 5: 587). See also *Cart. Ant.*, p. 84; and *C.A.D.*, vol. 6, no. 4066. The abbey precincts were moated (*Mon. Angl.*, 5: 587).

[51] *Papal Letters*, 1: 342.

[52] *C.P.R.*, AD 1307-13, pp. 152, 159. Widespread flooding was reported in 1307 (Britton, *Meteorological Chronology*, p. 131).

[53] *Docs. R.*, p. 57: "the walls which the monks and their associates (*comparticipes*) made round the marsh."

[54] Ibid., pp. 89-90.

[55] The abbot of Holm Cultram allowed certain benefactors of the house "*seminare et imbladare mariscum quantum pertinet ad dictam dominiam infra fossatum de Burgo*" (*Mon. Angl.*, 5: 607-8). Note also the reference to "*duas acras terrae arabilis cum pertinentiis in*

formidable task, and land that was almost useless in winter might provide very good grazing in summer. The Yorkshire houses used large areas of marsh, particularly for cattle, and similar evidence survives for other parts of the country. Thus Swineshead was confirmed (1154-89) in fen-grazing for twenty cows and possessed a vaccary "*in marisco juxta abbatiam.*" Vaudey (before 1189) could feed 140 head of cattle in the marshes of East Deeping, and Kirkstead's right of pasture (1169) for 1200 sheep, seven teams of oxen and ten cows in Branston also involved the use of marshland. Boxley had pasture for sheep and cattle in the Medway marshes, and similarly Holm Cultram along the shores of the Solway.

Good meadow was often more valuable than arable. In 1281 Sawtry had fifteen acres of meadow "newly reclaimed from the fen." Louth Park was confirmed (1314) in four selions of land with "all the meadow thereto belonging through the middle of the fen." Some of Fountains' meadow in Dishforth and in Acaster had been drained. The same house had 'water meadow' along the Wiske, the Swale, and the Ouse, and in 1456-7 it was obliged to reduce the rent on meadow that had been partly destroyed by floods along the Derwent. Other references to water meadow occur in the records of Beaulieu, Byland, Jervaulx, Warden, St. Mary Graces, Combermere, Furness, Quarr, Holm Cultram, Stanley (1189), Bruern, Rufford (ca. 1146), Kingswood, Bordesley and Thame.

Unimproved marsh was useful as a source of fuel (turbary), reeds, fish, water fowl, and, along the coast, salt. The monks of Stanlaw owned fisheries in the marshes of the Mersey. Sawtry's foundation grant included "*marisco et piscariis versus Witlemare.*" Fountains used a marsh near the abbey as a fish-pond (*vivarium*), and the abbot of Kirkstead could hunt, fish and fowl in Wildmore. Common salt was the main preservative and an important article of commerce during the Middle Ages. Holm Cultram owned salt-pans along both sides of the Solway from at least the end of the twelfth century. The neighbouring house of Calder likewise evaporated brine, but not to the same extent. Before 1300, Quarr (Isle of Wight) was granted a "salt pit in a marsh ... in the manor of Lymington" (on the mainland facing the Solent). Furness had salt-works in Angerton Moss (Ulverston), and Byland (1190-1216) possessed a 'salt house' at Coatham on the estuary of the river Tees. Charters to Newminster (ca. 1150), Jervaulx (1228) and Louth Park (1314) also mention their salterns.

---

marisco de Burgo," and a grant to Kirkstall of "*3 particatas terrae arabilis in loco qui vocatur mariscus*" (ibid., p. 539).

Royal Forests

The English royal forests probably reached their widest extent during the latter half of the twelfth century. The first considerable list, of 1222, contains over sixty names,[56] but many of these are known from earlier references; the Pipe Roll of 1169-70 mentions twenty-seven, and fourteen are given under *Pasnagium Forestarium Totius Anglie* in 1184-5. About 1189, when the number of Cistercian houses was still increasing (eighteen were subsequently founded), the area under forest law may have amounted to one-third of the country.[57]

The 'forests' (Fig. 14) included the widest possible range of terrain and primeval vegetation, as well as cropped land, a fact which their common organisation as hunting preserves has tended to conceal. An important group of forests almost surrounded the Hampshire basin, from the Chalk plateau southward; another followed the dip slope of the Ooltic escarpment; and a third occupied a large part of the middle Severn valley. The forest of Essex, most of the Midland forests and those bordering the Bristol Channel and around the upper Thames were chiefly upon heavy clays. The drift-covered plains of the Solway, of Lancashire and of Cheshire incorporate a wide range of soils, from intractable boulder clay to light sands and gravels. Marshy conditions must have prevailed, particularly in winter, along the Fenland margin of the forest of Huntingdon, in parts of the Vales of York and Pickering, within the Fylde of Lancashire and along the Essex coast. Pickering was a notable example of a forest extending across a number of physical zones, from sandstone moorlands, rising to over 1000 feet, in the north, through a narrow vale of Oxford Clay and the succeeding Corallian slope to, finally, the marshy *carrs* and *ings* of the Vale itself.

References to woodland occur in connection with assarting and grants of timber. The Midland forests in particular appear to have contained considerable stands. 'Waste' (unimproved heath, moor, scrub and marshland) also is frequently mentioned. Stanley held the "*mora de Alfletemore*" in the forest of Chippenham, and received 211 acres of 'waste' in Pewsham. In 1324 Beaulieu was assessed for 223 acres of 'waste' in the New Forest, and the monks could take whatever heath vegetation (*brueria*) they needed. Rufford enjoyed a similar right in Sherwood. Stratford Langthorn

[56] *C.P.R.*, AD 1216-25, pp. 360-62.

[57] A. L. Poole, *From Domesday Book to Magna Carta* (Oxford, 1951), p. 29. See also C. R. Young, 'English Royal Forests under the Angevin Kings,' *Journal of British Studies*, 12 (1972-73): 1-14.

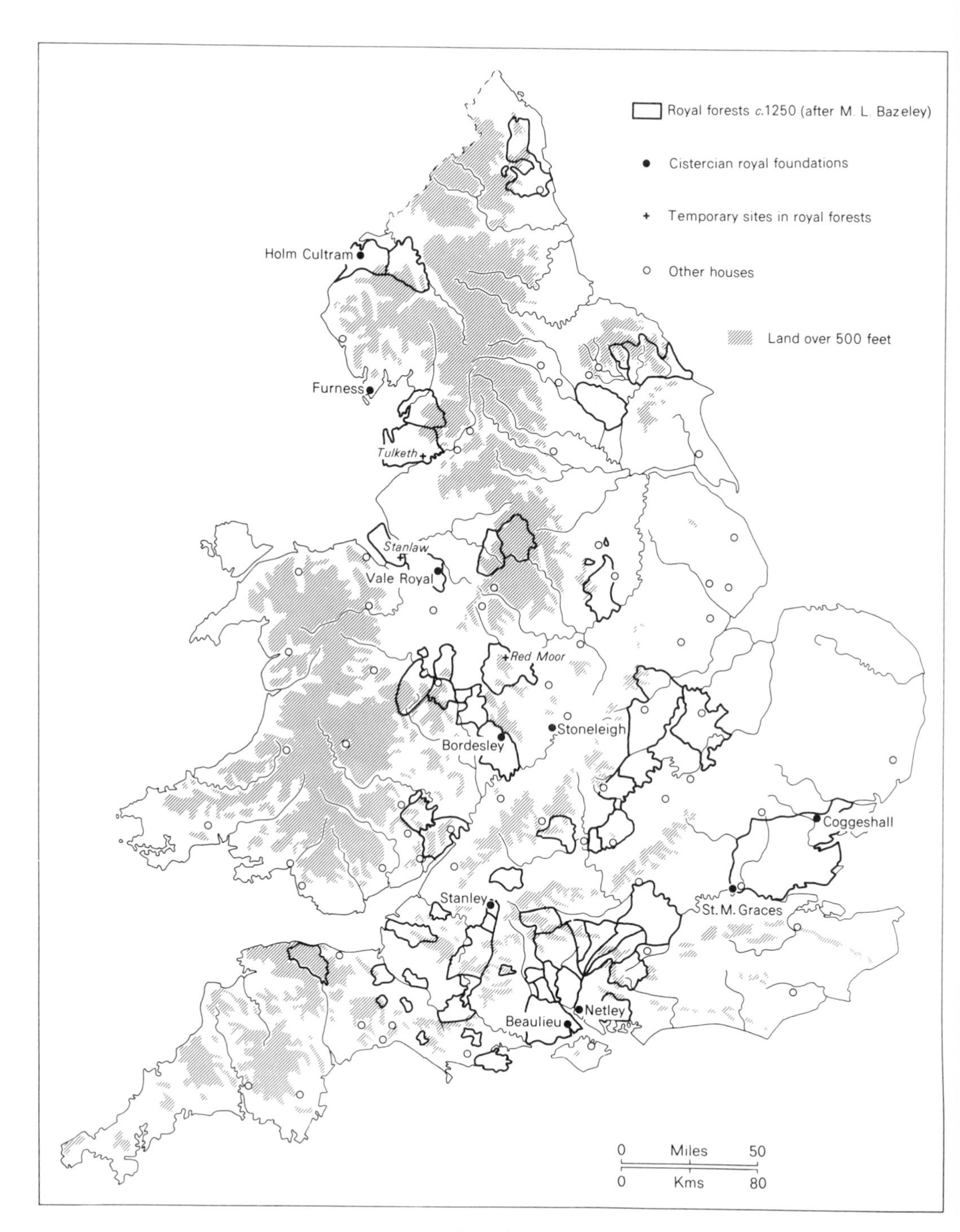

FIG. 14

Royal forests and Cistercian royal foundations.

(1189) could pasture 960 sheep on the heath of Walthamstow in the forest of Essex, and Coggeshall (1257) obtained the right to enclose both heath and woodland there.

An early grant to Sawtry in the forest of Huntingdon refers to the *marisco de Saltre.* Rievaulx had marshland rights in the forest of Pickering from the time of Henry II. Stretches of bog lay between Holm Cultram and the centre of the forest of Allerdale. About the beginning of the thirteenth century, the same house was allowed to cultivate a certain *landa* (lawn or glade) in Inglewood where, a hundred years later, grazing accounted for half of the forest revenue. The extent of the 'lawn' at Benefield in the forest of Rockingham can be judged from the fact that Pipewell was permitted to graze 250 animals there in 1252.

Cistercian Houses and the Royal Forests

Approximately one-third of the Cistercian houses founded by 1250 lay within royal forests.

TABLE 4: CISTERCIAN HOUSES AND THE ROYAL FORESTS

	Cistercian houses in England	In or near royal forests	Royal foundations	In or near royal forests
1250	58	19	8	6
Total*	61	20	10	8

* Excluding Rewley, established as an Oxford college in 1281, and St. Bernard's College, Oxford, 1437.

The community at Red Moor (1141) in the forest of Cannock was removed to Stoneleigh ca. 1154-5, and Tulketh (1124-7), the forerunner of Furness, stood within the forest of Lonsdale. With the addition of these two houses, all the Cistercian (or Savignac) royal foundations were sited within or very close to the boundaries of royal forests. The association between other Cistercian houses and afforested districts, particularly notable in the South East and the south Midlands, probably arose through the economic restrictions imposed upon private landowners by the operation of the forest laws.

Woodland and Supplies of Timber

A monastic community was in constant need of timber. Louth Park, we are told, purchased the wood of Cockerington "at great expense" (1226-46). Beaulieu, along with others, was once accused of cutting timber to the value of £200. By contrast, Roche in 1347 petitioned the king "that they may have again one oak in the park or woods of Hatfield by reason of the tithe."

Conventual buildings were at first made of wood. Beams from an earlier castle were used in the construction of the original abbey of Meaux. According to the Cistercian statutes, bell towers were always to be of wood. And the amount of timber needed for the sheds, barns, mills and living accommodation of granges together perhaps exceeded that employed at the abbey itself. Meaux (1235-49) used "incorruptible oak" (*quercus imputribilis*) for its farm buildings. In 1269 Furness was granted ten oaks annually for the construction and repair of Beaumont grange. Certain woods in the forest of Rockingham belonging to Pipewell were set aside for granges, and an inquiry revealed that timber had been cut for barns, cotes and bercaries. There are also many references to stands of timber around grange buildings. Meaux's grange of Croo in Holderness was established (1235-49) amid thick (*densae et altae*) woodland of oak and ash. About a hundred years later many trees had been cut down and it was possible to see for three to four miles around.

Woodland: The ownership of woodland within the royal forests was not confined to houses within or very close to the boundaries. Thus Basingwerk (Flintshire) possessed woods in the Peak forest and Warden (Bedfordshire) in the forest of Huntingdon. The importance of such woodland is sometimes very apparent. Bordesley gave 100 marks in 1230 in return for the confirmation of "the woods of Hallow, Tutnall and Tardebigge in the forest of Feckenham." In 1362 the grange of *Cnotteshull* in Feckenham comprised 120 acres of arable (valued at 40 shillings), ten acres of meadow (10s), twenty-four acres of 'waste' (worth nothing for it was held in common) and 185 acres of woodland (92s).[58] Rufford (1206-07) paid ten marks for permission to erect a house whereby to protect its woods in Sherwood, but apparently this was soon destroyed by men from the neighbouring vill of Wellow.[59] When Flaxley was deprived of an

[58] *C.M.I.*, 3: nos. 486, 489.

[59] *Pipe Roll 1206-7*, P.R.S., new ser., 22 (1946), p. 124, and *Pipe Roll 1208-09*, P.R.S., new ser., 24 (1949), p. 118.

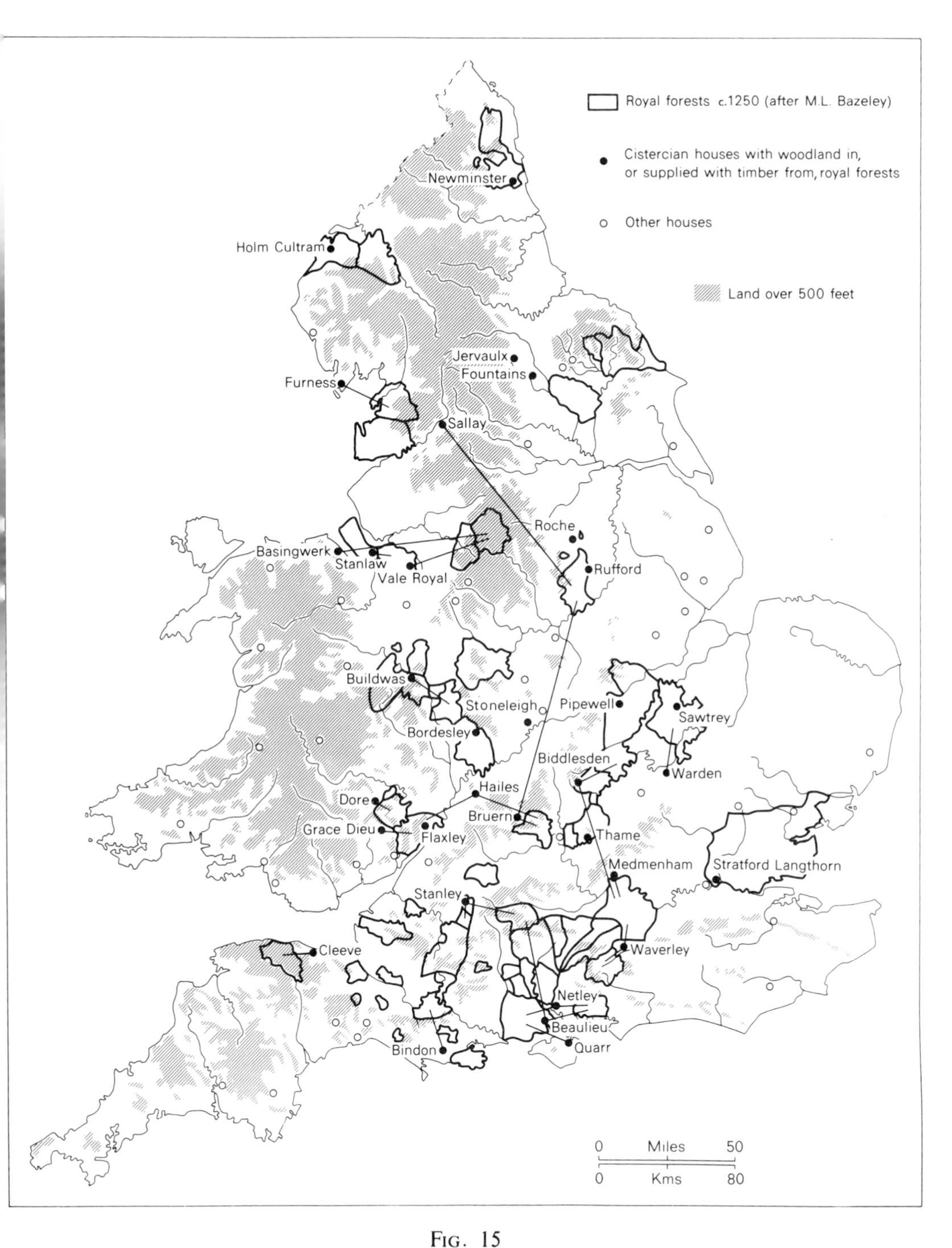

FIG. 15

Cistercian houses with woodland in, or supplied with timber from, royal forests.

allowance of two oaks per week from the forest of Dean, as much as 800 acres of woodland were granted in compensation.[60]

Woodland is sometimes mentioned along with licences to enclose. Bordesley (1238) was prepared to pay £20 for the right to enclose its woods, and the abbot of Coggeshall owed forty marks on the same account in 1203-4. Pipewell (1238) obtained permission "to enclose permanently [the] wood of Oldfield (in the forest of Rockingham) provided that the king's deer shal have free entrance and exit." Sawtry owed forty marks in 1206-7 "for enclosing the whole wood of Sawtry with a ditch and hedge (*fossatum et haia*)," by which it ceased to be commonable. The above-mentioned grant of 800 acres of woodland to Flaxley included the provision that only a tenth was to be enclosed at any one time. Enclosure was often the prelude to assarting. Thus Warden (1206-7) was permitted to enclose the wood of Midloe (grange) in the forest of Huntingdon and then to assart it.[61] Edward I allowed Waverley to enclose forty acres of woodland in Wolmer, and his successor "to assart and reduce it to cultivation."[62]

Supplies of timber: By about the middle of the fourteenth century some forests were far less wooded than they had been. Timber sent to Vale Royal (founded in 1281) was to be cut where it did "least damage" and be used solely for building.[63] Some earlier houses had been generously supplied.[64] Holm Cultram (Inglewood), Flaxley (Dean), Stratford Langthorn (Essex), Stanley and Stoneleigh obtained timber during the reign of Henry II and most probably from their foundation. All but the last named were forest-sited. The needs of the Yorkshire houses were partly met from private chases.[65]

Underwood (*subboscum*), twigs (*virgas*), windfalls (*cableicium*) and dead wood were sometimes included in grants of timber, or were gathered as *husbote* or *haybote* and used for hedges and fences, as firewood, and in making charcoal. Some grants of mature timber involved only one or two trunks; the average was about ten, and two cases of as many as sixty have

[60] *Chart. Fl.*, p. 32.

[61] *Cart. Ant.*, p. 114 (1206-07); *Chart. W.*, pp. 143-44, 291-94.

[62] *Rot. Orig.*, 2: 73.

[63] *Register*, pp. 3, 8 (1351).

[64] Grants of timber from royal forests are tabulated in R. A. Donkin, 'The Cistercian settlement and the English royal forests,' *Citeaux: Commentarii Cistercienses*, 11 (1960): 52-55.

[65] Jervaulx in Wensleydale (*Mon. Angl.*, 5: 569); Fountains in Kirkby Malzeard and Nidderdale (*Chart. F.*, 2: 706; *E.Y.C.*, 1: 73); Rievaulx in Helmsley and Teesdale (*Chart. R.*, pp. 157, 186).

been found — to Bindon from the forest of Blackmore in 1233, and to Hailes from the forest of Dean in 1246.[66] The need was probably greatest in the first half-century or so. Beaulieu (founded in 1204) had received at least 128 trunks by 1251, and Netley (1239) eighty-six by 1291. Some large grants went towards extensive repairs — thirty oaks to Buildwas out of Shirlet in 1232, forty to Stoneleigh in 1241, and twenty to Grace Dieu in 1235, the last two after outbreaks of fire. It was often stipulated that the trunks supplied should be "fit for timber" (*ad maeremium*), that is for constructional purposes. Rufford in 1229 and Beaulieu in 1232 were supplied with material for rafters (*ad cheverones*). Stalls (*stalla chori, stalla conversorum*) are mentioned in grants to Biddlesden, Cleeve, Beaulieu, Stanley and Thame, and oak for the church as a whole in others to Jervaulx (1227), Flaxley (1229), Waverley (1231), Buildwas (1232), Bruern (1232), Bindon (1233), Biddlesden (1235), Netley (1251) and Stanley (1251). Following the letter of the statutes of the order, Stanley obtained timber from the forest of Chippenham "*ad turrim ecclesie sue*" (1237). The abbot's lodge at Flaxley and at Bruern (four oaks) were specified in 1232 and 1263 respectively.

Waverley (1225-6, 1234-5), Bruern (1251), Medmenham (1232) and Stanley (1223) took trunks for their hearths ("*bona robora ad focum suum*"), and several other houses had the right to "reasonable estovers." Bruern, sometime during the twelfth century, was allowed two cart loads of wood per day from Wychwood, and this was supplemented by a third load of "*mortuum boscum et ramos*" and "*subboscum ad focum suum*" in 1216. Later (1254) there was an inquiry into the *husbote* and *haybote* of the same abbey in Wychwood. Henry II confirmed Quarr in the right to two loads of dead wood per annum in the New Forest, and Vale Royal was given all the dead wood in the forest of Peak (thirty miles away) over a period of five years commencing in 1302.

Holm Cultram (1199) was permitted to take bark (*cortices lignorum*) in the forest of Inglewood, presumably for tanning.[67] Flaxley worked the iron deposits of the forest of Dean, and in 1227 woodland around the abbey was granted for fuel. Two years later, the monks were allowed dead wood, underwood and old trunks (*vetera robora*), while instructed to keep their itinerant forge in the thorn tickets (*spissitudinibus*) on the margins of the forest. Other grants included eight oaks to Fountains (1227) from Knaresborough for the repair of a bridge; six 'batons' to Stratford

[66] *C.Cl.R.*, AD 1231-34, p. 195, and AD 1242-47, p. 404.
[67] *C.Ch.R.*, AD 1300-26, p. 80 (*conf.*). Tintern exercised the same privilege in the earl of Pembroke's forest of lower Went (co. Monmouth) (ibid., p. 99 (*conf.*)).

Langthorn (1225) for a mill; as many as thirty oaks to Thame (1236) "*ad fabricam cancelli sui*"; and timber from the forest of Lancaster to repair a fishery on the river Lune belonging to Furness.

Timber known to have been brought to the abbey itself is set out in the table below which gives the number of 'units' (oaks, logs, trunks) supplied and the approximate distance from the abbey to the boundary of the respective forest.

TABLE 5: TIMBER SUPPLIES

		Forest	Units	Miles
Beaulieu	1233	Bere	20	20
Biddlesden	1234	Henley (Park)	50	36
	1237	Salcey	5	6
Bindon	1233	Blackmore	60	12
Buildwas	1255	Kinver		13
Hailes	1246	Dean	60	20
Jervaulx	1227	Knaresborough	20	26
Medmenham	1232	Windsor	25	
Netley	1251	New Forest	15	2
	1251	Bere	15	7
	1254	New Forest	20	2
	1271	Bere	5	7
Stanley	1246	Melksham	2	2
Stoneleigh	1241	Kenilworth (Park)	40	4
Waverley	1231	Windsor		2
	1235	Aliceholt	5	2

The distances involved may commonly have been much greater, notwithstanding the uncertainty over forest limits. The ten oaks from Sherwood granted to Sallay in 1255[68] were probably taken to the abbey itself, but, in any event, its estates were not particularly extensive and a considerable cross-country journey is indicated.

There is very little information on how and by whom the timber was transported. A detailed statement of building expenses at Vale Royal for 1278-81[69] includes the cost of bringing logs from various parts of Delamere forest to the site of the abbey. In one year, six men with horses made a journey each day for eighteen days (108 journeys in all), and there are other references to 200 journeys and 360 journeys. The great waggons can be pictured from an entry in the chamberlain of Chester's accounts for 1312: "for men of the abbot of Vale Royal with a certain waggon with twenty oxen in the same waggon for boon days, carrying beams and other

[68] *C.Cl.R.*, AD 1254-56, p. 116.
[69] *Ledger V.R.*, pp. 192 ff.

great timber ... from Delamere forest to Chester castle for fourteen days in July."[70] Bordesley once brought fifty oaks from the royal park of Henley, about thirty-six miles away, and may have made use of the Thames. Buildwas had convenient access to the forest of Kinver along the Severn where it possessed a place "for loading and unloading boats."

Cistercian houses were occasionally permitted to sell or to make gifts from their woodland. Examples include Waverley in 1253 and 1260, Biddlesden in 1255, and Stratford Langthorn in 1280. When, in 1336, the monks of Rufford were permitted to supply twelve oaks from Sherwood to the bishop of Lincoln, it was stipulated that the grantee should arrange for the cutting and carriage. Secondary growth, such as scrub from assarts, was also sold. *Subboscum* appears among Tintern's assets in the *Taxatio Ecclesiastica* ca. 1291. Rufford in 1280 profited from the sale of undergrowth, and windfalls and dry roots were collected for use and for sale on other occasions.

Assarts and Assarting

Information about assarting in the royal forests by Cistercian houses may be found in the Pipe Rolls, especially of the twelfth century, and in the Chancery Rolls and certain chartularies, which are particularly valuable for the thirteenth century. The Pipe Roll entries are summarized in Table 6. Unfortunately, few amounts relate to assarts alone: Rievaulx was excused £2.3.6. *de assart* in 1155-6, and similarly Sawtry £3.6.8. *de assartis* in 1159-60. Pipewell in 1197-8 faced a charge of fourteen marks (£9.6.8.) "*pro bosco suo de Rohal' essartando.*" But assarts[71] were more usually combined with 'waste' (felling rather than the complete removal of trees and shrubs)[72] and sometimes with 'purprestures', which covered a wide range of encroachments.[73] *Wastum*, in particular, may often have been followed by assarting and cultivation.

Before 1184-5, the information is fairly uniform; later there is greater variety in the charges preferred, under the general heading of forest pleas, and 'assarting' is rarely specifically mentioned.

[70] F. H. Crossley, *Timber Building in England from Early Times to the End of the Seventeenth Century* (London, 1951), p. 2.

[71] See 'Dialogus de Scaccario' (1178-9) in T. Madox, *History and Antiquities of the Exchequer of the Kings of England* (London, 1769), 1: 396.

[72] *Introduction to the Study of the Pipe Rolls*, P.R.S. Publs. 3 (1884), p. 70 (under *assartum*).

[73] For example, Rufford was accused of purpresture in making a pond within Sherwood in 1268 (*C.P.R.*, AD 1266-72, p. 211; *Rot. Hund.*, 2: 303).

Table 6: Assarts and other Encroachments in the Royal Forests

							a £ s	*b* £ s
Rievaulx		A			1155-56	Yorks		2. 4
Sawtry		A			1159-60	Hunts	23. 7	3. 7
Buckfast	F				1159-60	Devon	7. 13	3. 7
Coggeshall	F	A	W		1167-68	Essex	204. 1	1. 14
Sawtry	F		W		1168-69	Hunts		1.
Buildwas		A	W		1169-70	Salop	90. 9	3. 7
Combermere		A	W		1169-70	Staffs	109. 5	3. 7
Bordesley	F	A	W		1169-70	Worcs	84. 2	13
Byland	F	A	W		1169-70	Yorks	217. 5	1. 5
Kirkstall	F	A	W		1169-70	Yorks	217. 5	7. 10
Pipewell	F				1169-70	Northants		2.
Kingswood	F				1170-71	Glos	40. 13	7. 10
Waverley	F	A	W		1171-72	Hants	25. 17	7.
Rufford		A	W		1171-72	Notts/Derby	13. 7	13. 6
Kirkstall	F	A	W		1174-75	Yorks	371. 14	1. 15
Stratford	F	A	W		1174-75	Berks	100. 6	0. 13
Waverley	F	A	W		1176-77	Hants	76. 8	7. 5
		A	W		1176-77	Hants	88. 8	19. 17
	F	A	W		1176-77	Surrey	39. 5	3. 7
		A		P	1176-77	Surrey	55. 5	4. 2
Pipewell		A	W		1177-78	Northants	243. 15	8. 1
Kirkstall	F	A	W		1177-78	Yorks	87. 18	3
Rufford	F	A	W		1177-78	Notts/Derby	58. 2	17
Pipewell	F	A	W	P	1180-81	Northants	96.	7. 3
Waverley	F	A	W	P	1181-82	Hants	43. 15	10.
		A	W	P	1181-82	Surrey	16. 19	2.
Kirkstall	F				1184-85	Yorks		7. 10
Rufford	F			P	1184-85	Notts/Derby		1. (1)
	F		W		1184-85	Notts/Derby		1
Stratford	F			P	1185-86	Berks		7
Rufford	F		W		1186-87	Notts/Derby		13
Pipewell	F			P	1197-98	Northants		6. 13
		A			1197-98	Northants		9. 7
Stanley	F				1203-4	Wilts		33. 7
Furness	F				1205-6	Lancs		133. 7 (2)
Waverley	F			P	1207-8	Surrey		7
Swineshead	F				1208-9	Lincs		7
Pipewell	F				1208-9	Northants		7
Basingwerk	F		W		1211-2	Derby		13
Beaulieu	F		W		1211-2	Berks		6. 13
	F		W		1211-2	Hants		2.

Payments, debts and remissions for 'encroachments' recorded in the Pipe Rolls (P.R.S.) — (F) specifically a forest fine, under assarting (A), waste (W) or purpresture (P). Col. *a* — the total sum accountable; col *b* — the amount relating to the respective Cistercian house (to the nearest shilling). The counties are those in which the offences were committed.

(1) The sum of three separate amounts.

(2) A debt of 200 marks; the fine was of 500 marks but 300 were remitted.[74]

[74] W. Farrer, ed., *The Lancashire Pipe Rolls* (Liverpool, 1902), p. 204.

The importance of the Pipe Roll entries concerning encroachments upon the royal forests lies in their early date and in the fact that they refer to a substantially higher proportion of Cistercian houses than of other monastic communities. Moreover, the activities of the houses that appear most often can generally be followed through the thirteenth century. Kirkstall, mentioned, among other occasions, in 1169-70 (with Byland) and 1174-5, when the Yorkshire forests accounted for very large sums, is the chief exception.

In the event of timber and undergrowth being completely removed, as when Rufford was allowed to "fell, root up and carry away ... all the heath, trunks and dry roots within their wood in the king's forest of Sherwood," there was every prospect of cultivation. What exactly followed 'disafforestation' is not always clear, but "there can be no doubt that [assarting] profited by it."[75] Darnhall could "assart and till" in the disafforested manor of Weaverham. Vale Royal (transferred from Darnhall in 1281) held all its lands disafforested and was permitted "*boscos illos assartare et in culturam redigere*." To be exempt from the triennial survey of encroachments known as the 'regard' was an important step towards disafforestation. The monks of Basingwerk were exempt from the regard in the forest of Peak "so that they may bring into tillage the soil of the said woods and waste." If an encroachment of some sort had been made, and freedom from the regard was subsequently obtained, the way was generally clear for cultivation. Thus we read "that the purpresture at *Cnotteshull* in Feckenham forest shall be quit of waste and regard and view of verderers and regarders so that they (the monks of Bordesley) may till the land without impediment."[76] On the other hand, when some of the abbey's woods in Feckenham were placed outside the regard it was on condition that no assarts were to be made therein.

In the regard of Pickering forest in 1334[77] all 'encroachments' (assarts and enclosures) made after 1217 were noted. There were seventy-four in all, and the lay population was for the most part responsible. The majority were quite small, about five acres, but a few amounted to twenty acres. The Cistercian nunnery of Rosedale had enclosed eighteen acres (sown) and elsewhere twenty acres. Rievaulx is not mentioned, although an important grant to the house by Henry II was accompanied by the right to

[75] R. Koebner, "The Settlement and Colonization of Europe,' in *The Cambridge Economic History of Europe*, 2nd ed., ed. M. M. Postan (Cambridge, 1966), 1: 81.

[76] *C.Ch.R.*, AD 1257-1300 (1267), p. 73.

[77] R. B. Turton, ed., *The Honor and Forest of Pickering*, North Riding Record Society, Publs., new ser., 3 (1896), pp. 28-200.

cultivate at will — "*et terram suam ibidem excolere et exercere pro voluntate sua.*" The land was then 'waste,' probably marsh, sedge and rough pasture; but the Hundred Rolls of 1275-6 tell us that there were 300 acres of arable at the grange of *Kekemareys* in the Vale, four miles south of Pickering and near the present Marishes.[78] Very likely all of this had been assarted, drained and ploughed up by the *conversi.*

The majority of references to forest clearings concern very small areas, under an acre; such, for example, as the perch reclaimed by Netley in Wychwood (sixty miles away) in 1246. On the other hand, some assarts amounted to fifty acres or more, and large-scale operations were perhaps more characteristic of the forests than elsewhere. Buildwas in 1277 obtained "a licence, after inquisition *ad quod damnum*, to assart sixty acres of [its] own soil in Stirchley" (forest of Wrekin). The Pipe Roll of 1207-8 refers to two assarts belonging to Pipewell in the forest of Rockingham, one of eighty acres (dating apparently from 1197-8) and the other of 140 acres; later (1237) it was observed that the monks had cleared woodland chiefly for tillage — "*omnes causas transcendit.*" Henry III (1253) gave Netley three carucates in the New Forest with permission "to enclose, assart and cultivate." Likewise the monks of Dore (1198-9) held 300 acres of woodland in the forest of Trivel, therein "*assartare, excolere et tractare.*" They also owed £20 on being freed from the regard in respect of 100 acres of "old assarts."[79] Beaulieu enclosed over 1000 acres in the New Forest between 1236 and 1324.[80]

Grants of forest assarts occupy a prominent place in the records of several Cistercian houses. Flaxley, soon after its foundation in 1151, was given 200 acres of assarts and 100 acres "which have been and remain to be assarted" in the forest of Dean. Together they formed the nucleus of the grange of Wallmore. The chartulary of Fountains preserves a "licence by King John to Richard Malbisse to break up and bring into cultivation eighty acres of pasture in the king's forest between the Ouse and the Derwent in Wheldrake" where Fountains had a grange. Later, Richard granted to the monks "the assart which John gave him." Netley in 1248 was permitted to hold about thirteen acres of assarts made by the abbot of

[78] Over the period 1266/7-1285 Pickering was a (private) chase rather than a royal forest.

[79] *Pipe Roll 1198-9*, P.R.S., new ser., 10 (1933), p. 219, and *1199-1200*, P.R.S., new ser., 12 (1934), p. 241. See also *Pipe Roll 1205-6*, P.R.S., new ser., 20 (1942), p. 69: fine of 840 marks for assarting 500 acres of woodland.

[80] *Chart. Bl.*, p. lvii. In 1299 the monks obtained permission "*includere et in culturam redigere*" 60 acres in the New Forest (ibid., p. 77).

Leicester at Wellow (*Welew*, within either the New or Milcet forest) and released to the Cistercian community which was in a better position to work the land.

Grazing

Parts of all the royal forests were used as pasture, and from time to time some well-placed Cistercian houses were accused of over-grazing — for example, Netley in the New Forest in 1271, and Flaxley in the forest of Dean ca. 1282.

Goats were rarely, if ever, included in a right of pasture and occasionally were specifically excluded (*exceptis capris*). They consumed young woody growth and seedlings and consequently checked regeneration. Sheep also were considered harmful and were almost as unwelcome as goats. In 1251 an agreement was concluded between Fountains and Sallay by which the latter was allowed to pasture 740 sheep in Litton "outside the forest of Littondale." Comparatively few grants were framed in terms of sheep. The royal house of Beaulieu (1230) was allowed to turn both sheep and cattle into the New Forest; and in 1393 the monks were confirmed in the right to keep all their animals (except goats) there and in the forest of Bere-Porchester "in covert and open, in the fence month (two weeks before and after midsummer day) as at other times." When Stanley was given a tract of 'waste' in the forest of Pewsham, fifteen acres were described as being "without the gate of the abbot's sheep-fold." Merevale occasionally kept sheep in the Peak forest; likewise Bordesley in Feckenham, and Rievaulx in Pickering.

Pipewell (1235) could graze up to 250 beasts on the *lawnd* of Benefield in Rockingham. About 1300, the hay of the 'lawn' was worth £25 per annum and the grazing £10. The abbot complained in 1331 that three haywains and a variety of large animals (nine horses, sixty oxen, ten bullocks, thirty cows and ten heifers), all belonging to the monastery, had been unlawfully removed from Benefield. Forest vaccaries are mentioned in the early Pipe Rolls; there were at least ten in the New Forest in 1186-7, each worth thirty shillings per annum. Holm Cultram's vaccary in Inglewood supported forty cows. The Yorkshire houses similarly exploited the private chases of the Pennine dales (*supra*, p. 75).

Horse-breeding was a prominent feature of some forests. Biddlesden was allowed to have a horse-pen (*haratium*) in Whittlewood (1234), and similarly Holm Cultram in Inglewood (1218-9). Merevale and Basingwerk each had permanent studs in the Peak about the middle of the thirteenth century. Horses belonging to Grace Dieu and Tintern were kept in the forest of Dean. Pigs thrived in oak and beech woods and pannage dues from the royal forests amounted to a considerable sum before the end of the twelfth century. In addition to grants of pasture for pigs, notices have survived of pigsties (*porcarias*) belonging to Stanley in Chippenham (1289) and to Bordesley in Feckenham (1189).

Other Activities

A variety of other activities are mentioned in connection with the royal forests. Vale Royal gathered ferns (*feugera*) for glass-making[81] and had a bee-keeper in Delamere. Flaxley collected the tithe of chestnuts in the forest of Dean. Many houses cut turbary and quarried stone. In 1215 Stanley obtained the right to take stone in Chippenham "*ad fabricam ecclesie sue*"; and between 1292 and 1297 the monks could work the king's quarry in the forest of Pewsham "to build the houses of the abbey and a wall round about." Grants of timber also often refer to "materials for building" which presumably included stone.

At least three Cistercian houses worked iron deposits within royal forests: Flaxley and Grace Dieu in the forest of Dean, and Stanley in Chippenham. Stanley was authorized to dig ironstone on its demesne lands in the forest in 1294. Flaxley began mining in the forest of Dean soon after its foundation (1151) and ultimately possessed a permanent forge and a number of itinerant forges. From 1227 Grace Dieu could take ore for two itinerant forges. Mineral deposits within the chases of the southern and eastern Pennines were worked by the Cistercian houses of Yorkshire and Lincolnshire.

By the beginning of the thirteenth century the value of the royal forests to the crown was chiefly financial. Timber and pasture brought in a considerable revenue and the expansion of arable was controlled as much in the interests of the Exchequer as of the chase. Indeed the work of assarting is nowhere more clearly recorded, whether in the form of special franchises or of infringements of the *lex forestae*. Cistercian houses enjoyed important privileges from the middle of the twelfth century and about one-third of the order, including several royal foundations, were active improvers or otherwise exploited a wide variety of natural products in the ensuing one hundred and fifty years.

[81] *C.Cl.R.*, AD 1279-88, p. 264. Fern ash mixed with sand formed the base.

5

Towns and Trade

"*Multa de mercatoribus nostris querela est, multa confusio*" (1134)[1]

The Disposal of Wool

Information about the disposal of Cistercian wool is typically fragmentary: references to fulling mills and to the manufacture of cloth, contracts stipulating delivery in a particular port or town, and a number of licences to export. Since, however, wool had few if any competitors as an article of Cistercian commerce during the twelfth and thirteenth centuries, we are probably justified in taking into account other evidence, even though a connection with the wool trade cannot be conclusively demonstrated: toll exemptions and other trading advantages, the possession of ships, unexplained dealings with foreign merchants, the setting-up of markets and fairs, and the acquisition of urban property.

Cloth and Fulling Mills

As early as 1193 the wool of the English Cistercians was described as "the chief part of their substance."[2] The bulk of this was probably exported. No references to sales to local clothiers have come to light. Yet it is very probable that there were such transactions even before the export trade declined and the native cloth industry expanded in the second half of the fourteenth century. Wool-working towns such as Beverley, Louth and

[1] *Statuta*, 1: 24.

[2] William of Newburgh, *Historia rerum Anglicarum*, in *Chronicles of the Reigns of Stephen, Henry II, and Richard I*, ed. R. Howlett, R. S. 82 (London, 1885), 1: 399. See also Matthew Paris, *Chronica majora*, ed. H. R. Luard, R. S. 57 (London, 1880), 5: 553.

Coggeshall lay in close proximity to Cistercian communities. At the same time it is fairly certain that the monasteries themselves were not important centres of cloth manufacture.[3]

Meaux, we are told, had a stone building at Wawne grange where wool was woven and cloth fulled for the use of "the monks, the *conversi* and the poor of the neighbourhood" (1235-49). The Close Rolls for 1296 include an "order to restore to the abbot and convent of Beaulieu ten sacks [of wool] of the thirty lately bought ... for the king's use, as the king has granted to them that they shall have ten sacks in order to make cloth for their own use."[4] Fountains (1457-8) and apparently Kirkstall also had weaving establishments.[5]

A twelfth-century grant to Vaudey was made on condition that the house supplied the benefactor with linen and woollen clothing (*lineo et laneo*) and also lamb-skins (*pellibus agninis*), but the cloth was probably purchased by the monks. Similarly, Furness, in return for a quitclaim to land (1251-2), furnished goods including "seven ells of cloth, green or dyed, six ells of bluett and one fur of lamb." Kingswood was buying cloth from at least the middle of the thirteenth century — cloth for harness, for coverlets, for shoes and capes.[6] In a list of wages paid by the abbey in 1255, shepherds are mentioned but not weavers. From the end of the fourteenth century to the time of the Dissolution (when most of the monastic fulling mills were leased out) many other houses are known to have bought cloth.

Fig. 16 shows the Cistercian houses that are known to have possessed at least one fulling mill (Appendix 5). The distribution is undoubtedly incomplete. A mill is often mentioned without any indication as to whether it was used for corn or cloth. While the majority of such notices almost certainly refer to the more common corn mills, some fulling mills have probably been overlooked. Stanlaw by an undated charter was granted a stream and a piece of land to erect either a tannery or a fulling mill.

[3] Concerning continental Europe, see G. F. von Schmoller, *Die Strassburger Tucher- und Weberzunft und die Deutsche Weberei von* XIII-XVIII *Jahrhundert* (Strassburg, 1879), 9ff.; J. W. Thompson, 'The Cistercian Order and colonization in mediaeval Germany,' *Amer. Jour. Theol.*, 24 (1920): 86; P. Boissonade, *Life and Work in Mediaeval Europe* (London, 1927), p. 188. G. Espinas, *La draperie dans la Flandre française au moyen-âge* (Paris, 1923), vol. 1, devotes a section to 'la draperie des organismes religieux.'

[4] See also *Account B.*, pp. 32, 39, 214-24 (1269-70).

[5] *Mem. F.*, 3: 49; D. E. Owen et al., *Kirkstall Abbey Excavations, 1950-1954*, Thoresby Soc. Publs. 43 (1955): ix.

[6] *Docs. K.*, pp. 193-99 (1240), 215-16 (1262).

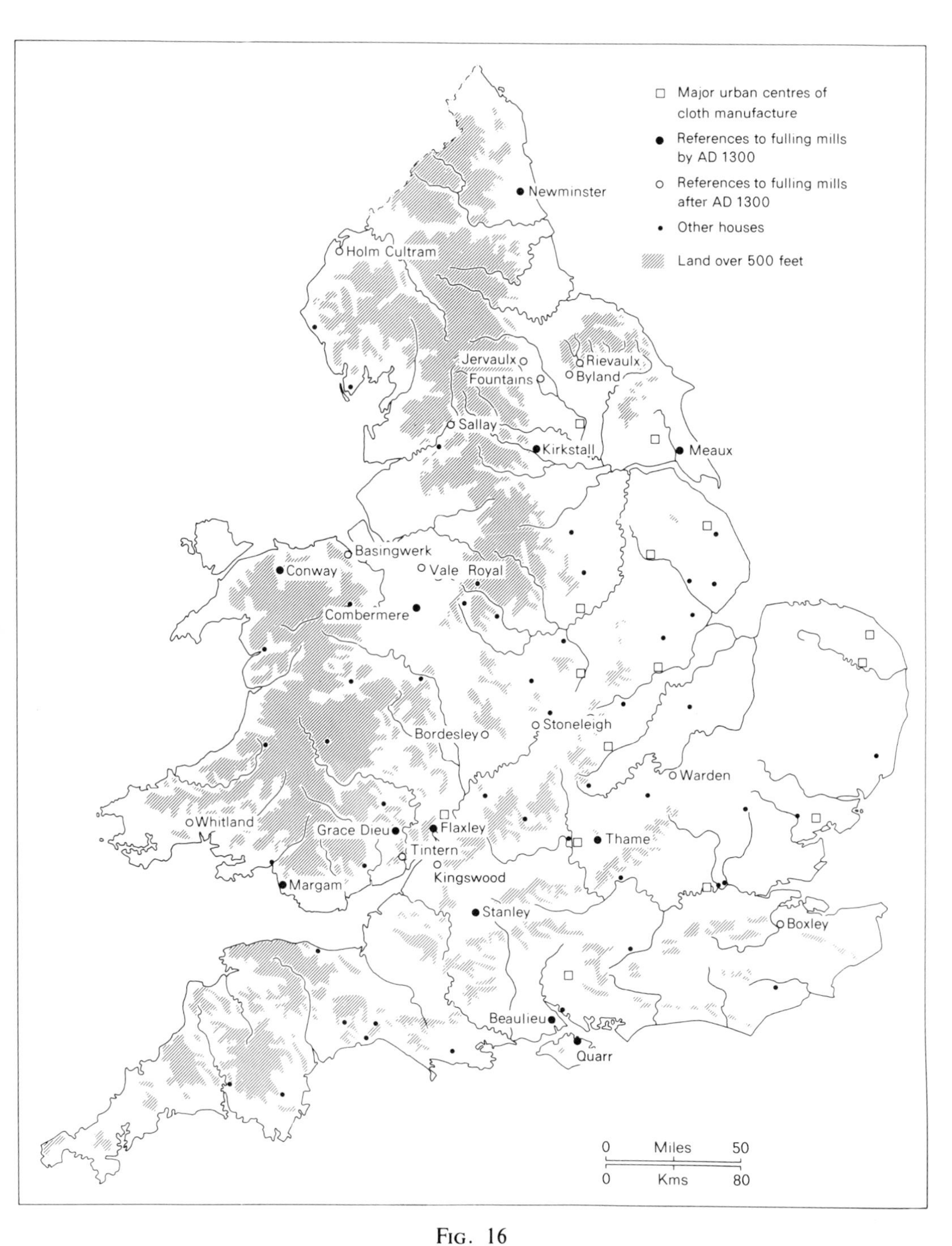

FIG. 16

Cistercian houses with fulling mills (Appendix 5) and the distribution of the major urban centres of cloth manufacture.

Only two twelfth-century examples of Cistercian fulling mills have been found. The statutes of the order forbidding the acquisition of mills (1157) applied also *de fullonibus*, although houses only recently united to Cîteaux (chiefly Savigny and its colonies, 1147) were permitted to keep those that they already possessed.[7] Stanley had a *molendinum fullericum* ca. 1189-90, and a fulling mill was granted to Thame in 1197.[8] Possibly before the end of the century, Newminster was confirmed in land near the river Wansbeck "*ad molendinum fulrez.*" Five fulling mills are mentioned in the chartulary of Newminster, but not all of these were necessarily in use at the same time. Two stood near the abbey on the banks of the Wansbeck; one at Sturton grange (1252); another at Caistron grange; and one at Hepden, almost thirty miles away on a head-water of the river Coquet and within the pastoral lordship of Kidland.[9] The presence of fulling mills on outlying estates, including granges, should be taken into account in referring to the distribution by houses.[10]

Toll Exemptions and Other Commercial Advantages

The Cistercians were often obliged to carry their wool to a port or to some place convenient to the buyer. In so doing, they had important advantages, such as toll exemptions, the use of granges for purposes of accommodation and storage,[11] and ample means of conveyance.

Wool was transported by pack-horse and by cart. In 1275 Vaudey was suspected of taking wool to Boston, "partly by cart and partly by water." Dore sent several cart-loads of wool to Windsor in 1216, and likewise Basingwerk to London in 1277. When Combermere received letters of

[7] *Statuta*, 1: 67. See also n. 9 *infra*.

[8] The earliest reference to a fulling mill in England belongs to the last quarter of the twelfth century: E. M. Carus-Wilson, 'An industrial revolution of the thirteenth century,' *Eco. Hist. Rev.*, 11 (1941): 44 (1185); R. Lennard, 'Early fulling mills: additional examples,' ibid., 2nd ser., 3 (1950-51): 342-43 (?1174-80).

[9] Chart. N., p. 78. Fountains worked a fulling mill at the grange of Kilnsey on the upper Wharfe (*Mem. F.*, 1: 376), also the centre of an important pastoral district. Since this was written, two early references to mills belonging to houses not listed in Appendix 5 or shown in Fig. 16 have been found: (a) confirmation (1154-89) to Kirkstead of a fulling mill at Kirkby on Bain (Stenton, *Documents ... Danelaw*, p. 117); (b) Pipewell's fulling mill at Great Barford, 1228 (Joyce Godber, ed., *The Cartulary of Newnham Priory*, Beds. Hist. Rec. Soc. Publs., 43 (Bedford, 1963), 1: 96).

[10] Of the thirteen fulling mills noted by Aleksandr Savin[e] in the *Valor Ecclesiasticus*, three belonged to Cistercian houses (*English Monasteries on the Eve of the Dissolution* (Oxford, 1909), pp. 125-26.

[11] On one occasion the Scottish house of Dundrennan stored eight and a half sacks of wool at a grange belonging to Holm Cultram (*Rot. Parl.*, 1: 471).

protection to transport wool "and other of the abbot's necessaries" to Boston, horses and carts were specified. A concession to Holm Cultram indicates that some of its wool was loaded upon carts and taken to Newcastle: "*liberos introitus et exitus per totam terram suam cum plaustris* (waggons) *sumagiis* (pack-horses) *et carettis suis* (carts), *eundo et redeundo de domo sua de Holm versus Novum Castrum cum lanis et totis bonis suis.*" In 1263 the abbey's carts were hindered at the bridge of Hexham on the way to Newcastle.[12] Carts were more convenient than pack-horses when returning with an assortment of goods, and it may be that the former were used to an even greater extent than by the ordinary wool merchant. The monasteries had to meet a variety of day-to-day demands as well as the seasonal requirements of the wool clip; it is, therefore, not surprising that they were sometimes called upon to assist the king. In 1304 a cart and four horses were required from each of twenty abbeys "to take the Exchequer from York to Westminster." Rufford and all the Yorkshire Cistercian houses except Jervaulx were named. Fountains, Jervaulx, Meaux and Whalley were among the eight religious houses asked to supply carts for Edward III's Scottish expedition of 1332-3.

There were several stages in the transport of wool from the monastic estates to the ports. R. A. Pelham concluded that "cart traffic [for wool] was the rule rather than the exception at this period [the fourteenth century]; ... a sack of wool sewn up in its canvas container weighed over three hundredweights, so the pack-horse can have been of use only in the preliminary stages of collection."[13] Horses were probably used between the shearing stations and the abbey wool shed (*lanaria*) where the clip was cleaned, sorted and packed into sacks.

Exemption from toll (Appendix 6 and Fig. 17) was an important commercial advantage. The principal heads under which exemption was allowed, other than simply toll (*thelonium*), were passage or right of way or use of a ferry (*passagium*), toll at a bridge (*pontagium*), pavage (*pavagium*), murage (*muragium*), and foot passage or entry (*pedagium*). The grant to Vale Royal in 1299 was typical of the concessions enjoyed; it conferred "freedom from toll for their own goods and merchandise and for things which they bought for themselves or sold belonging to themselves in fairs, markets and at all bridges throughout the land."

[12] *Cal. Docs. Scot.*, 1: 462.

[13] 'The early wool trade of Warwickshire and the rise of the merchant middle class,' *Trans. Birm. Arch. Soc.*, 63 (1944): 50. See also T. H. Lloyd, 'The medieval wool-sack: a study in economic history,' *Textile History*, 3 (1972): 92-99.

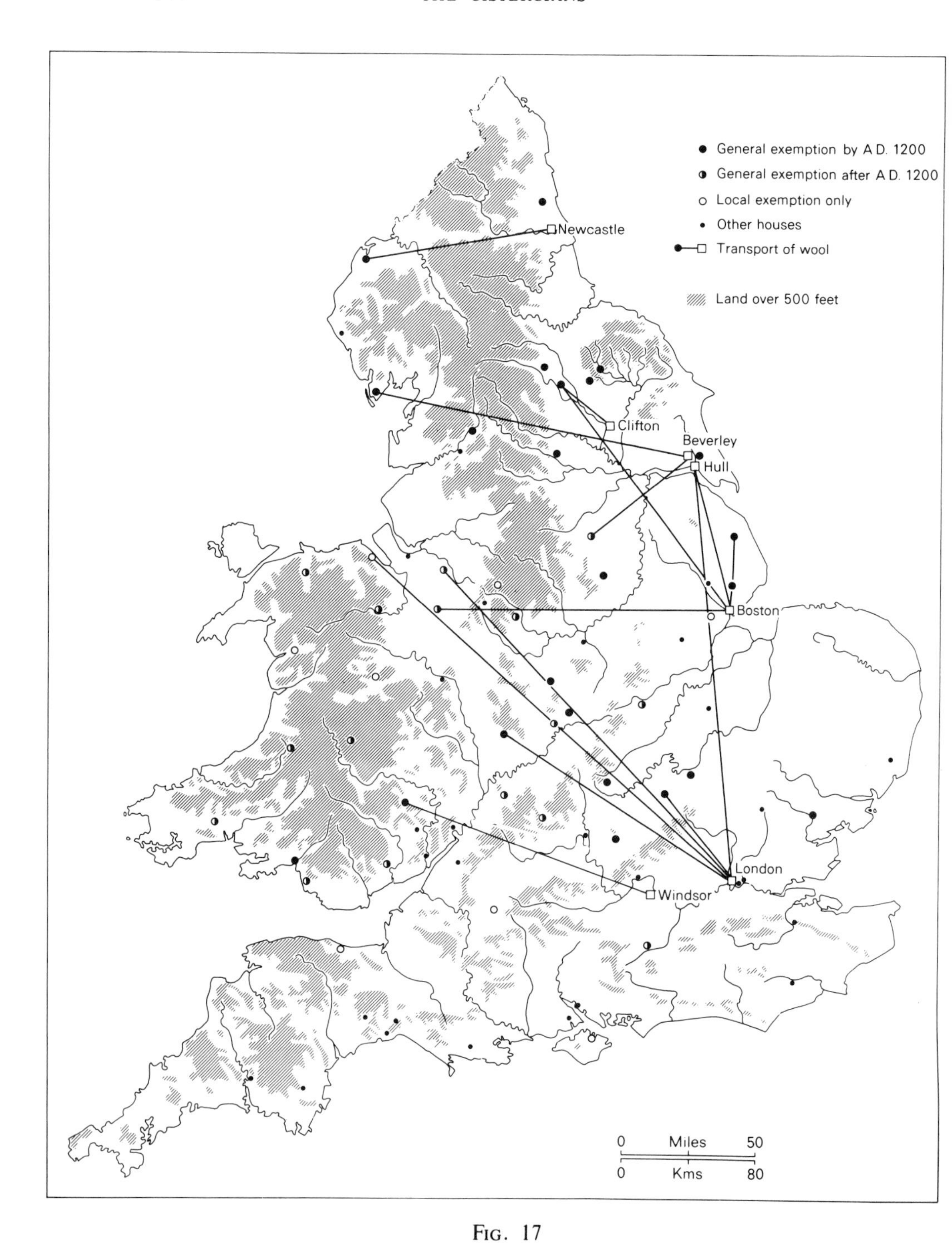

FIG. 17

Cistercian houses with toll exemptions and/or transporting wool (Appendices 6 and 7).

The majority of exemptions refer to England and Wales with, in some cases, particular Continental ports or Ireland. The rest were of local extent or restricted in some way. Thus Dieulacres was exempt "*per totam terram*" of the earl of Chester and Lincoln (1217-32), and similarly Stanley in the city of Bristol. Strata Marcella had freedom from toll "for all things intended for their own use" throughout the kingdom except London. Most houses appear to have been privileged within the lands of their founders.

At least twenty-three houses, mostly in eastern England, had secured general exemption from tolls before 1200. Seven of the eight Yorkshire houses were granted freedom by either Henry I (Rievaulx) or Henry II.[14] Coggeshall, Furness, Merevale, Thame, Louth Park, Neath, Revesby, Tintern, Woburn and probably Newminster, also had charters of exemption by 1189. The remaining notices mostly belong to the late twelfth or to the thirteenth century when the Cistercians were most actively involved in the wool trade.

Particular tolls varied somewhat in amount from place to place. Murage on a sack of wool, for example, was usually between 2d. and 4d. These seem trifling sums, but often there were many sacks of wool, and in a journey across England the aggregate total would quickly mount. Consequently it was very desirable that a house with freedom from toll should carry its own wool, for if the merchant was obliged to do so he would certainly offer less per sack. The merchant would also have to pay hired men, whereas a monastery could employ the unsalaried *conversi*. The advantages of exemption are perhaps best illustrated by the protests raised against abuses. The most persistent of these was the marketing of nonmonastic wool by servants or lay brothers.[15] Louth Park, Kirkstead and Revesby were accused in 1275 of buying-up "wool and other merchandise" over a period of fifteen years to sell to foreign merchants. As a result, the city of Lincoln had been 'damaged' to the extent of 100 marks, the amount that would have accrued from the tolls and customs normally due.[16]

[14] Clairvaux, with many affiliated houses in eastern England, was granted freedom from tolls throughout the lands of Henry II (*Mem. F.*, 2: 3). Les Dunes (Flanders) was also exempt by right of a charter of Henry II (E. Berger, *Recueil des actes de Henri II*, revised ed. (Paris, 1920), 2: 279.

[15] When the tenants of a monastery were included in the terms of a grant, it was usually on condition that they did not act as "common merchants."

[16] *Rot. Hund.*, 1: 317.

Transport of Wool

A large proportion of England's internal trade during the Middle Ages was river-borne. Wool and other heavy commodities could be carried more cheaply be water than by road, and evidence survives of the use of rivers by Cistercian houses, especially during the thirteenth century. The rivers Ure and Ouse between Boroughbridge and York were toll-free to Fountains (1155) and Jervaulx (confirmed 1236); the latter enjoyed "the liberty of the water ... so that they may bring and take all things needful to them in one ship." Fountains had 'free passage' on the river Swale, and similarly Meaux on the Hull. A charter to Rievaulx permitted the monks "to load and unload their ships [on the Ouse] in going and returning from markets (*nundinae*)." Ships used to pass along the Derwent to Stamford Bridge, but by 1332 the channel was obstructed by weirs and the abbot of Fountains was one of the aggrieved parties. In 1275 Kirkstead was accused of appropriating two acres of land at Calcroft where, in the time of Henry III, Lincoln mariners loaded and unloaded wool. Newminster had a shipping point on the Tyne, Roche on the Trent, and Byland on the Ouse in a suburb of York. Part of Furness's "chain of stations between the abbey and Boston"[17] was a house at York, "*a regia strata de Skeldergate ante usque ad aquam de Ouse retro.*"

There are references to the carriage of wool by at least fourteen Cistercian houses[18] (Appendix 7 and Fig. 17). The delivery points were either major ports, chiefly London and Boston, or river wharfs. In only one case (Vaudey, 1275) is water transport over part of the route specified, although it can be assumed that wool delivered by Fountains at Clifton on the Ouse, and that taken to Windsor by Dore, continued its journey by water. Monasteries under obligation to deliver wool are included in Fig. 17, as well as three instances of wool already at a port but still belonging to the house in question. Delivery to centres along the east coast strongly suggests that the wool was destined for overseas markets. It is, however, not improbable that the wool of Furness and of Roche taken into custody at Beverley in 1224 was bound for the important cloth industry of the town. References to the transport of wool are mostly later than this and eleven of the seventeen dated examples belong to the last quarter of the

[17] *Coucher F.*, 6: xvii.

[18] In contrast, only one reference to Cistercian wool carried by a merchant has been found: "Safe conduct until Christmas (1277) for Orlandinus de Podio, king's merchant, and his men bringing 20 sacks of wool to Chester which he bought of the abbot of Aberconway" (*C.P.R.*, AD 1272-81, p. 235).

thirteenth century. The arrangements were often very precise. The abbot of Woburn had "until All Saints day (1275) ... to carry his wools to London (and) store them there." In the same year Darnhall was obliged to "cause [its] wool (twelve sacks) to be carried to the city of London (from Hereford where the wool was dressed) at their cost and their peril and risk ... and shall there cause it to be delivered at Gile's lodgings before the feast of St. Peter at the beginning of August, 1276."

Overseas Trade

By about the middle of the twelfth century at least a dozen Cistercian houses enjoyed toll concessions in Continental ports from Barfleur to Dieppe.[19] These privileges usually applied to "men, horses and property" and point more to private journeying, usually to Cîteaux or on behalf of the king,[20] than to trading ventures.

Several monasteries possessed ships of one kind or other (Appendix 8), vessels of up to 200 tons; but usually little more is known than their names, such as *La Mariote* (1254) and *La Stoyle* (1268, 1272) belonging to Beaulieu, *La Russynole* (1271) to Netley, and the *Hule* (1235) to Neath. Beaulieu and Quarr were sometimes obliged to supply "sea-going vessels" for the sovereign's use. Thus an order was issued in 1254 "to let the smaller ship of the abbot of La Quarer come and go where the abbot will ... keeping his greater ship for the Queen's crossing." When in 1321 the bailiffs of twelve towns of the South and South West were requested to send as many ships as possible to Ireland, the abbot of Beaulieu was asked to dispatch his to Drogheda. The same two houses were also involved in overseas trading. In 1221 a lay brother (*frater*) of Beaulieu had collected a ship-load of grain "*in partibus borealibus*" for the use of the abbey. A ship belonging to Quarr and laden with wine was in Southampton in 1252. And under the year 1281 we find — "protection and safe conduct for the abbey and convent of Beaulieu taking a ship loaded with corn and other goods from time to time to Gascony and other places within the king's power and bringing thence wine and goods." Neath (Glamorgan) in

[19] Byland (1154-89), Coggeshall (ca. 1150), Fountains (1155), Furness (1154-89), Jervaulx (1165-73), Kirkstall (1154-89), Meaux (1154-61), Newminster (ca. 1165), Revesby (1155-8), Thame (ca. 1155), Woburn (1155-8).

[20] See S. Wood, *English Monasteries and their Patrons in the Thirteenth Century* (Oxford, 1955), p. 120; and A. M. Cooke, 'A study in twelfth century religious revival and reform,' *Bull. John Rylands Library*, 9 (1925): 163, 167. The Cistercians were accused (1153-74) of "being always on the road."

1234 received a licence "to buy and transport corn from England" and, the following year, permission "for a ship ... to come in safely to England with merchandise to trade." A ship belonging to the neighbouring house of Margam was seized in 1234 at Bristol.[21]

There was a considerable amount of trade between the abbeys of the North West and places in Ireland; the evidence chiefly takes the form of licences to import corn or victuals into England (Appendix 8B). Holm Cultram was also importing victuals (presumably wine) from Gascony at the close of the thirteenth century.[22] The abbey held the port of Skinburness by royal charter from 1301.[23] In 1278 Vale Royal sent Robert de Baru of Chester to Ireland for victuals, and, shortly afterwards, the monks commissioned a burgess of Chester to purchase 100 tuns of wine.[24] But the practice of employing regular merchants (*negotiatores*) did not, apparently, commend itself widely to the English Cistercians.

The wool trade dominates the picture that we have of Cistercian overseas activity. The licences to export (Appendix 9) state or clearly imply that the monasteries were to ship their own wool; there is no suggestion that they acted merely as carriers. Fourteen houses are shown in Fig. 18. Ten belonged to the northern group of leading wool producers, and at least eight of these also obtained toll exemptions during the twelfth or thirteenth century. The shipment of wool to Flanders from the monasteries of north-east England was relatively easy. On the other hand, Furness, Strata Florida and Holm Cultram were three of the more isolated houses. Perhaps disposing of their wool through itinerant merchants proved so unsatisfactory that permission to export was sought. Strata Florida (which does not appear in Pegolotti's list of monasteries with wool for sale) was allowed to arrange shipments over a period of three years (1213-6). More often, a house was limited to a single ship-load. Garendon (1225) was permitted to export to "Flanders or other areas not under the control of the king of France." Flanders was the only destination specifically mentioned and almost certainly the bulk of Cistercian wool at this time was landed there. Licences were usually addressed simply, "*Rex ballivis por-*

[21] The statutes of the order refer in 1190 to the ships of Les Dunes (Flanders). Lyse Kloster (Norway), a daughter of Fountains, traded with England; and the Scottish houses too ventured abroad (C. H. Talbot, *The Cistercian Abbeys of Scotland* (London, 1939), p. 9). The German houses had shipping in the Baltic in the thirteenth century (F. Winter, *Die Cistercienser des nordöstlichen Deutschlands* (Gotha, 1868), 1: 114).

[22] *C.P.R.*, AD 1281-92, p. 426.

[23] *Reg.H.C.*, p. 126. In 1297 Holm Cultram and Furness were included in a list of ports (*C.Cl.R.*, AD 1296-1302, pp. 82-82, 101, 121).

[24] *C.P.R.*, AD 1272-81, pp. 265, 315.

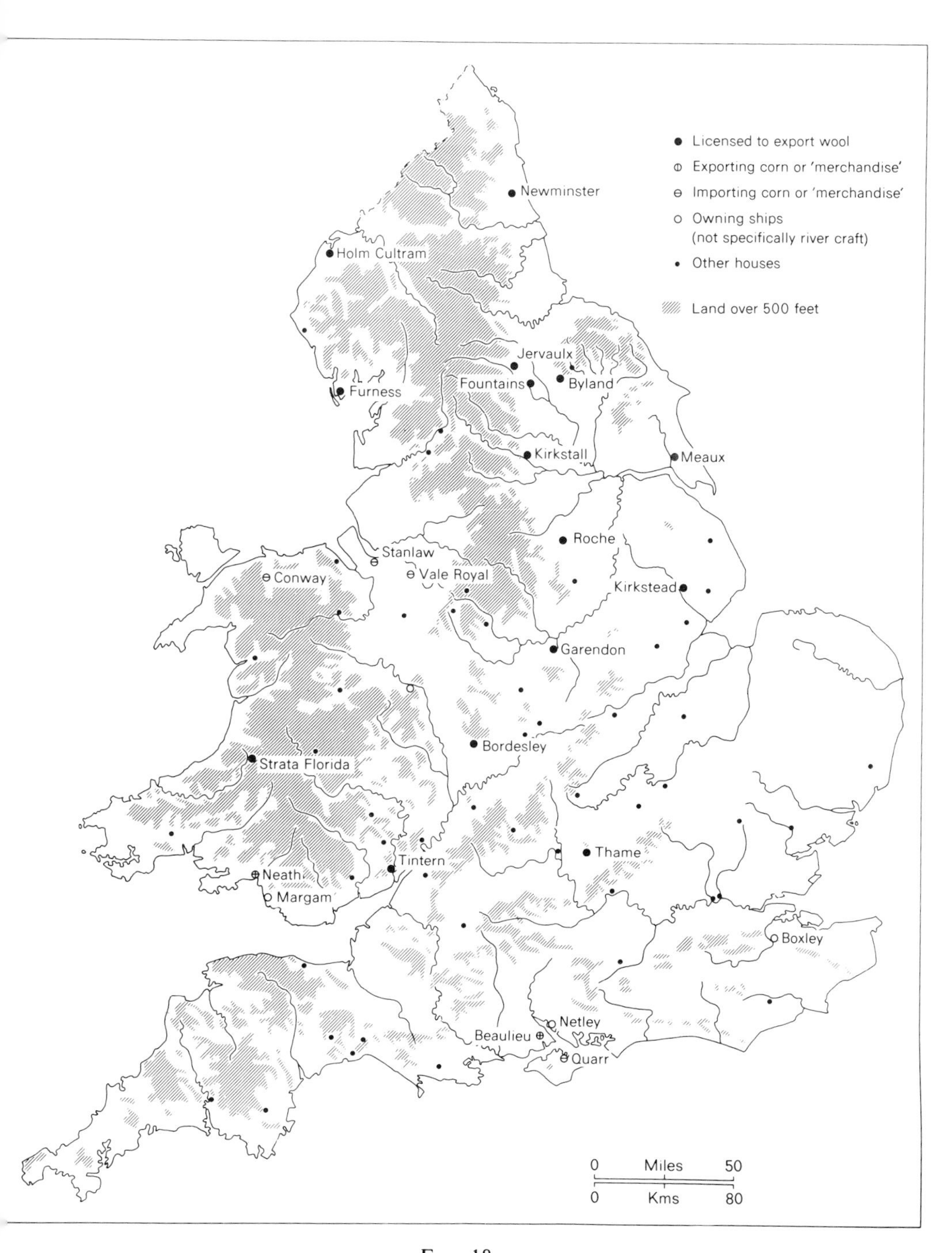

FIG. 18

Cistercian houses trading abroad and/or with sea-going ships (Appendices 8 and 9).

tuum maris Anglie." Bordesley had thirteen sacks of wool lying in London in 1224 and was given leave to export it, presumably from the same port. The licences to Garendon, Byland and Jervaulx were addressed to the officials of the Cinque ports. The wool in question may not have been brought south by land; ships out from Boston or Hull sometimes called at one or other of the Cinque ports before crossing the Channel. The licences to Fountains and Kirkstall were forwarded to the king's controller at York, and that granted to Kirkstead to the port officer at Lynn. Until 1293 the port of *Wyke* (later known as Kingston upon Hull) belonged to Meaux. It was handling wool, some, very likely, from the Meaux estates, in the latter part of the twelfth century.[25]

All but one of the known licences to export wool belong to 1224 or 1225. The evidence of negotiations with foreign merchants increases noticeably from the second quarter of the thirteenth century; similarly the references to monasteries obliged to deliver wool at certain places belong very largely to the period 1225-1300. Much later (1418-23) Furness was suspected of loading wool at *Le Peele de Foddray* (on Walney island) for transit to *Ernemuthe en Zeeland.* In 1390 an enquiry had been held into the unauthorized export of wool from Cumberland, Westmorland and Furness.

Wool Ports and Wool Merchants

The ports that handled the bulk of England's wool lay along the eastern and southern seaboards (Fig. 19),[26] opposite the great Flanders market. As we have seen, when Cistercian houses undertook to deliver their wool, this most commonly involved a journey to Boston or to London.

From the close of the thirteenth century attempts were made to control the wool trade by naming certain towns as staples. In 1297 shippers were restricted to nine English ports, but the first true staple (Antwerp then St Omer) dates only from 1313. It was replaced by home staples in 1326, although not permanently. When home staples were enforced only native merchants could operate outside these *entrepôts* without special permission.

[25] J. N. Bilson, 'Wyke-upon-Hull in 1293,' *Trans. E. Riding Ant. Soc.*, 26 (1926-28): 40-41.

[26] Shipments are tabulated in E. M. Carus-Wilson and O. Coleman, *England's Export Trade, 1275-1547* (Oxford, 1963), and the figures are mapped in R. A. Donkin, 'Changes in the Early Middle Ages,' in *A New Historical Geography of England*, ed. H. C. Darby (Cambridge, 1973), Fig. 30.

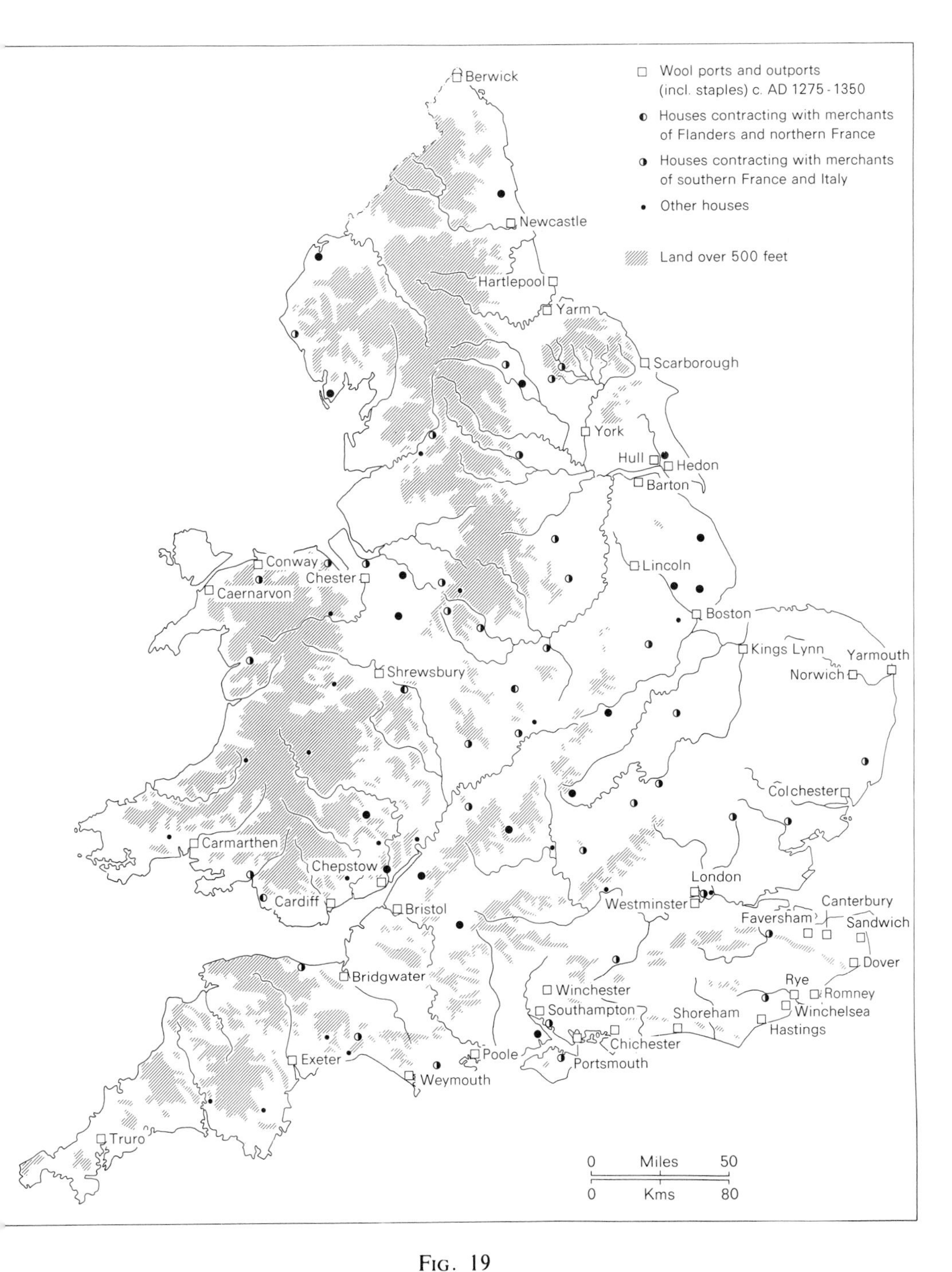

Fig. 19

Cistercian houses contracting with foreign wool merchants (Appendix 10) and the distribution of the chief wool-exporting ports.

Most of the leading wool suppliers lay within easy reach of the wool ports of the North East (Newcastle, Hull, Boston) or of Southampton or Bristol. There was no concentration around London; the city itself may have taken some Cistercian wool but that grown to the north-east, south and south-west of the capital was generally considered 'coarse' and fetched a relatively low price. Houses with a considerable surplus in Dorset, Wiltshire and the four northern counties were also within coarse wool districts, but they were apparently able to market their wool at a price above or just a fraction below the average for the order as a whole, possibly on account of local improvements or superior sorting. The monasteries disposing of a low surplus at a high price lay principally within the south Midlands and the march of South Wales.

Evidence linking Cistercian houses and English merchants is disappointingly small. Flaxley was in debt to both native and alien merchants in 1277. Warden owed 500 marks to John de Triple, merchant of London in 1320, and Combe, twelve years later, £140 to a citizen of Coventry, John of Meryton. More interestingly, Combe (according to an action dated 1364) contracted to deliver forty-two sacks of wool to Richard de Stoke and Richard de Buttre of Coventry;[27] and Meaux, some time between 1349 and 1353, sold 100 sacks of wool to Thomas de Holmo Beverlaco (a burgess of Beverley) and Richard, his son.[28] From the middle of the fourteenth century the trade in wool fell more and more into the hands of Englishmen. Over the period ca. 1150-1325 the disposal of the Cistercian product was largely controlled by foreigners — men from northern France, Flanders and Italy.

In 1273 licences were issued for the export of 32,743 sacks of wool, 34.9 per cent by Englishmen, 24.4 per cent by Italians, 16.1 per cent by merchants of northern France, 11.2 per cent by Brabanters, and 5.7 per cent by merchants of southern France.[29] Italians and Brabanters were also well represented in the licences to export wool issued in 1277-8.[30] Flemish wool merchants frequented London as early as the tenth century, and it is

[27] *C.P.R.*, AD 1361-4, p. 526.

[28] *Chron. Melsa*, 3: 85. Before 1166 Roche and Louth Park raised money on wool through the English financier William Cade (Hilary Jenkinson, 'William Cade, a financier of the twelfth century,' *E.H.R.*, 28 (1913): 221). High quality wool from the Scottish house of Newbattle was being exported by a local merchant as late as 1490 (*Reg. Newbattle*, p. xxxviii).

[29] A. Schaube, 'Die Wollausfuhr Englands vom Jahr 1273,' *Vierteljahrschrift für Sozial- und Wirtschaftsgeschichte* 6 (1908): 68. See *C.P.R.*, AD 1272-81, pp. 13-26, 33-39.

[30] *C.C.R. (V)*, pp. 1-11.

well known that the cloth industry of Flanders, supreme throughout the twelfth and most of the thirteenth centuries, depended very heavily on fine English wool. The Cistercian statutes for 1206 refer to "*querela Bergensium* (Bergues) *contra abbates Angliae de venditione lanarum.*"[31] Spanish wool also was used to some extent in Flanders and, more important, up to the last quarter of the thirteenth century it "supplied the greater part of the needs of Florentine manufacture."[32] Thereafter the Italians, who also had long been active in London, began to oust the Flemings and the French in the export of English wool, until "at the end of the century they possessed the virtual monopoly of the staple commodity of the country."[33] The finishing of northern cloth flourished in Genoa, Lucca and Florence from the late twelfth century, but by the last years of the thirteenth century Florence, surpassing all other Tuscan cities, was as much involved in weaving as in finishing imported cloth. The Italian industry reached its zenith about 1350 when 30,000 men are reputed to have been employed in Florence alone and cloth produced in Italy was marketed in the cities of the Near East. These developments — first Flemish and then Italian predominance — can be followed in relation to the English and Welsh Cistercian houses.

References to merchants of Flanders and northern France fall within the period 1212-1275 — men of St. Omer, Cambrai, Ypres, Ghent and Douai. A thirteenth-century list of English wool-producing monasteries (inferior to that of Pegolotti) is preserved among the archives of Douai.[34] Frenchmen from Montpellier, Cahors[35] and Bordeaux make an appearance between 1275 and 1323, and Italians from Genoa, Florence, Lucca, Pistoia and Chieri between 1275 and 1344 (Appendix 10 and Figs. 19 and 20). No significant German interest in the marketing of Cistercian wool has been found.[36]

[31] *Statuta*, 1: 332. Similarly ibid., p. 362 (1209): "*Querela Arnulphi Canis de monachis de Querchetele* (Quarr) *qui lanam suam praevendiderunt, committitur abbati de Fontanis* (Fountains)."

[32] R. S. Lopez, 'The trade of medieval Europe: the south,' in *The Cambridge Economic History of Europe*, ed. M. M. Postan and E. E. Rich (Cambridge, 1952), 2: 329.

[33] R. J. Whitwell, 'Italian bankers and the English crown,' *T.R.H.S.*, 2nd ser., 17 (1903): 175, 216.

[34] G. Espinas, *La vie urbaine de Douai au moyen âge* (Paris, 1913), 3: 232-34. Merchants from Douai are known to have been at Boston fair in 1289 (Hall, *Select Cases*, pp. 63-64).

[35] See P. Wolff, 'Le problème des Cahorsins," *Annales du Midi*, 62 (1950): 229-38; N. Denholm-Young, 'The merchants of Cahors,' *Medievalia et Humanistica*, 4 (1946): 37-44.

[36] M. M. Postan has written: "for a time in the thirteenth century [the Cologners] even succeeded in penetrating into the Anglo-French wool trade and interposing themselves be-

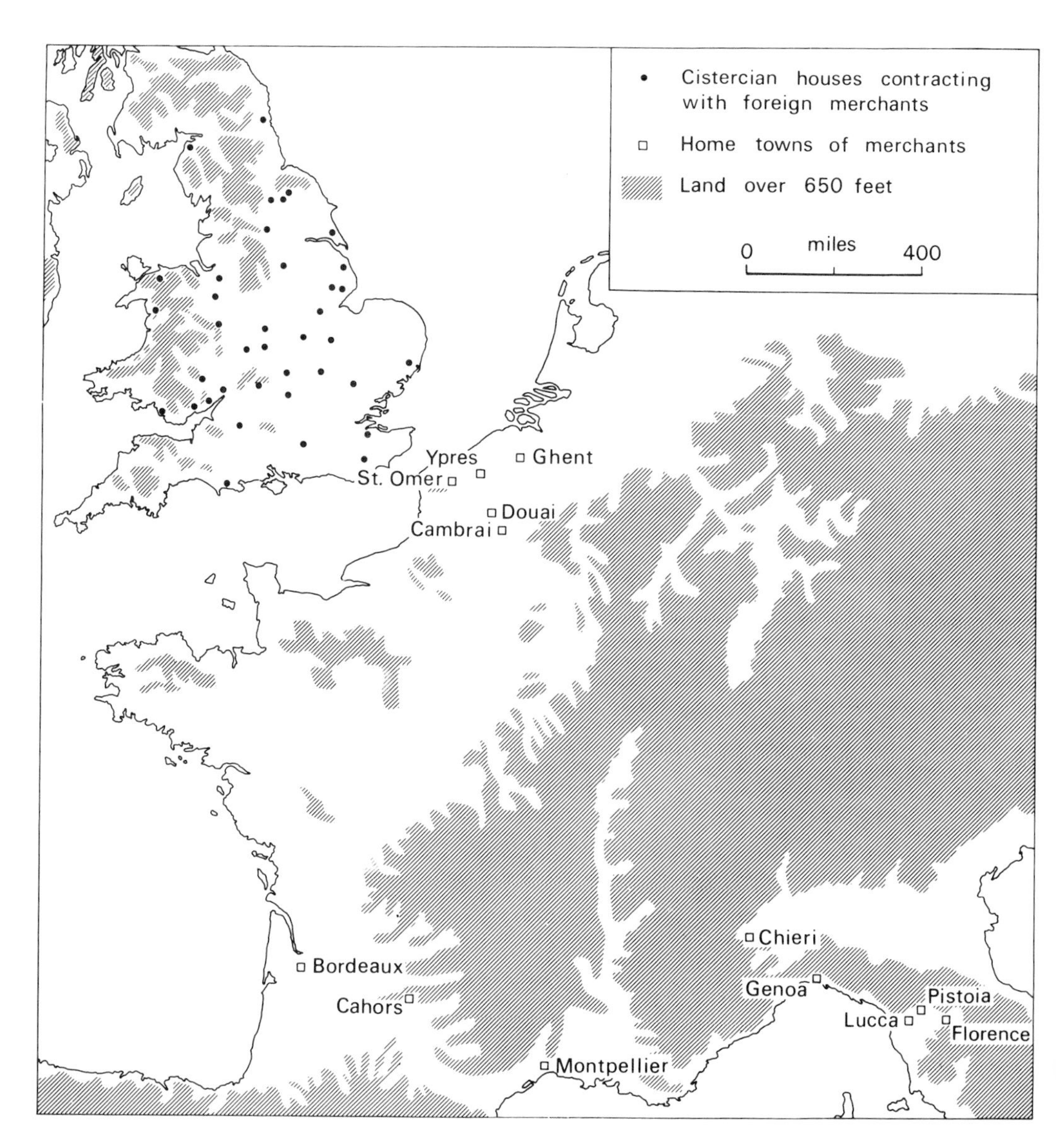

Fig. 20

Home towns of foreign wool merchants contracting with Cistercian houses in England and Wales.

Only about a third of the notices collected specifically mention wool; those belonging to the fourteenth century are mostly records of debts (obligations which, incidently, must have made it difficult to turn from the sale of wool to the working of cloth).[37] Although merchants or the agents often visited monasteries to initiate agreements, negotiations might be concluded far from the monastic precincts. In 1272 Newminster, Kingswood, Pipewell, Beaulieu and Biddlesden were in contact with Flemish merchants in London.[38] Three years later the abbot of Darnhall "sold for himself and his convent in the city of London ... to Giles de Ayre, attorney of John Wermond of Cambrai, twelve sacks of good wool." This was apparently a forward contract as no wool changed hands at the time. In 1276 Fountains agreed to supply sixty-two sacks of wool to certain Florentine exporters; the latter paid 697½ marks in London, and the monastery undertook to deliver wool at Clifton (near York) over a period of three years.

Most of the Italians who were associated with the English and Welsh Cistercian houses belonged either to Lucca or to Florence. They included members of some of the great merchant firms — the Peruzzi, the Pulci, the Mozzi, the Society of Mark Reyner, the Bardi, the Black Circle (*circuli nigri*), the White Circle (*circuli albi*), the Frescobaldi and the Spini, all of Florence; the Ricardi, the Betti and the Society of the Sons of Betori, of Lucca. Details of contracts negotiated in 1294 by eight Florentine and two Luchese firms refer to 133 religious houses in England and Wales, of which no less than forty-nine were Cistercian (apart from eight nunneries).[39] Entries in the Close Rolls give the names of many of the individual merchants; some recur several times, the surname Simonet[ti] frequently between 1323 and 1334. Asselin[us] Simonet[ti] of Lucca, occasionally in association with Bindus Gyle of Florence, did business with Vaudey in 1323, 1326 and 1332; with Sibton in 1334; with Waverley in 1329 and 1334; with Bindon and Biddlesden in 1334. Michael Simonetti was in contact with Kirkstead about the middle of the century, and

---

tween the English wool growers and the Flemish cloth markets" ('The trade of medieval Europe: the north,' *The Cambridge Economic History of Europe* (Cambridge, 1952), 2: 185).

[37] Not only was wool often paid for in advance, but a loan was sometimes repayable in wool (*Rot. Parl.*, 1: 1 (Bordesley)).

[38] *C.P.R.*, AD 1266-72, pp. 648, 700, 709. Journeys to London, Gloucester and Bristol by the abbot or monks of Kingswood (1240-63) are mentioned in *Docs. K.*, pp. 193-99, 216-17, 219-21.

[39] Lloyd, *The Movement of Wool Prices*, p. 9 and table 5.

Nicholas and Guitenello Simonetti with one or other of the above-named houses.

Fig. 19 probably shows most if not all of the Cistercian houses with the strongest overseas connections. They include twenty-five of the twenty-six leading producers, twenty-two of the twenty-four supplying first quality wool at a price above that of the order as a whole, and sixteen of the seventeen supplying superior 'middle' wool. Darnhall negotiated with men from Cambrai in 1275; according to Pegolotti it marketed only six sacks, but the price is unrecorded. The remaining houses with French or Flemish connections were either large producers or supplied very fine wool. The wool of Dore, Tintern, and Combermere, three of the more westerly houses, was notable for its quality rather than quantity; on the other hand, Margam (Glamorgan) could be expected to have a large quantity (twenty-five sacks) of medium quality wool for sale.

The Italians appear to have operated very largely within the same areas as the Flemings, but they also contracted with several undistinguished houses of the South East[40] and of North Wales. Competition for supplies increased towards the end of the thirteenth century and for a decade or two beyond this. Italian merchants were not unknown even in Scotland; in 1306 the jurors in an inquisition before the bailiffs of Newcastle declared that although there was no member of the Society of Pulci or Rembertini of Florence in the city, there was a report of one in Scotland who had bought wool of the Cistercian abbots of Coupar Angus and Melrose.[41]

Where wool merchants were numerous, wool prices were likely to rise through competition.[42] Foreign traders congregated in the chief ports and in the county towns behind the eastern and southern seaboards. English wool merchants, too, were mainly associated with towns in the south-eastern half of the country, including the south Midlands (Fig. 21).[43] If the prices quoted for Cistercian wool (according to Pegolotti) are compared with those fixed in 1337 for the various counties,[44] there is perhaps

[40] According to Pegolotti, Robertsbridge (Sussex) had a surplus of three sacks; the only price quoted was nine marks. Sibton (Suffolk) was credited with ten sacks at prices ranging from five to fourteen marks.

[41] *C.M.I.*, AD 1219-1307, no. 2007. John Juntino of the Peruzzi was in Newcastle in 1331 (*C.Cl.R.*, AD 1330-3, p. 374).

[42] R. S. Lopez observed ('The trade of medieval Europe: the south,' p. 318) that "in the larger part of France and England the Florentine and Milanese buyers of wool aroused the antagonism of the petty local craftsmen and wool merchants by outbidding them."

[43] *C.P.R.*, AD 1272-78 (1273-4), pp. 13-26, 33-39; *C.C.R. (V)*, (1277-78), pp. 1-11; *C.Cl.R.*, AD 1327-30 (1327), p. 237. J. C. Davies, 'An assembly of wool merchants in 1332,' *E.H.R.*, 31 (1916): 596-606.

[44] *C.P.R.*, AD 1334-38 (1337), pp. 480-83.

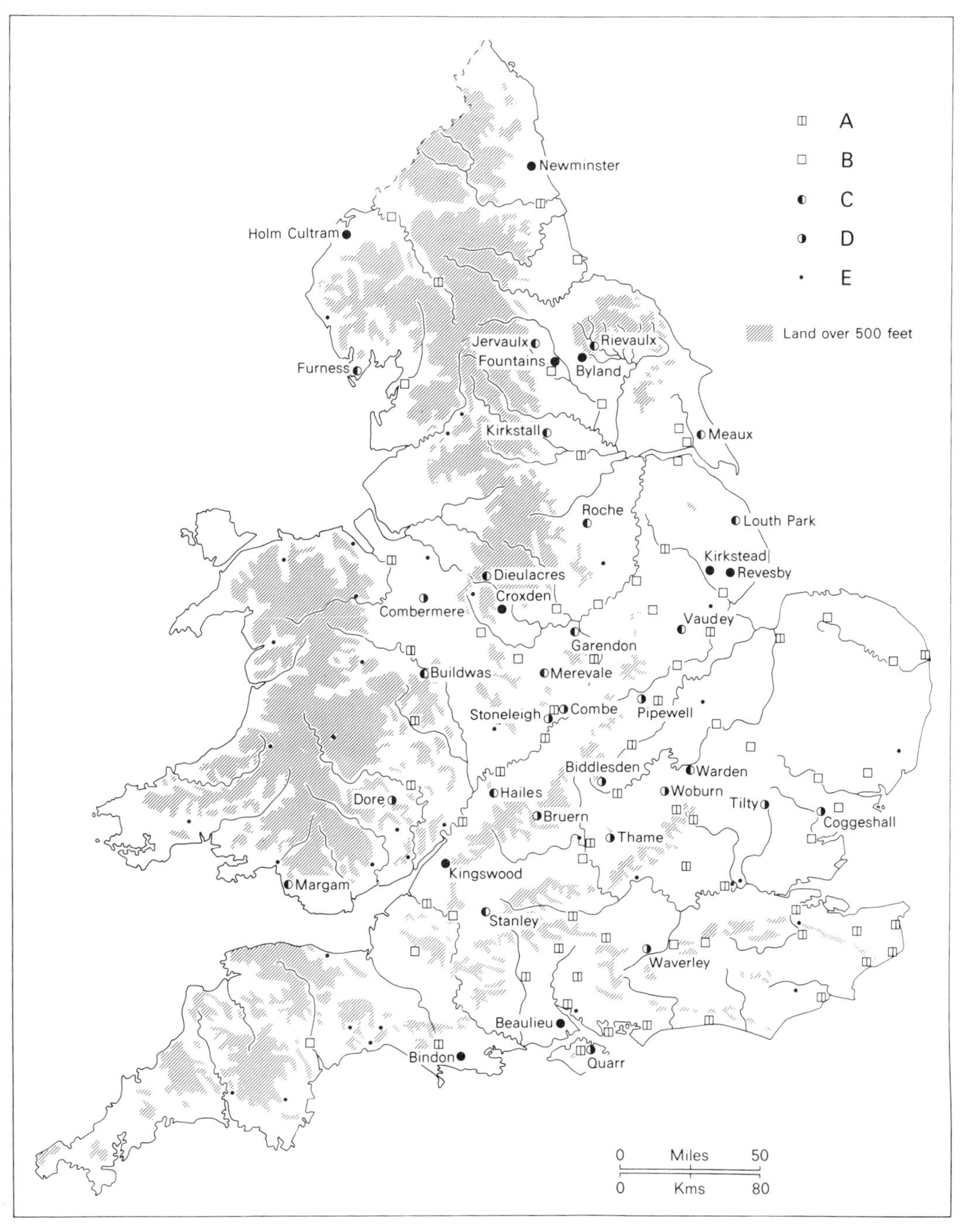

FIG. 21

Cistercian houses with wool surpluses (after F. B. Pegolotti) and the distribution of towns with wool merchants:

A: towns with merchants licensed to export wool, 1273 and/or 1277-8.

B: other towns with wool merchants, 1327.

C: Cistercian houses with more than the average quantity of wool for sale.

D: Cistercian houses with 'best' and/or 'middle' wool exceeding the average price difference between Cistercian (ca. 1300) and county (1337) wool.

E: other Cistercian houses.

some evidence of the effects of competition, most notably in a zone extending from Lincolnshire south-westward along the Cotswolds where merchants based upon Boston, London, Southampton and Bristol sought supplies.

Markets and Fairs

In the course of the thirteenth century there was a notable increase in the number of places where it was lawful to hold a market or fair. Between "1199 and 1483 over 2800 grants of markets were made by the crown, more than half of these in the first seventy-four years of that period."[45] At least thirty-one Cistercian houses in England and Wales were permitted to organize a market or fair (Appendix 11).[46] A few were claimed as prescriptive; others, no doubt, were started without permission and a royal grant simply gave them legal status.[47] Some probably remained irregular; Buckfast, for example, never appears to have received a charter for the market it held ("*nesciunt quo warranto*") at Cheristow.

A charter generally authorized both a weekly market and an annual fair. Richard I's confirmation of Boxley's market at Hoo in 1189-90 is the earliest reference discovered. It is, in fact, the only firm evidence from the twelfth century, although the market which Furness had at Dalton *ab antiquo* may well be equally early. Only four markets and six fairs clearly date from the first half of the thirteenth century. During the next fifty years, however, at least twenty markets and the same number of fairs were sanctioned, and thereafter fourteen markets and twenty-three fairs, closing with the grant of two two-day fairs to Woburn in 1530. In all, about sixty per cent antedate 1300.[48]

[45] Great Britain, Ministry of Agriculture, *Markets and Fairs in England and Wales*, Economic Series, 13 (London, 1927), 1: 17.

[46] For lack of documentary evidence the following are not included: a fair at Axminster belonging to Newenham (C. Oliver, *Historic Collections, Relating to the Monasteries of Devon* (Exeter, 1820), p. 59); and a fair three times a year at Mevenydd belonging to Strata Florida (T. Jones Pierce, 'Strata Florida abbey,' *Ceredigion*, 1 (1950): 30). E. A. Lewis noted the "reluctance on the part of English sovereigns to permit the enjoyment of market and fair privileges in districts subject to a Welsh prince" ('The development of industry and commerce in Wales,' *T.R.H.S.*, 2nd ser., 17 (1903): 131).

[47] "The claim of the crown to create markets was fully established by the 13th century" (L. F. Salzman, 'The legal status of markets,' *Camb. Hist. Jour.*, 2 (1926-28): 209). See also *Regesta Regum Anglo-Normannorum, 2: Regesta Henrici Prima, 1100-1135*, ed. C. Johnson and H. A. Cronne (Oxford, 1956), p. xxiv.

[48] "All the market grants made to the German Cistercians date from the middle of the 13th century" (J. W. Thompson, 'The Cistercian Order,' pp. 91-92).

With one exception (the unauthorized gathering at Ford in 1410) all markets were held on a week-day.[49] No example of a bi-weekly market has been found, but there was a change of day on at least two occasions. Fairs usually occupied three days, although a few continued for only two. Holm Cultram's fair at *Kirkeby Johannis* (now Newton Arlosh) was arranged for the vigil of the Nativity of St. John the Baptist (June 23) and the following sixteen days. At the same time (1305) *Kirkeby* was styled a free borough and replaced *Skinburness* which had been partly destroyed by the sea. The fair at *Wyke*, granted to Meaux in 1278-9, extended over fifteen days.[50] These, however, were exceptional. The longer fairs (eight days or more) all belonged to houses in the North or the Midlands: Stoneleigh, 1284; Rufford, confirmed 1285; Dieulacres, 1293; Jervaulx, 1307, in addition to the two already mentioned. Forde had a six-day fair at Thorncombe (1312). Swineshead's fair at Swineshead (1298) and Vale Royal's at Kirkham (1287) each lasted five days.

Most fairs were held on certain fixed days, usually during the period of a saint's feast.[51] One in Easter week, another related to Ascension day and four to Trinity Sunday or to Whitsunday are the only known exceptions. The fair 'season' stretched from March to November. The great majority fell in the second half of the year: June (six), before the main harvest; July (eleven), August (seven), September (seven), and October (five), coinciding with or just after the harvest; and November (four). Of the fairs held in October or November, all but one belonged to northern houses — Dieulacres, Furness, Meaux, Rufford, Revesby and Whalley — where the harvest was likely to be late. The only significant change of date was at Charmouth belonging to Forde, from July 31-August 2 to September 20-22. In a few places fairs were held more than once per year:

[49] After 1488-9 Sunday markets were only permitted during the four weeks of harvest (Royal Commission on Market Rights and Tolls, *Report* (London, 1889), 1: 223). Changes from Sunday to a week-day became common in the time of Henry III; J. L. Cate noted thirty over the period 1218-40 ('The church and market reform in England during the reign of Henry III,' in *Mediaeval and Historiographical Essays in Honor of James Westfall Thompson*, ed. J. L. Cate and E. N. Anderson (Chicago, 1938), p. 27).

[50] When Edward I acquired *Wyke*, renaming it Kingston upon Hull, another grant was made (1299): a bi-weekly market and a fair of thirty days (*C.Ch.R.*, AD 1257-1300, p. 476).

[51] Vale Royal's fair at Kirkham was due on the eve, day and morrow of midsummer and the two following days, and thus included the vigil and feast (June 24) of the Nativity of St. John the Baptist. Waverley's fair (1512) at Wanborough, Surrey, was held on August 23, 24 (St. Bartholomew's day) and 25.

TABLE 7: FAIRS

Beaulieu	Faringdon	1222	2 days	October
		1260	1 day	May-June[52]
Cleeve	Cleeve	1466	4 days	July
		1466	4 days	September
Furness	Dalton	1239	3 days	October-November
		1246	3 days	October[53]
Jervaulx	East Witton	1307	8 days	August
		1307	2 days	November[54]
Stratford Langthorn	Billericay	1476	3 days	July
		1476	3 days	August
Woburn	Woburn	1242	3 days	September
		1530	2 days	July
		1530	2 days	March

It appears that the fairs of Furness at Dalton and those of Stratford at Billericay closely followed one another. Moreover, the latter's fair at Burstead, only three miles from Billericay, was also held in July. Other houses controlled two or more fairs but in different townships. Basingwerk had fairs at Charlesworth, Glossop (both in July) and Holywell; Dunkeswell at Buckland Brewer and Broadhembury, both in August; Buckfast at Kingsbridge (July), Buckfastleigh (August) and South Brent (September). The fairs belonging to Buckland (April and June), Sallay (June and September), and Forde (March-April and September) were more widely spaced.

Some markets and fairs were held in places far from the monastery (Fig. 22). Conversely, it occasionally happened that a person other than the abbot and convent enjoyed rights in the nearest settlement. John de Boeles had a market and fair at Warden, and Roger Mortimer of Chirk a market and two fairs at Old Whitland, each about one mile from the abbeys of Warden and Whitland respectively. At Swineshead, Robert Greslay was granted a fair in 1227 extending from the 20th to 22nd of September; that later granted to the abbey "at the chapel of St Saviour, Swineshead" fell in May or June on the vigil, feast and morrow of Holy Trinity and the two following days. The bishop of Lincoln claimed (1351) that he and his

[52] See Appendix 11, n. 1.

[53] Possibly a substitute for the former (*V.C.H. (Lancashire)*, 3: 314). This is not clear from *C.Ch.R.*, AD 1226-57 (1246), p. 295, but a confirmation of Richard II (1398) mentions only the latter (*Coucher F.*, 1: 135).

[54] See Appendix 11, n. 2.

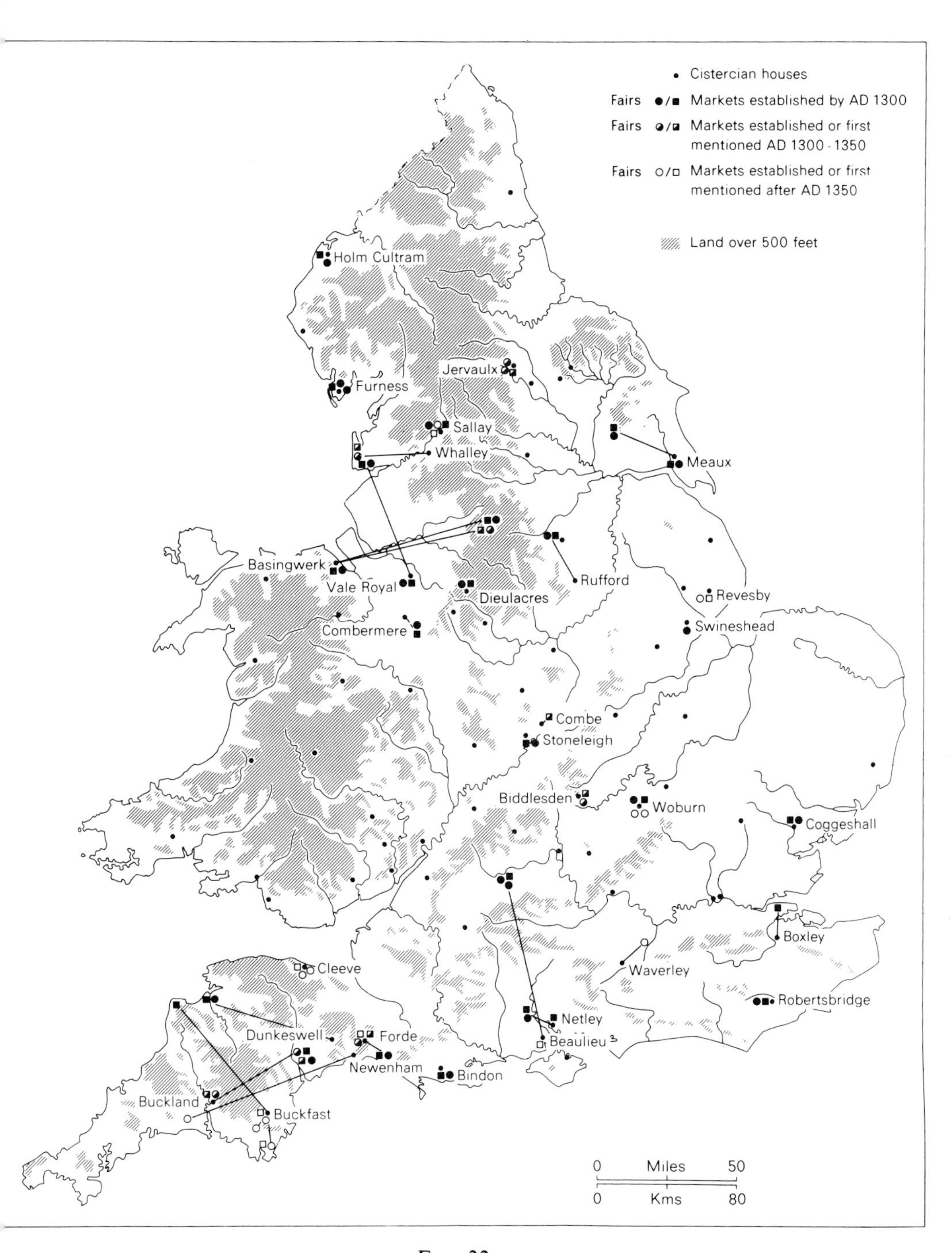

FIG. 22

Markets and fairs belonging to Cistercian houses in England and Wales (Appendix 11).

predecessors had had a market at Thame "time out of mind."[55] At Bolton, Sallay shared control with John de Pudsay.

We are not usually told exactly where within a township a particular market or fair was to take place. Woburn's market (1242), like that at Swineshead, was held near the chapel. Buckfast's fair at South Brent occupied "a place called *Brentedowne*" — possibly the slopes of Brent Hill. The abbot of Holm Cultram was allowed to select a place at *Wavermouth*, and this was probably the usual procedure. At least two late markets were sited within or just outside the monastic precincts.[56] Beaulieu's market (1468) was to be "within the site and close of the monastery"; and a commission was appointed in 1410 to enquire into a report that the abbot of Forde "has raised a market at the gate of the abbey and long held it there every Sunday, and still holds it, taking tolls, stallages, picages and other profits without licence ... to the damage of the neighbouring markets."[57]

Authorized gatherings, other than those at the monastery itself, were rarely associated with estates managed as granges.[58] Rights seem to have been mostly exercised in places where the monks held a considerable interest but were prepared to accept the existing tenurial arrangements, or where they had or wished to establish a borough. The latter were comparatively few.[59]

Markets and fairs brought in revenue in the form of fees and tolls, and this, for the monks, was probably their chief attraction. When Vale Royal established (1296) a 'free borough' and 'free guild' at Kirkham the abbot reserved for himself "stallages, amercements of bread and drink, and tolls of markets and fairs." In 1388 Furness was claiming 4d. on every horse-

[55] *Register*, 4: 7. The Cistercian monastery of the same name, founded in 1140, lay a mile and a half from the town.

[56] An entry in the statutes of the order (1: 340) under 1207 appears to forbid this in the case of a Spanish house, Carracedo: "*Prohibetur abbati Carrazeti [Carracetum] ne circum abbatiam suam nundinas patiatur ulterius convenire.*" An ancient Benedictine foundation, Carracedo became Cistercian in 1203.

[57] Normally a royal grant expressly safeguarded established markets and fairs. Markets were only permitted at Coupar Angus (Perthshire) at the discretion of the burgesses of Dundee (*Chart. C.*, 2: 98 (1329-71).

[58] The following are known cases: Wellow (fair 1251, grange ca. 1291—*Tax. Eccles.*, p. 214) belonging to Netley; Burstead (market and fair 1253, grange according to Knowles and Hadcock, p. 129) belonging to Stratford Langthorn; and Wanborough (fair 1512, grange 1205—*Rot. Ch.*, p. 161) belonging to Waverley. Dalton appears to have included parts of two or more granges (*Coucher F.*, 1: 633).

[59] Leek (Dieulacres), Kingsbridge (Buckfast), *Wavermouth*, *Skinburness*, *Kirkeby Johannis* (Holm Cultram), and possibly also Faringdon (Beaulieu) and Dalton (Furness). See *infra*, pp. 161-2.

load of merchandise brought to Dalton fair.[60] Newenham received directly the profits of a fair at Axminster while the market there was leased out for as much as sixty shillings per annum. Cleeve's market and fairs in the township of the same name helped towards "the liquidation of expenses connected with the re-erection of a church ... which had been wholly destroyed by flood."[61] The financial benefits are suggested in other ways too. When the monks of Revesby acquired the manor of Mareham it was already the scene of a weekly market and an annual fair, and they took care to have these confirmed. Holm Cultram paid 100 marks (£66.13.4) and Jervaulx £20 for rights in *Skinburness*[62] and East Witton respectively. In 1301 Meaux claimed damages of 1000 marks from Roger son of Remegius de Pocklington for holding a market and fair at Pocklington where they (also) had this right, but judgment was given for the defendant.[63]

The monks' markets and fairs probably handled little of the export trade in wool. A great wool house with a market or fair was rather exceptional. Only three of the eight Yorkshire houses and two out of five in Lincolnshire are known to have possessed either. Two concentrations of houses are apparent in Fig. 22, one in the north-western counties (Cumberland, Lancashire, Cheshire and Flintshire), the other in the South West, broadly coinciding with a group of relatively late foundations. The former included only two important wool houses, Furness and Holm Cultram, and the latter one, Forde. The export trade normally justified special arrangements, with negotiations conducted either at the monastery itself or some great mart. The North West and the South West customarily produced only poor to moderately good wool and perhaps markets and

[60] [Great Britain, Parliamentary Papers], *Reports from Commissioners, Inspectors, and Others: 1875*, vol. 27: *The Thirty-Sixth Annual Report of the Deputy Keeper of the Public Records* (London, 1875), Appendix 1, p. 176. Earlier (1257, 1320) the house permitted certain tenants to use Dalton market to buy goods for their own use without payment of toll (*Coucher F.*, 1: 212-14, and 2: 458). The toll-free market at Ulverston (1280), less than five miles away, attracted men from Dalton, and it appears that the abbot succeeded in having the franchise annulled (*V.C.H.* (*Lancashire*, 1914), 8: 350).

[61] T. Hugo, 'On the charters and other archives of Cleeve abbey,' *Proc. Somerset Arch. Nat. Hist. Soc.*, 6 (1856): 41; N. F. Hulbert, 'A survey of the Somerset fairs,' ibid., 82 (1936): 148.

[62] *Rot. Parl.*, 1: 161 (but possibly also taking into account the creation of a free borough: *C.Ch.R.*, AD 1300-26, p. 2).

[63] W. P. Baildon, *Notes on the Religious and Secular Houses of Yorkshire*, Yorks. Arch. Soc. Rec. Ser., 81 (London, 1931), 2: 27. Meaux obtained land in Pocklington in exchange for *Wyke*, 1293-4 (*C.Ch.R.*, AD 1257-1300, p. 455). For Roger's charter, see ibid., AD 1226-57 (1245), p. 288, and AD 1257-1300, pp. 179, 480.

fairs served the local cloth industry. Elsewhere, too, home demand merited some attention, especially from the middle of the fourteenth century, but in most cases existing marketing arrangements probably proved adequate. Fountains lay only three miles from Ripon which had an important fair from the beginning of the twelfth century, and Rievaulx and Byland were closer still to the markets and fairs of Helmsley (1353) and Coxwold respectively.

There is, however, another possible connection between monastic markets and the wool trade. Some houses, particularly those enjoying toll exemptions, purchased wool to supplement their own stocks. A directly-controlled market or fair would facilitate this, for since such trafficking in wool was unpopular with townsfolk who were deprived of revenue it was desirable that the *conversi* should work as unobtrusively as possible.

A neighbouring market would also make available a useful range of household articles,[64] and fairs may have been used to dispose of commodities such as grain and hides.[65] The marketing of corn through local centres increased in volume over about the same period as market franchises multiplied.[66] While the monks themselves farmed, a surplus in some years was almost inevitable, and in the case of a well-endowed house an excess over internal needs was probably normal. Conversely, as estates were leased out, the need to buy grain regularly would arise. Kingswood sold nineteen sacks of grain in 1242. The more distant granges of Beaulieu disposed of their surplus grain and rendered cash to the abbey.[67] The chronicler of Croxden occasionally commented on prevailing prices,[68] and in 1347 we are told that "the bishop of Winchester ... bought for his stock all the crops that the abbot and convent of Thame [could] spare."[69]

[64] At Woburn "the needs of the abbey created a town" (*V.C.H.* (*Bedfordshire*, 1912), 3: 459).

[65] In 1300 Meaux had some unspecified goods at Pocklington market and fair (*C.P.R.*, AD 1292-1301, p. 550). In 1502 the York Mercers and Merchant Adventurers wrote to the abbot of Fountains thus: "We understand that you occupy beying and sellyng lede and other merchandise as a fre marchaunt, contrary to Godds lawis and mans ... and so your occupying is grett damage and hurte to us merchaunds in thies parties ..." (*The York Mercers and Merchant Adventurers, 1356-1917*, ed. M. Sellers, Surtees Soc. Publs., 129 (London, 1918), pp. 110-111).

[66] N.S.B. Gras, *The Evolution of the English Corn Market from the Twelfth to the Eighteenth Century* (Cambridge, Mass., 1915), pp. 18, 23, 46.

[67] *Account B.*, pp. 14, 23-26 (1269-70).

[68] C. Lynam, *The Abbey of St. Mary, Croxden, Staffordshire* (London, 1911), Appendix 7 (1317-8), and 12 (1368).

[69] *Register*, 1: 123.

But it is characteristic that the details of the decentralized trade in grain passed largely unrecorded.

Boroughs and Urban Property

Boroughs

The Cistercians occupy but a small place in the history of English towns.[70] They established or held a few 'boroughs', but each was some distance from the respective abbey. Dieulacres was founded in 1214 and soon held "*totum manerium de Lec.*" "Richard, the first abbot, gave a charter to the burgesses [of Leek] which was a copy of that given (1209-28) by Earl Ralph with [certain] omissions."[71] A successor of the abbot appears as lord of the township in the *Nomina Villarum* (1316). The same inquest names the abbot of Buckfast as lord of the 'borough' of Kingsbridge. Kingsbridge was taxed at the higher (i.e. urban) rate over the period 1306-36, being described as a 'borough' on eight occasions.[72] In 1300 Edward I allowed Holm Cultram to hold *Wavermouth* as a free borough. This franchise probably lapsed when *Skinburness* was granted a similar status (1301), only to give way in turn to *Kirkeby Johannis* (Newton Arlosh).[73] In each case the abbot acquired the right to a Thursday market and an annual fair of seventeen days. Vale Royal's vill of Kirkham was elevated to a borough in 1296; and ca. 1300 Edward I agreed that "there [should] be a free borough" in the abbey's manor of Over.[74] Kirkham had a regular market and fair from 1287 (which the abbot continued to enjoy after 1296) and Over from 1280. Beaulieu from its foundation (1203-4) owned a large part of Great Faringdon which in the latter half of the thirteenth century, and possibly earlier, was known as a

[70] See N. M. Trenholme, *The English Monastic Boroughs*, University of Missouri Studies, vol. 2, no. 3 (Columbia, 1927). Cf. C. Higounet, 'Cisterciens et Bastides,' *Le Moyen Age*, 4ᵉ sér., 5/vol. 56 (1950): 69-84.

[71] A. Ballard, *British Borough Charters 1042-1216* (Cambridge, 1913), pp. xxix,xxxv.

[72] J. F. Willard, 'Taxation boroughs and Parliamentary boroughs,' in *Historical Essays in Honour of James Tait*, ed. J. G. Edwards, et al. (Manchester, 1913), p. 431. It was described as the "manor or borough" of Kingsbridge in 1557 (J. Youings, ed., *Devon Monastic Lands: a Calendar of Particulars for Grants 1536-58*, Devon and Cornwall Rec. Soc. new ser., 1 (Torquay, 1955), p. 123).

[73] *C.Ch.R.*, AD 1300-26 (1305), p. 55. There is some doubt concerning the whereabouts of *Wavermouth* and *Skinburness*, but both lay "within the metes of the island of Holm Cultram"; *Skinburness* was partly destroyed by the sea.

[74] *Ledger V. R.*, pp. 187-89.

'borough', although no charter has been found.[75] The case of Dalton is similar. Furness eventually held the whole township, but it has been suggested that the title of 'borough' (again no charter exists) antedates the foundation of the abbey.[76] A burgess of Dalton is mentioned in 1276.[77]

The English Cistercian houses neither settled in towns[78] nor encouraged towns to develop immediately outside their precincts.[79] Occasionally, places under local mesne lords grew up near by,[80] and from the thirteenth century, as we have seen, some monasteries also established boroughs. These, however, remained small, and it is clear that the Cistercian *plantatio* had little influence on the rise and growth of urban communities. More important was the acquisition by the monks of property in established centres.

Urban Property

"In domibus quae in villis aut castellis vel civitatibus sunt, non habitent monachi vel conversi" (1134).[81]

Property in the greater towns facilitated trade, furnished temporary lodging, and could be leased out to bring in revenue. In 1300 one-fifth of Oxford was owned by four (non-Cistercian) monasteries.[82] Before the

[75] *V.C.H.* (*Berkshire*, 1924), 4: 491-92. Beaulieu had a market (1218) and fair (1222) and in 1322 held twenty messuages here (*C.Cl.R.*, AD 1318-23, p. 614).

[76] *V.C.H.* (*Lancashire*, 1914), 8: 313.

[77] [Great Britain, Parliamentary Papers], *Reports from Commissioners, Inspectors, and Others: 1875*, vol. 27: *The Thirty-Sixth Annual Report of the Deputy Keeper of the Public Records* (London, 1875). Appendix 1, p. 169; *Coucher F.*, 1: 331. See also ibid., p. 168, and 2: 200 (burgages, 1371). Before the end of the thirteenth century the abbot had the right to a market and fair.

[78] St. Mary Graces (1350) in the eastern suburbs of London was the only exception.

[79] In Scotland there appears to have been a closer connection. In 1497 James IV allowed the monastery of Kinloss to style Kinloss ("*situatam et jacentem ante portas dicti nostri monasterii*") a "free burgh of barony" (*Recs. K.*, p. 135). A town developed around Culross (Talbot, *The Cistercian Abbeys of Scotland*, p. 58). There was also a burgh at Coupar Angus (J. L. Morgan, *The Economic Administration of Coupar Angus Abbey* (doctoral thesis, University of Glasgow, 1929), 3: 273); and a charter of James IV created Keithick (less than a mile from the same abbey) a free burgh (*Chart. C.*, p. 98).

[80] Morpeth (one mile from Newminster), a borough, 1188-1239; Leeds (three miles from Kirkstall), 1209; Helmsley (two and a half miles from Rievaulx), 1186-1227; Neath (one mile from Neath abbey), 1147-73.

[81] *Statuta*, 1: 30.

[82] H. E. Salter, 'The city of Oxford in the middle ages,' *History*, n.s., 14 (1929-30): 97.

Dissolution two-thirds of London[83] and a "considerable proportion of Lincoln"[84] were in the hands of religious bodies of all kinds.

It is well known that many 'grants' to the monasteries were in fact sales. The monks also openly purchased property. Thus Warden was confirmed (1175-1200) in land which it had bought in Norwich; Furness purchased a toft in York (ca. 1228); and Holm Cultram bought land in Newcastle. After the Statute of Mortmain was passed (1279) some houses paid heavy fines for permission to acquire urban property.

Fig. 23 shows the wide distribution of Cistercian monasteries known to have owned land in London, Westminster or Southwark (in the last-named only Netley, Beaulieu and Waverley, all south of the capital). There were at least seventeen before 1300, including Vale Royal, a late (1274-81) and distant house, founded by Edward I. The Yorkshire houses had tenements in Boston, Lincoln and York (Fig. 24), but not, apparently, in the capital.[85] Through the sea and river ports of the east coast passed much of the wool destined for Flanders. Some houses held property in quite minor ports[86] — Grimsby, Hedon, Barton, Yarm, Scarborough — from which wool was occasionally exported uncustomed.[87] There was also the need to ensure supplies of fish, an important item in the diet of the monks. We find Boxley (1225) dispatching a ship to Berwick for herrings,[88] and Waverley (1284) sending to Yarmouth with similar purpose. The *Taxatio Ecclesiastica* ca. 1291 reveals that Waverley owned land in Great Yarmouth, and Beaulieu and Boxley houses and fisheries in Little Yarmouth, where Robertsbridge too had property (1272-1307). A slightly earlier notice (1267) records that Fountains bought herrings and other supplies in Redcar.

[83] M. B. Honeybourne, *The Extent and Value of the Property in London and Southwark Occupied by the Religious Houses ... Before the Dissolution of the Monasteries*' (M. A. thesis, University of London, 1929-30), p. 8; W. G. Bell, *Fleet Street during Seven Centuries* (London, 1912), p. 206 (map: 1538-40).

[84] J. M. F. Hill, *Mediaeval Lincoln* (Cambridge, 1948), p. 152.

[85] According to Bell (*Fleet Sreet*, p. 53), Rievaulx in 1310 held property (without the king's permission) in Shoe-lane; nothing has been found to support this.

[86] Figs. 23 and 24 are based on evidence tabulated in R. A. Donkin, 'The urban property of the Cistercians in medieval England,' *A.S.O.C.*, 15 (1959): 115-29. Fig. 24 takes account of holdings in all (including Welsh) seaports. Inland, many smaller places (Pontefract, Ripon, Bridgnorth, for example) could also have been shown.

[87] *C.F.R.*, AD 1272-1307 (1275), p. 44; *Rot. Parl.*, 1: 423 (1324); A. Rowntree, *The History of Scarborough* (London, 1931), pp. 167-68; C. Frost, *Notices Relative to the Early History of the Town and Port of Hull* (London, 1827), pp. 100-1.

[88] *C.P.R.*, AD 1216-25, p. 505.

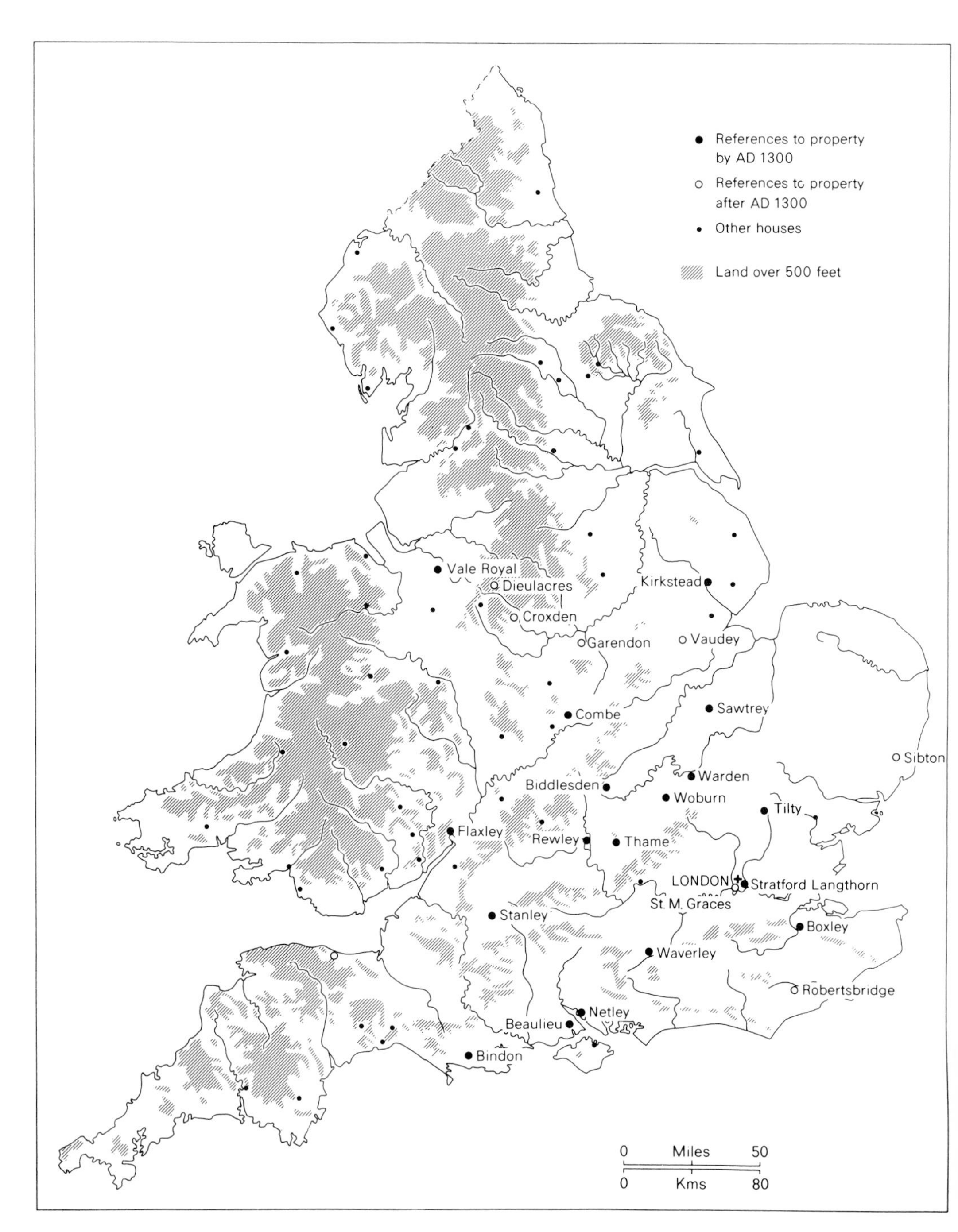

FIG. 23

Cistercian houses with property in London.

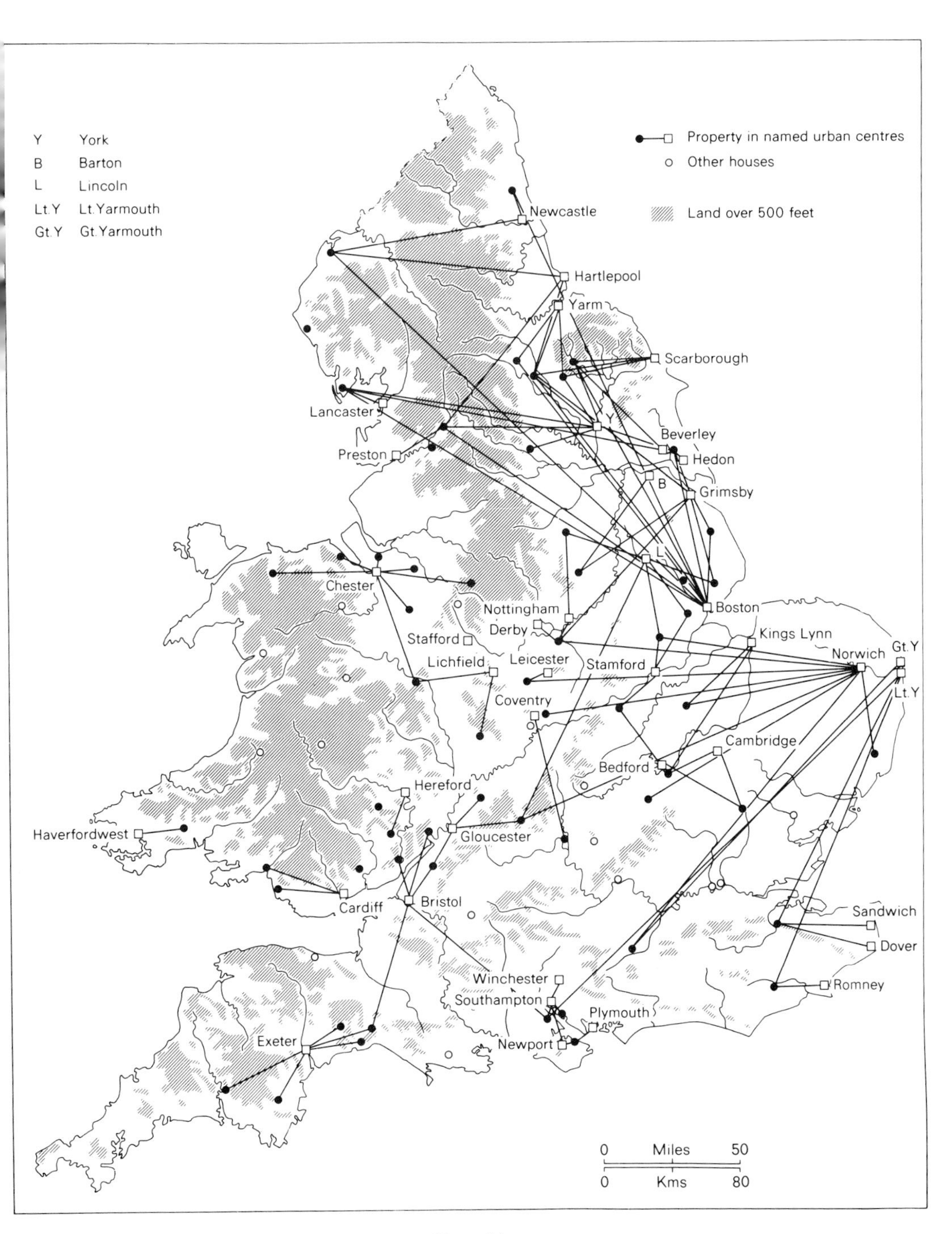

FIG. 24

Cistercian houses with property in selected urban centres.

Chester, Bristol and Exeter were important locally, but not leading wool ports, and no far-distant house held property in these cities.[89] Norwich and Yarmouth served houses in the South and the Midlands, Boston in the North, North East, and North West. The Coucher Book of Furness includes grants in Boston and a confirmation of a right of way that specially mentions the period of the great fair of St. Botolph. York, Lynn and Lincoln attracted a few houses outside their respective regions; Southampton, on the other hand, was of only local importance.

Many houses had acquired urban property by the end of the twelfth century, long before the ownership of markets and fairs became common. Stanlaw had land in Chester six years after its foundation in 1172 and possibly earlier. Stratford Langthorn owned property in London by 1154-89; Kirkstead (1156-8), Sallay (1199-1216), Meaux (1197-1210) and Fountains (1199) in Boston; Rievaulx (1180-1203), Kirkstall (1147-82), Byland (1154-89), Meaux (1182-97) and Fountains (1199) in York; Fountains in Scarborough (1175-94), Yarm and Hartlepool (1199); Revesby (1189-99) and Fountains (1199) in Grimsby; Meaux in Beverley (1182-97) and Hedon (1150-60); Boxley in Dover and London (1189); Warden in London (1190-1210), Bedford (1180-90) and Norwich (1175-1200); Buildwas in Chester (1189-99); Revesby in Lincoln (1189-99); Bordesley in Lichfield (1189); Forde in Exeter (1189-99); and Waverley in Great Yarmouth (1189-99). During the thirteenth century, holdings were extended and improved and almost every house had an urban foothold of some kind; thereafter, grants and purchases declined but never entirely ceased.

We are often told in which parish or street particular properties lay. Access to a main thoroughfare or a navigable river was clearly desirable. Rievaulx was once accused of encroaching upon the land of the Dean and Chapter of York "lying buttyng opon the water [the river Foss] in Laierthorp [Layerthorp] in the suburbes [of York]." In the same city, Fountains and Furness had tenements extending to the river Ouse, and the former had a house on the principal bridge. Other holdings lay beyond the walls — in Fishergate, Gillygate and the marsh of Hungate (1180-1203). In

[89] Dieulacres (Staffordshire, but formerly at Poulton, Cheshire) had land in Chester (*Chart. D.*, p. 331). The abbot of Tintern was a member of the staple of Bristol, and the Bristol Channel was plied "by innumerable boats ... of Tintern" (E. M. Carus-Wilson, 'The overseas trade of Bristol,' in *English Trade in the Fifteenth Century*, ed. E. Power and M. M. Postan (London, 1933), p. 187).

Boston, Fountains owned property in Wormgate (parallel to the river Witham) which it could approach with waggons and horses.[90]

Nine holders of free tenements (*libera tenementa*) in Norwich failed to appear before the justices on the first day of the Eyre, 1286; eight were Cistercian abbots and "several are known to have had holdings by the riverside, presumably for the export of wool."[91] The monks of Garendon had a number of messuages in Conisford leading to the north bank of the river Wensum. A deed of the time of Henry III gave them rights in land "lying in Nether Conesford, extending from the king's highway to the [river] bank (*ripam*) of Norwich." The same monastery had houses in the market places of Nottingham (*foro cotidiano*) and Derby. Before the end of the twelfth century, Warden received the "temporary gift" of a house by the bridge of Bedford. Kingswood had a messuage "between the bridges" of Gloucester; and Newenham owned a house "*juxta barbicanum*" in Exeter. The accounts of Fountains for 1458-9 mention the repair of some property in the horse-fair at Ripon.

In London, some monasteries had land near the river: Stratford Langthorn and Flaxley (1291 and 1292, Thames-street), Sawtry (ca. 1291, parish of St. Michael *ad Ripam* or Queenhithe), Woburn (1386, parish of St. Benet Paul's Wharf) and St. Mary Graces (1362, parish of St. Michael Queenhithe, and, 1425, St. Magnus). Others owned property in the parishes of (from east to west) All Hallows Staining, St. Dionis Backchurch, St. Antonine, St. Thomas Apostle, St. Nicholas Olave and St. Nicholas Coleabbey, all well within the walls. But the possessions of the distant monasteries mostly lay in the outlying, less heavily built-up parishes: St. Clement Danes (Combe, 1293), St. Mary le Strand (Combe, 1293, Vale Royal, 1299), St. Andrew Holburn (Kirkstead, 1292), and Fleet-street in St. Bride's (Thame, 1322). Garendon also had an interest in Fleet-street (1347), and Vale Royal in Westminster and Islington (1299).

Church land and buildings predominated in parts of most medieval towns. In London "nearly every tenement is described as being bounded on three sides by other ecclesiastical property."[92] Warden had land in front of St. Martin le Grande "next to [that] of Woburn on the south" (1190-1210). The town house of the abbot of Buckfast in Exeter was "in

[90] *Chart. F.*, 1: 115, 118; P. Thompson, *The History and Antiquities of Boston* (London, 1856), pp. 216-17.

[91] W. Hudson and J. C. Tingey, eds., *Records of the City of Norwich* (London, 1906), 1: 214.

[92] Honeybourne, 'Extent and value,' p. 8.

the close, surrounded on three sides by the archdeaconary houses of Barnstaple, Totnes and Cornwall."[93] In Chester, Stanlaw owned a "house next to the church of St. Michael" and land alongside a tenement of the canons of Lilleshall. In 1498 the corporation of Gloucester confirmed some property belonging to the Benedictine abbey of St. Peter; Hailes held the land on one side and the Augustinian abbey of St. Mary, Cirencester, on the other.[94] Grants to (or purchases by) a particular religious house often adjoined property it already owned or leased. The monastic interest in urban real estate steadily expanded and no town of any size and few parts of London were quite unaffected by the Dissolution.[95]

The monks acquired numerous dwelling houses (*mansio, mesuagium, burgagium, tenementum*), some with storage space for wool or other commodities. On one occasion, Netley leased out several houses in Melcombe, "except a soller and cellar in which they stored their grain."[96] Beaulieu owned a "great house, *le Wollehouse*" in Southampton.[97] Warden had a "stone house" in Norwich (1180-1200), Rievaulx in Beverley, and Fountains in Scarborough.

A building used to accommodate monks and *conversi* was usually known as a hospice (*hospitium, hospicium*). M. B. Honeybourne estimated that there were about thirty-eight in London alone,[98] four or five belonging to Cistercian communities (Beaulieu, Stratford Langthorn, Kirkstead, Waverley and probably Vale Royal).[99] Edward I gave Vale Royal two messuages in Shoe-lane, property which included shops, cellars and gardens in 1384, and once described as the abbot's inn.[100] For a time

[93] G. Oliver, *Historic Collections, Relating to the Monasteries in Devon* (Exeter, 1820), pp. 58, 69; J. A. Youings, 'The city of Exeter and the property of the dissolved monasteries,' *Reps. Trans. Devon Assoc.*, 84 (1952): 125.

[94] W. H. Stevenson, *Calendar of the Records of the Corporation of Gloucester* (Gloucester, 1893), p. 419. A. Raine (*Mediaeval York* (London, 1955), p. 52) noted that four religious houses had their York headquarters along Aldwark.

[95] For Cistercian monasteries in Scotland and Ireland, see *Rental C.*, p. 147 (Coupar Angus: *hospitia* at Perth and Dundee); *Liber M.*, 1: 17 (Melrose: in Berwick near the Tweed, 1165-1214, and Edinburgh); *Reg. Newbattle*, p. 123 (in Edinburgh); *Chart. B.*, pp. 19, 25 (Balmerino: in Dundee, 1268, and Perth); *Recs. K.*, p. 102 (Kinloss: in Aberdeen, 1370); *Chart. Duiske*, p. 17 (in Wexford, 1207, and Kilkenny).

[96] *C.A.D.*, 3: D. 63.

[97] A. B. Wallis Chapman, ed., *The Black Book of Southampton*, Southampton Rec. Soc. Publs., 17 (Southampton, 1915), 3: 10 (1455).

[98] Summary of thesis in *B.I.H.R.*, 9 (1931-32): 57.

[99] M. B. Honeybourne, 'The abbey of St. Mary Graces, Tower Hill,' *Trans. London and Middlesex Arch. Soc.*, n.s., 11 (1952): 21.

[100] M. B. Honeybourne, *Extent and Value*, p. 342. It was bounded on the south by tenements of the abbot of Garendon.

Warden and Dieulacres also had hospices in the city. The latter, when disposing of some property "*infra muros London et extra*" added "*salvo nobis et nostris hospitio nostro in capitali managio* (in Wood-street) *ad proprias expensas nostras quando London veniemus.*" But many abbots who passed through the capital *en route* for the annual Chapter General at Cîteaux probably lodged at Stratford Langthorn or, after 1350, at St. Mary Graces.

An undated deed records the grant to Dore of "a piece of land that they may have a hostel when they come to Hereford." As early as 1177-8 Kirkstall obtained a messuage in Pontefract "*ad hospitium habendum.*"[101] This was demised a few years later, but the abbot made sure that he could stay there whenever he wished. Between 1235 and 1245 the monks of Sallay leased out some property in Micklegate, York, reserving "the hall and kitchen for use when visiting [the city]." Again, when they restored to Jervaulx some buildings in Wormgate, Boston, the latter undertook to provide them with a room, stable and kitchen for up to fifteen days during the period of Boston fair.[102]

The ownership of shops, stalls and booths was fairly common from the middle of the thirteenth century. The abbot of Coggeshall built a house "in the high street and market of Coggeshall" which served as his shop (1336). However most shops were almost certainly leased out; sometimes the number alone suggests this. Vale Royal (1299) owned thirteen or more shops (eleven "called cobblers' shops") in Chester, Rewley (1376) twenty-three in Coventry, and Furness (1333-4) at least six in Drogheda.

Accommodation in towns must have been needed long before the last quarter of the twelfth century when evidence first becomes widely available. In visiting daughter settlements, granges could generally be used, but in journeys to and from the Continent overnight halts in ports were inevitable. What induced the monasteries to seek their own premises was probably their growing interest in the marketing of wool. Figs. 23 and 24 include some of the early centres of cloth manufacture — Lincoln, Nottingham, Beverley, Leicester, Winchester, Stamford, York and London — but in the thirteenth century most houses were predominantly concerned with the export trade. Negotiations were often conducted in neigh-

[101] *E.Y.C.*, 3: 202; W. H. Turner, *Calendar of Charters and Rolls preserved in the Bodleian Library* (Oxford, 1878), pp. 614-15. Even earlier, perhaps, Margam had a house in Bristol *ad hospitium* (*Cartae Glam.*, 1: 11 (1147-82)).

[102] A rental (1485) of the abbot of Combermere includes "John Wybunbury for the swan [inn, Nantwich]... IXd" (*Book Comb.*, p. 63). Perhaps this replaced a monastic hospice.

bouring towns or in the principal ports and here Cistercian property was chiefly concentrated. When the overseas wool trade declined from about the middle of the fourteenth century a *pied à terre* was still useful for abbots and monks travelled about more than ever.[103] At the same time, much urban property was advantageously leased out and, like an increasing proportion of agricultural land, became only an item in the annual account roll.

[103] The accounts of the bursar of Robertsbridge for 1416, 1426-7 and 1437-8 list expenses incurred in London (*Docs. R.*, pp. 164, 169-70).

Plate 4

St Bernard directing the building of a church.
Original in Neuberg a.d. Mürz, Austria.

6

Postscript

The Cistercian order spread by a process of colonization from existing houses. The sites chosen represented a convergence of interest on the part of local benefactors and of the monks themselves. The preference of the order for secluded locations was well known, and founders could only benefit by the improvement of tracts of waste that formed part of their estates. So far as the houses of England and Wales were concerned, this meant working within the existing 'frontiers' of rural settlement, except perhaps in limited areas of the Pennines, the North Yorkshire Moors and Wales.

Contacts between houses were maintained by a system of regular visitation and through the annual Chapter General at Cîteaux to which all abbots were summoned. Irregularities and absenteeism notwithstanding, this comprehensive organization presumably facilitated the diffusion of new ideas, of specific items of technology and of architectural design.

It is generally acknowledged that the houses of northern England played an important part in the transformation of Anglo-Norman Romanesque in the direction of early Gothic. Rievaulx especially shows the influence of Burgundy, and at this daughter house of Clairvaux we find "the first use of the pointed arch in England, except for the high vaults of Durham nave."[1] The church at Fountains combines Anglo-Norman and Burgundian features. At Kirkstall too there are pointed barrel vaults and a ribbed vault over the presbytery. "This vault" observed Geoffrey Webb, "has a special importance in the study of early Gothic vaulting, as it seems to be technically in the Anglo-Norman descent from the

[1] G. Webb, *Architecture in Britain: The Middle Ages*, Pelican History of Art (Harmondsworth, 1956), p. 44.

Durham vaults and, in its combination of the vault rib and the pointed arch, it suggests a development parallel to that of the Ile-de-France but independent of it." The Cistercians were clearly not the first to use the ribbed vault, either in England[2] or on the Continent, but they were partly responsible for its wide dissemination.

Towards the close of the twelfth century architectural ideas emanating from northern France began to be felt in England; and, interestingly, "the first signs of north French Gothic are to be found at Roche" (ca. 1170).[3] Somewhat later buildings at Byland, Jervaulx and Furness show similar influence. Cistercian architecture at once reflected and enriched the whole development of Gothic and thus, in the words of Henri Focillon, "contributed to the maintenance and extension of the overriding unity of the West."[4]

Innovations connected with agriculture and rural industry have generally been associated with large estates, particularly, during the Middle Ages, monastic estates. It is not clear that the Cistercians were responsible for introducing to England any such innovations, but again they were probably important agents of diffusion. The fulling mill (*supra*, 138) is found upon a Cistercian estate within a decade or less of the earliest known reference to such a mill in England. The monks of Kirkstall may have been among the first to build a water-driven hammer forge,[5] and several Cistercian houses had tanning mills before the close of the twelfth century.[6]

[2] Earlier examples survive at Durham (1096), Winchester (after 1107), Peterborough (1118), and Gloucester (1100-20). On the other hand, the white monks "seem to have been the first in England to adopt the corbel (a Burgundian motif) as a means of support to the springers of a vault" (A. Clapham, *English Romanesque Architecture After the Conquest* (Oxford, 1934), p. 83.

[3] Webb, *Architecture in Britain*, p. 82.

[4] *The Art of the West in the Middle Ages* (London, 1963), 2: 21-22. There is a considerable literature on Cistercian architecture (Donkin, *Check-list*, pp. 23-26). See particularly M. Aubert, 'Existe-t-il une architecture cistercienne?' *Cahiers de civilisation médiévale X^{e}-XIIe siècles*, 1 (1958): 153-58, and F. Bucher, 'Cistercian architectural purism,' *Comparative Studies in Society and History*, 3 (1960): 89-105.

[5] *Mon. Angl.*, 5: 536 ("*forgiam et terram*," confirmed 1154-89). "The Cistercians," observed R. J. Forbes, "pioneered the use of water-mills in iron metallurgy, not only in France but in Germany, Denmark and Britain. Out of 30 French documents of the twelfth century concerned with hammer-forges and iron metallurgy 25 were drawn up by Cistercian monks as producers" ('Power,' in *A History of Technology*, ed. C. Singer, et al. (Oxford, 1956), 2: 610.

[6] At the time of the rebuilding of Clairvaux, 1135-6, there were apparently water-powered mills (*aquarum ad molas*) for fulling (*fullones*), tanning (*coriarii*) and iron-working (*fabri*) (*Sancti Bernardi Abbatis Clarae-Vallensis Vita et Res Gestae*, Migne, *Pat. Lat.*, 185: col. 285).

The earliest reference to a windmill anywhere in the West is usually dated ca. 1180.[7] It is mentioned in connection with a grant to the Benedictine abbey of St Sauveur-le-Vicomte in Normandy. There is a similar but unfortunately suspicious reference to a *molendinum ad ventum* (1170-80) in a confirmatory charter to Swineshead (Lincolnshire)[8] which had Norman connections as a member of the order of Savigny (united to Cîteaux in 1147). Apart from this, the first known record of a Cistercian windmill in England belongs to the period 1220-40 and concerns either Stanlaw (Cheshire)[9] or Thame (Oxfordshire);[10] the latter house also had one of the only two Cistercian fulling mills documented from the twelfth century.

Another development associated with the close of the twelfth century was the increasing use of the horse for ploughing.[11] The white monks may well have contributed to this,[12] especially in the North where several houses (notably Jervaulx) specialized in horse-rearing and all maintained large arable granges.

More significant, and certainly more distinctively Cistercian, was the recruitment of a special monastic work-force — the *conversi*, a kind of enlarged *famuli*. Without lay brothers the typical Cistercian grange — an island of advanced organization in a sea of peasant tenements and feudal demesne — would hardly have been possible. But in the process of forming such estates, partly by evictions and exchanges of property and partly by assarting and general reclamation, contact with the surrounding population was inevitable. Indeed many granges, and most other holdings, always depended on additional non-monastic labour. The ideal of isolation from the world of ordinary men, forcefully enjoined in the early statutes,

[7] L. Delisle, 'On the origin of windmills in Normandy and England,' *Jour.Brit. Arch.Assoc.*, 6 (1851): 403-06; J. C. Notebaart, *Windmühlen* (Den Haag, 1972), pp. 372, 374.

[8] *C.Ch.R.*, AD 1300-26 (1316), p. 319. See L. White, *Medieval Technology and Social Change* (Oxford, 1962), p. 162 n.1. The earliest secure dates are 1185 (B. A. Lees, ed., *Records of the Templars in England in the Twelfth Century: the Inquest of 1185*, Records of the Social and Economic History of England and Wales, 9 (London, 1935), pp. 131, 135) and 1191-2 (*The Chronicle of Jocelin of Brakelond*, ed. and trans. H. E. Butler (London, 1949), pp. 59-60).

[9] *Coucher W.*, 2: 509—grant (?) ca. 1230 of a *molendinum ventricium* at Ince (Lancashire).

[10] *Chart T.*, 1: 13—grant "*aliam acram propinquiorem molendino ad ventum dictorum monachorum*" (ca. 1237). See also *Chart N.*, p. 18 (? early thirteenth century), and *Reg. Con.*, p. 8.

[11] White, *Medieval Technology*, pp. 64-65; R. Lennard, 'The composition of demesne plough teams in twelfth-century England,' *E.H.R.*, 75 (1960): 193-207, especially p. 201.

[12] For the number of horses on Beaulieu's estates (1269-70) see *Account B.*, p. 29.

soon proved impracticable and was finally abandoned in a growing preoccupation with commercial affairs. The asceticism and lofty principles that initially attracted gifts of all kinds ironically placed the white monks on the road to great wealth and influence. The fundamental change that took place in the character of the order in no more than a century and a half is strikingly reflected in the fact that ca. 1300 Cistercian abbots were being regularly called to debate affairs of state in parliament.

Lords in Parliament

By the close of the thirteenth century all religious superiors of the rank of abbot or prior were liable to be called to parliament. Even the most privileged communities owed fealty to the Crown. Royal houses, founded in frankalmoigne and holding land by divine service, owed fealty to their immediate lord, the king, while the rest (by far the majority) were bound by simple allegiance.

A. F. Pollard maintained, correctly in principle, that spiritual lords were "liable to summons because they held land *per baroniam*, by military tenure in chief of the Crown."[13] This would have permanently excluded all Cistercian houses and all but twenty-four Benedictine foundations.[14] In practice, however, "tenurial considerations played a steadily diminishing part in determining the composition of the clerical element in the councils and parliaments of John, Henry III and Edward I"[15] which included many abbots and priors with estates held of mesne lords only. Under Edward II and Edward III a decreasing number of superiors were called and some of these claimed and won exemption on the grounds that they held nothing *per baroniam*. Beaulieu, a royal foundation, was thus discharged (1341), "unless their presence was necessary or opportune."[16] Of course not all lords who were summoned actually attended parliament, especially in the late thirteenth and early fourteenth centuries.[17] Attendance was regarded

[13] *The Evolution of Parliament*, 1st ed. (London, 1920), p. 64, following L. O. Pike, *A Constitutional History of the House of Lords* (London, 1894), p. 156. See P. Spufford, *Origins of the English Parliament* (London, 1967), p. 77: *Modus Tenendi Parliamentum* (ca. 1321-4).

[14] A. M. Reich, *The Parliamentary Abbots to 1470*, University of California Publications in History, vol. 7, no. 4 (Berkeley and Los Angeles, 1941), pp. 293 ff.

[15] H. M. Chew, *The English Ecclesiastical Tenants-in-Chief and Knight Service* (London, 1932), p. 170.

[16] *C.Cl.R.*, AD 1341-3, p. 201.

[17] See D. B. Wiske, 'The attitude of the English clergy in the thirteenth and fourteenth centuries towards the obligation of attendance on convocations and parliaments,' in *Essays*

as a disagreeable duty; it was also difficult to enforce, which doubtless was one reason for the decline in the number of writs issued until, under Richard II, there were only twenty-seven established parliamentary abbots, largely Benedictine.

Some heads of houses were summoned regularly, a greater number infrequently, and others escaped entirely. There was no simple pattern, but it is inconceivable that selection was entirely arbitrary. Cistercian abbots were occasionally consulted during the reign of Henry III and even earlier. There were seventeen among the 102 religious summoned by Simon de Montfort in 1264-5.[18] However detailed and regular information is only available from the latter part of Edward I's reign (1295). The superiors of forty-four Cistercian houses (59 per cent of the order in England and Wales) were at some time summoned between 1295 and 1307; twenty-five (33 per cent) between 1307 and 1327; and only seven (9 per cent) between 1327 and 1377.[19] At least forty-six houses were selected under the three Edwards, compared with forty-five Benedictine, eighteen Premonstratensian and twelve Augustinian foundations.

Many Cistercian houses received eight or more writs under Edward I and several on double this number of occasions under his successor. Beaulieu was called twenty times under Edward II and eighteen times between 1327 and 1341. Few houses were troubled after the great parliament of 1322. The present discussion therefore mainly concerns a period of less than thirty years, decades around the turn of the thirteenth century when the members of the Cistercian order had accumulated much the greater part of their estates and were still actively involved in the wool trade.

The heads of four of the five houses founded by reigning sovereigns (Stoneleigh, Beaulieu, Netley and Vale Royal) were summoned at one time or other. Furness (founded by Stephen, later king), Holm Cultram (founded by Henry, son of David I of Scotland) and Stanley (founded by the Empress Maud and Prince Henry, later Henry II) also received writs, but the abbots of two other houses with close royal connections (Bordesley and Conway) were apparently never required to attend parliament. Cer-

---

in History and Political Theory in Honor of Charles Howard McIlwain, ed. C. F. Wittke (Cambridge, Mass., 1936), pp. 77-108; R. S. Roskell, 'The problem of the attendance of the lords in medieval parliaments,' *B.I.H.R.*, 29 (1956): 153-204.

[18] *Foedera*, 1: 449; Reich, *Parliamentary Abbots*, p. 362.

[19] Inventories compiled from *Parl. Writs* (vols. 1 and 2) generally agree with the lists for each reign published by Reich, *Parliamentary Abbots*, pp. 362-65. Reich overlooks Buckland and mistakenly identifies *Blanca Landa* (Whitland) as a Premonstratensian house (Blanchland). For other lists, see *Rot. Parl.*, 1: 188-91, and *Docs. Eng. Hist.*, pp. 333-40.

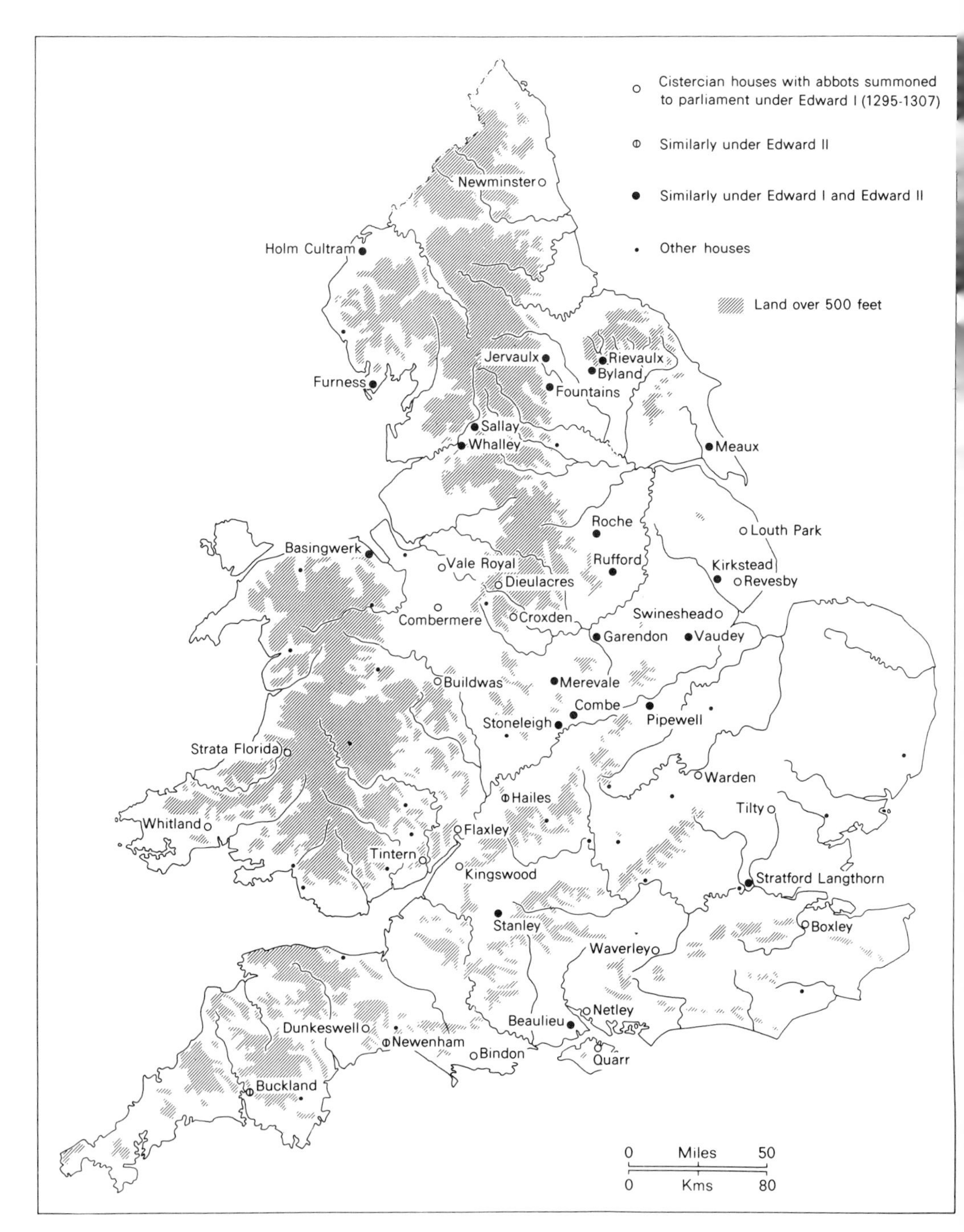

FIG. 25

Cistercian houses with abbots summoned to parliament 1295-1327.

tainly, then, a summons was not an inevitable consequence of royal origin.[20] Nor does age of origin appear to have been a vital consideration; abbots of houses founded before 1150 were called in about the same proportion as others.

Military operations in France, Scotland and Wales were, periodically, a heavy financial burden on the royal Exchequer, and the magnates, and particularly by clergy, were summoned to parliament chiefly in the hope that they would grant a subsidy. Edward I was in great difficulties on all three fronts when the 'Model Parliament', "the most comprehensive assembly yet summoned in England,"[21] met in November 1295. In June 1294 the king had appropriated all "the wool, wool-fells and hides" of England, and in 1297 stocks of more than five sacks were seized. (There was something of a precedent for this: in 1193-4 the wool of the Cistercians, Premonstratensians and Gilbertines was taken to meet the ransom of Richard I who, appropriately in the circumstances, was an honorary brother of Cîteaux). Customs on the export of wool were first imposed in 1275.[22] The question then arises whether, in nominating particular abbots for parliament, there was a clear preference for those in charge of relatively wealthy houses and in particular of houses with substantial surpluses of wool, the most realizable of assets apart from treasure.

The *Taxatio Ecclesiastica* (ca. 1291) serves as a general guide to the value of the temporalities of the Cistercian communities of England and Wales, and Pegolotti's approximately contemporary compilation gives the amounts of wool that were customarily available from sixty-four members of the order. Twenty-nine houses (39 per cent) exceeded the average valuation, and twenty-six (41 per cent) marketed more than the average quantity of wool. Of the houses that received writs between 1295 and 1307, 45 per cent belonged to the 'wealthier' group and 52 per cent were important wool producers; during Edward II's reign the proportions were 60 per cent and 64 per cent respectively, and over the period 1327-41, 86 per cent in each case. The tendency to select the leading houses (according to both criteria) increased as the number of writs declined. Altogether the superiors of twenty-three (79 per cent) of the 'wealthier' houses and no less than twenty-five (96 per cent) of the more important wool producers were summoned to parliament, usually on many occasions.

[20] No Cistercian abbot received the mitre before the fifteenth century. Jervaulx (1409), followed closely by St. Mary Graces (1415), were the first to be so honoured (*Papal Letters*, 6: 159, 465).

[21] F. M. Powicke, *The Thirteenth Century, 1216-1307*, 2nd ed. (Oxford, 1962), p. 673.

[22] For Edward III's heavy dependence on revenue from wool, see F. R. Barnes, 'The taxation of wool, 1327-1348,' in *Finance and Trade under Edward III*, ed. G. Unwin (Manchester, 1918), pp. 137-177.

The Cistercian houses that most frequently received writs lay predominantly to the north-west of a line from the lower Severn to the Wash (Fig. 25). The territorial imbalance was more marked than would have been the case if all the 'wealthier' houses or even if all the leading wool producers (and no others) had been called. Furthermore, the distribution of Cistercian (and Premonstratensian) summonses was broadly complementary to that of the Benedictine (and Augustinian), and for some time there was a tendency to select one group or the other.[23] Possibly the choice depended on what subjects were to be discussed or where the parliament was held (often in some place other than Westminster and commonly in York). In any event, it seems likely that the territorial interests and connections of the two leading orders were taken into account, if only in association with economic and other considerations.

The Cistercians are particularly associated with northern England, not because of any marked concentration of former houses there (Fig. 5), but rather on account of the extent and magnificence of the remains at particular sites. In the twelfth and thirteenth centuries too the northern houses enjoyed a special collective reputation. This arose from their work and achievements in what was a comparatively undeveloped region. Here donations were more generous and there was more scope for sheep- and cattle-rearing at a time when England became a leading wool and hide exporter. Above all, perhaps, the Cistercian houses of the North were largely outside the fields of influence of long established religious foundations (interestingly, no house was founded within the palatinate of Durham). It is possible to refer to a Benedictine 'province' in the South and East and to a Cistercian 'province' in the North and West (including Wales), corresponding respectively to zones of greater and lesser population and wealth.[24] Such differences were less marked in 1300 than in 1100 and for this the Cistercians were in some way responsible. The pioneer, even entrepreneurial, character of the order was only fully realised in the North, and it was upon this that its reputation chiefly rested.

[23] Reich, *Parliamentary Abbots*, p. 343.

[24] See R. A. Donkin, 'Changes in the early Middle Ages,' in *A New Historical Geography of England*, ed. H. C. Darby (Cambridge, 1973), pp. 78-81.

Appendix 1

SITE CHANGES

Final Sites	Earlier Sites
Caernarvonshire	
Conway 2 (Maenan), ca. 1283	Rhedynog-felen, 1186 [Knowles and Hadcock, pp. 112, 118.]
	Conway 1 (Aberconway), ca. 1190, [Ibid., p. 114; *C.C.R. (V)*, p. 285; *C.Cl.R.*, AD 1279-88, p. 407.]
Cardiganshire	
Strata Florida 2, 1184-1201	Strata Florida 1, 1164 [Knowles and Hadcock, pp. 114, 126.]
Carmarthenshire	
Whitland, ca. 1151	? Treffgarn, 1140-4 [Ibid., pp. 115, 127.]
Cheshire	
Vale Royal, 1281	Darnhall, 1274 [*Ledger V.R.*, pp. 4-5; *C.Ch.R.*, AD 1257-1300, p. 215.]
Dorset	
Bindon, 1172	W. Lulworth, 1171-2 [Knowles and Hadcock, pp. 112, 116; *C.Ch.R.*, AD 1257-1300, pp. 216-17.]
Forde, 1141	Brightley, 1136 [Knowles and Hadcock, p. 112; *Mon. Angl.*, 5: 376.]
	Westford, [Ibid.]
Essex	
Stratford Langthorn	Stratford Langthorn, 1135 [*The Itinerary of John Leland*, ed. L. T. Smith (1910), vol. 5, pt. ix: 5.]
	? Burstead
Flintshire	
Basingwerk, 1157	? Coleshill (Hên Blas), 1131-2 [D. H. Williams, *Arch. Camb.*, 114 (1965): 10.]
Glamorgan	
Margam, *ante* 1151	? Pendar, 1147 [Knowles and Hadcock, p. 122.]
Gloucestershire	
Kingswood 2, ca. 1164 or 1166-ca. 1170	Kingswood 1, 1139 [*Mon. Angl.*, 5: 424.]
	Hazelton, ca. 1149-50 [Knowles and Hadcock, pp. 113, 121.]
	Kingswood 1, ca. 1150-54 [Ibid.]
	Tetbury, ca. 1150-54 [Ibid., pp. 114, 121; *Mon. Angl.*, 5: 424.]
Hampshire	
Beaulieu, 1204	Faringdon, 1203 [*Mon. Angl.*, 5: 682; *Chart. Bl.*, pp. xxxiv-xxxv.]
Lancashire	
Furness, 1127	Tulketh, 1124 [*Mon. Angl.*, 5: 244, 246; *Coucher F.*, 1: 8.]
Whalley, 1296	Stanlaw, 1172 [*Mon. Angl.*, 5: 639; T. Madox, *Formulare Anglicanum* (1702), p. 262.]

Final Sites	Earlier Sites
Leicestershire	
Garendon	Garendon, 1133 [T. R. Potter, *Charnwood Forest* (1842), p. 180.]
Lincolnshire	
Kirkstead 2, 1187	Kirkstead 1, 1139 [Knowles and Hadcock, pp. 113, 121; *Chart. F.*, 1: 67.]
Louth Park, 1139	Haverholme, 1139 [*Chron. L. P.*, pp. xxii-xxv.]
Vaudey, 1147-9	Bytham, 1147 [*Mon. Angl.*, 5: 489; Knowles and Hadcock, pp. 114, 127.]
Monmouthshire	
Grace Dieu 2, 1236	Grace Dieu 1, 1226 [*Ann. Wav.*, pp. 312, 317.]
Llantarnam, ? ca. 1272	Caerleon, 1175-79 [D. H. Williams, *Welsh Cistercians* (1969), p. 32.]
Montgomeryshire	
Strata Marcella 2, ? 1172	Strata Marcella 1, 1170 [Knowles and Hadcock, pp. 114, 126.]
Oxfordshire	
Thame, ca. 1140	Otley, 1137 [*Mon. Angl.*, 5: 403; Knowles and Hadcock, pp. 114, 126.]
Radnorshire	
Cwmhir, 1176	Ty Faenor, 1143 [*Roy. Comm. Anc. Mon. Wales* (1913), 3: 7.]
Staffordshire	
Croxden, 1178	Cotton, 1176 [*Mon. Angl.*, 5: 660-61.]
Dieulacres, 1214	Poulton, 1153-58 [Ibid., pp. 626-27; Knowles and Hadcock, pp. 112-113, 118, 123.]
Surrey	
Waverley	? Waverley, 1128 [*Mon. Angl.*, 5: 239; *Ann. Wav.*, p. 312.]
Sussex	
Robertsbridge, 13th century [? ca. 1250]	Salehurst, 1176 [*V.C.H.* (*Sussex*), 2: 71-72.]
Warwickshire	
Stoneleigh, 1154-55	Red Moor, ca. 1141 [Knowles and Hadcock, pp. 114, 124-125; *Mon. Angl.*, 5: 443, 446-447.]
	Cryfield, 1154-55 [Ibid.]
Wiltshire	
Stanley, 1154	Loxwell, 1151 [Knowles and Hadcock, pp. 114, 125.]
Yorkshire	
Byland, 1177	Calder, 1135 [*Mon. Angl.*, 5: 349-350; Knowles and Hadcock, pp. 112, 116.]
	Hood, 1138 [*Mon. Angl.*, 5: 351.]
	Byland 1, 1143 [Ibid.]
	Stocking, 1147 [Ibid.]
Jervaulx, 1156	Fors, 1145-50 [*Mem. F.*, 1: 131.]
Kirkstall, 1152	Barnoldswick, 1147 [Ibid., p. 93.]

Appendix 2

DEPOPULATION IN YORKSHIRE

Column 1 gives the name of the monastery and its foundation date (at the final site, but in the case of Byland the penultimate is also given). Places now 'lost' or represented by only a farmstead are in italics. The evidence of Domesday Book (D.B.) is arranged in four columns: W = 'waste', P = largely or partly 'waste'; next, the number of carucates for geld and the number of ploughlands (thus 3:2); where only a collective ratio can be given it is shown thus *3:2*, followed by the number of carucates for geld in the place itself. The following three columns indicate whether the place is mentioned (×) in Kirkby's Inquest (K.I., 1284-5), the Knights' Fees (K.F.) of 1303, and the *Nomina Villarum* (N.V., 1316). The figures under K.I. are the carucates allotted to the abbey and are shown in italics when they represent the total. Under N.V., L = lord of the vill, P = part lord.

The granges in italics were situated close by rather than in the same territory; the date is that of the earliest reference discovered.[1] Sometimes it is known that the monastic holding was complete, and this is shown in the final column (date of the reference wherever possible, otherwise ' × '); the phrasing varies somewhat — grant or possession of 'all the vill', 'all the place', 'all the land', or simply 'all'. *Conf.* = confirmed.

[1] R. A. Donkin, 'The Cistercian grange in England in the twelth and thirteenth centuries,' *Studia Monastica*, 6 (1964): 124-38.

Monastery	Place		D.B.		K.I.	K.F.	N.V.	Grange: Name	Grange: Date	Grange: All held
(a) *Settlements depopulated or probably depopulated*										
Byland 1147/77	Byland 1		6:3		*8*	—	—	Byland	1146	1142-3
Kirkstall 1152	Bracewell		6		×	×	×	Barnoldswick (Bracewell, E. Marton, W. Marton, Stock)	1152	1154-76 *conf.*
	E. Marton, W. Marton		6		×, ×	×, ×	×, ×			
	Stock		4		×	—	—			
Fountains 1132	Baldersby	W	*5:3*	3	×	—	—	Baldersby (Baldersby, *Birkou*, *Eseby*)	1189-99 *conf.*	1284-5
	Birkou		—		×	—	—			
	Eseby	W	4		×	—	—			
	Cayton		2		—	—	—	Cayton	1145-46 *conf.*	
	Greenbury		—		1	—	—	Greenbury	1189-99 *conf.*	×
	Thorpe Underwood	W	8:4		—	—	—	Thorpe	1189-99 *conf.*	1175-99
Meaux 1151	Meaux	P	*1:1*	2	—	—	—	N. Grange	1153-54 *conf.*	1154 *conf.*
(b) *The prospect of displacement*										
Rievaulx 1132	E. Heslerton	W	*1:1*	1½	×	×	×			
	Welburn		8:4		—	—	×	Welburn	1332 *conf.*	×
	Welbury		6:3		×	—	×	*Ingram*		
	Willerby	P	*2:1*	5	×	×	×			
(c) *PLaces possibly reduced*										
Fountains 1132	Arnford		2		—	×	—	Arnford	1189-99 *conf.*	
	Brimham	W	3½:2		—	—	—	Brimham	1189-99 *conf.*	×
	Caldwell	P	*7:4*	4	—	—	—	Marton	1162 *conf.*	×
	Cattal		5:2		—	×	—	*Kirk Hammerton*	1172	
	Dacre	W	*3:2*	3	—	—	—	Dacre	1145-46 *conf.*	×
	Dromonby		*17:8*	3	×	×	—	*Busby*	1180-90 *conf.*	
	Fixby		1		—	—	×	*Bradley*	1189-99 *conf.*	
	Herleshou	P	*4:3*	3	—	—	—	*Morker*	1156 *conf.*	1149-53 *conf.*
	Kirby (Hall)		2:2		—	—	×	*Thorpe*	1189-99 *conf.*	1206 *conf.*
	Kirby Wiske	W	8:4		4	—	×	Kirby Wiske	1189-99 *conf.*	

Monastery	Place		D.B.		K.I.	K.F.	N.V.	Grange: Name	Date	All held
[Fountains 1132]	L. Busby	P	1½:1		×	×	—	Busby	1180-90	
	Markenfield		5:3		—	—	—	*Morker*	1156 *conf.*	
	Ripplington		—		—	—	—	*Sleningford*	1189-99 *conf.*	×
	Thorpe, nr. Brereton	W	*2:1*	2	—	—	—	*Cayton*	1145-46 *conf.*	
	Upsland	W	3:2		×	—	—	*Sleningford*	1189-99 *conf.*	
	Warsil	W	2		—	—	—	Warsil	1145-46 *conf.*	
Kirkstall 1152	Birkby	W	*2:1*	1½	—	—	—	*Roundhay*	1177-85	
	Watecroft	W	*2:1*	½	—	—	—	*Roundhay*	1177-85	
Jervaulx 1156	Akebar		4:5		—	—	—	Akebar	1342	
	Clifton		3:2		×	—	—	*Ellington*	1286-7	
	Didderston		*11:10*	4	*3*	—	—	Didderston	1284-5	1284-5
	Fors	W	4:2		—	—	—	Fors		
	Hesselton		6:4		2	—	×	Akebar	1342	
	Rookwith	W	6:4		—	—	—	Rookwith	1301	1228 *conf.*
	Ruswick	W	2:2		*3*	—	—	Ruswick	1301	1228 *conf.*
Sallay 1148	Barrowby		1:1		—	×	—	Barrowby	1172 *conf.*	
			2:1	3						
	Ellenthorpe		1½		—	—	—	Ellenthorpe	1172 *conf.*	1148
	Sallay		—		—	—	—	Sallay	1172 *conf.*	1148
	Stainton	W	3		—	—	—	Stainton	1172 *conf.*	12th cent.
Meaux 1151	Arram		1:1		×	×	—	Arram	1197-1210	
	Hornsea Burton	P	*1:1*	2	×	×	P	*Wassand*	1197-1210	
	Myton	W	*6½:4*	1½	—	×	—	Myton	1172 *conf.*	
	Octon		14		×	×	×	Octon	1150-60	
	Rowton	P	2		×	×	—	Rowton	1286-1310	
	Wassand		2:2		×	×	L	Wassand	1197-1210	
Rievaulx 1132	Crosby	W	*17:9*	1	—	—	—	Crosby	1152	1153-7 *conf.*
	Flotmanby		*2:1*	6	×	×	×	*Hunmanby*	1147	
	Griff		2:1		—	—	—	Griff	1154	1132
	Hoveton	W	*24:7*	2	—	—	—	*Skiplam*		1151
	L. Broughton		*17:8*	8	×	×	×	L. Broughton	1180-88	
	Morton		3:1		—	—	—	Morton		
	Newton		2:1		*4*	—	—	Newton	12th-13th cent.	1284-5

Monastery	Place		D.B.		K.I.	K.F.	N.V.	Grange: Name	Grange: Date	Grange: All held
[Rievaulx 1132]	*Raventhorpe*	W	1:½		×	—	—	*Hesketh*	ca. 1145	
	Shitlington	W	*3:2*	3	—	×	×	Shitlington	1150-60	
	Steinton		—		—	—	—	*Bilsdale*	1280	1145-52
	Stilton	W	2:2		—	—	—	*Griff*	1154	1132
			1:½							
Byland 1147/77	Baxby	P	*4:3*	2	×	—	—	*Wildon*	12th cent.	
			2:1	6						
	Dale Town		3:2		×	—	×	*Murton*	1170-90	
		W	*2:1*	1½						
	Denby	W	3:2		—	×	L	Denby		
	Murton		6		*4*	—	—	Murton	1170-90	1165-85
	Osgodby		*4:3*	3	*4*	—	—	Osgodby	12th cent.	1284-5
		W	*5:3*	2½						
	Wildon		3:2		—	—	—	Wildon	12th cent.	12th cent.

(d) *Other places possibly reduced but not known to have formed part of a grange before 1300*
(grid references are given for those not listed by M. W. Beresford[2])

Byland: Cottam; Givendale; Iselbeck; Killerby; Tollesby; Laysthorpe (the abbey held the 2 carucates in 1284-5, and the abbot was lord of the place in 1316); Marderby (all 4 carucates held 1284-5 and the abbot was lord in 1316; the estate may have been organized with Osgodby grange, about 2 miles to the south); Stainsby (464160).

Fountains: *Yarnwick*; Goulton; *Aismunderby*; L. Newton (851579).

Jervaulx: Lazenby (site of village N.E. of the hall).

Kirkstall: Burdon (299438); Stub House; Wothersome (3 carucates were held from the abbot in 1284-5; Beresford thinks the settlement was small by the mid-14th cent.); Lofthouse (the abbey had 4.5 carucates here 1284-5). Neither Wothersome nor Lofthouse appear in the *Nomina Villarum*.

Meaux: *Gardham* (probably already small by the mid-14th cent. according to Beresford); *Raventhorpe*; Bewick (234394).

Rievaulx: Arden (520905); Riccal (about 3 miles E.N.E. of Newton grange); *Hathelton* (085385) — all except a bovate was confirmed to the abbey in 1332.

Roche: Bilham; Hellaby (515920); Wilsic (564959).

Sallay: Crook's House (868500) — all held (12th cent.); Painley (840500).

[2] 'The lost villages of Yorkshire,' *Yorks. Arch. Jour.*, 37 (1951): 474-491; 38 (1952-54): 44-70, 215-240, 280-309.

Appendix 3

VACCARIES

Monastery		
Beaulieu	1269-70	*Account B.*, pp. 62, 68, 135, 156.
	1316	*Chart. Bl.*, p. 229.
Biddlesden	ca. 1291	*Tax. Eccles.*, p. 54.
Byland	1140	*Mon. Angl.*, 5: 350.
Conway	ca. 1291	*Tax. Eccles.*, p. 289.
Fountains	1296	*Chart. F.*, 1: 111.
	1304	*Chart. F.*, 1: 62.
	1457-8	*Mem. F.*, 3: 42.
	1457-8	Ibid., p. 53 (four).
	1458-9	Ibid., p. 83 (two).
	1458-9	Ibid., p. 84.
	1458-9	Ibid., p. 86.
	1496	Ibid., 1: 343.
	1496	Ibid., p. 351.
	1525	Ibid., p. 321.
Furness	1292	*Coucher F.*, 3: 635 (four).
Holm Cultram	1215-6 *conf.*	*Mon. Angl.*, 5: 595.
	1227	*C.Ch.R.*, AD 1226-57, p. 32.
	1361	*Mon. Angl.*, 5: 593.
Jervaulx	ca. 1156	Ibid., p. 572; *E.Y.C.*, 4: 33.
	1253 *conf.*	*C.Ch.R.*, AD 1226-57, p. 418 (three).
	1280-1	*C.I.P.M.*, 2: 214 (thirteen).
Kirkstall	1155-62 *conf.*	*E.Y.C.*, 3: 152-53.
	ante 1166	*Mon. Angl.*, 5: 537.
	1166-94	*Coucher K.*, pp. 52-53.
	1327 *conf.*	*C.Ch.R.*, AD 1327-41, p. 46.
Kirkstead	1270	P. Thompson, *History of Boston*, p. 47.
	1323	*Inq. Dam.*, p. 268.
Louth Park	1275	*Rot. Hund.*, 1: 296.
	? 15th cent.	*Chron. L.P.*, p. 73.
Meaux	1151	*E.Y.C.*, 3: 93.
	1150-60	*Chron. M.*, 1: 109.
	1182-97	Ibid., p. 219 (two).
	1194-1216	Ibid., p. 346.
	1205	*Rot. Ch.*, p. 146.
	1235-49	*Chron. M.*, 2: 6.
	1235-49	Ibid., p. 65 (two).
	1396-9	Ibid., 3: 242.
Pipewell		*Mon. Angl.*, 5: 436.

MONASTERY		
Revesby	1222	P. Thompson, *History of Boston*, p. 47.
	ca. 1536	*Mon. Angl.*, 5: 456.
Rievaulx	1301	W. Brown, *Yorkshire Lay Subsidy*, p. 26.
Sallay	1189 *conf.*	*Chart. S.*, 1: 69.
Sawtry	1281	*Rot. Hund.*, 2: 663.
	ca. 1291	*Tax. Eccles.*, p. 51 (two).
Strata Marcella	*ante* 1282	*C.M.I.*, AD 1307-49, no. 732.
	1287 *conf.*	M. C. Jones, *Montgomeryshire Collections*, 4 (1871): 314.
	ca. 1291	*Tax. Eccles.*, p. 289.
	1322 *conf.*	*C.Ch.R.*, AD 1300-26, p. 440.
Swineshead	1154-89 *conf.*	*Mon. Angl.*, 5: 337.
	1316 *conf.*	*C.Ch.R.*, AD 1300-26, p. 319.
	1317 *conf.*	*C.P.R.*, AD 1313-17, p. 647.
	1537	*Mon. Angl.*, 5: 339.
Thame	ca. 1291	*Tax. Eccles.*, p. 43.
Valle Crucis	ca. 1291	Ibid., p. 289.
	1535	*Roy. Comm. Anc. Mon. Wales (Denbighshire)*, (1914) 4: 160.
Woburn	ca. 1291	*Tax. Eccles.*, p. 49.
	1337	*C.P.R.*, AD 1334-8, p. 493.

Appendix 4

TANNERIES

Monastery		
Beaulieu	1269-70	*Account B.*, pp. 37, 314.
Bruern	ca. 1536	*Mon. Angl.*, 5: 497.
	1538	Ibid., p. 500.
Dore	ca. 1291	*Tax. Eccles.*, p. 172.
Fountains	1491	*Mem. F.*, 1: 232.
Furness	1292	*Coucher F.*, 3: 635.
	ca. 1536	*Mon. Angl.*, 5: 251.
Hulton	ca. 1291	*Tax. Eccles.*, p. 252.
Jervaulx	ca. 1536	*Mon. Angl.*, 5: 577.
	1539	Ibid., p. 578.
Kirkstead	1538	Ibid., p. 423.
Margam	ca. 1291	*Tax. Eccles.*, p. 284.
Meaux	1235-49	*Chron. M.*, 2: 64.
	1372-96	Ibid., 3: 227.
Newminster	1537	*Mon. Angl.*, 5: 402.
	1547	*Chart. N.*, p. 310.
Quarr	ca. 1291	*Tax. Eccles.*, p. 214.
Robertsbridge	1417-18	G. M. Cooper, *Sussex Arch. Coll.*, 8 (1856): 166.
Sallay	ca. 1226	*Chart. S.*, 1: 141.
	ca. 1300	*Mon. Angl.*, 5: 641.
	1312	*Chart. S.*, 2: 51.
	1481	T. D. Whitaker, *History of Craven*, 3rd ed. (1878), p. 63.
Sibton	*ante* 1363-4	*Docs. S.*, p. 112.
Tintern	ca. 1291	*Tax. Eccles.*, p. 282.
Whalley	1478	T. D. Whitaker, *History of Whalley* (1806), p. 84.
	1521	Ibid.
	1538	*Mon. Angl.*, 5: 650.

Appendix 5

FULLING MILLS

Monastery		
Basingwerk	1535	*Mon. Angl.*, 5: 263.
Beaulieu	1269-70	*Account B.*, pp. 39, 219, 221, 279, 294, 301, 303.
Bordesley		*V.C.H.* (*Worcestershire* 1913), 3: 161.
Boxley	1535	*Mon. Angl.*, 5: 461.
Byland	1540	Ibid., p. 354.
Combermere	1255	*Rot. Hund.*, 2: 55.
Conway*	ca. 1291	*Tax. Eccles.*, p. 292.
Flaxley*	1291	*Chart. Fl.*, p. 46.
Fountains*	1540	*Mem. F.*, 1: 376.
Grace Dieu	ca. 1291	*Tax. Eccles.*, p. 172.
Holm Cultram*	1535	A. Savine, *English Monasteries*, pp. 125-26.
Jervaulx*	1535	*Mon. Angl.*, 5: 577.
Kingswood	1537	*Rental Kingswood*, p. 135.
Kirkstall	1288	E. M. Carus-Wilson, *Ec.H.R.*, 11 (1941): 45.
	1459	*Rental K.*, p. 13.
Margam	ca. 1291	*Tax. Eccles.*, p. 284.
	1336	*Cartae. Glam.*, 4: 153-54.
Meaux*	1235-49	*Chron. M.*, 2: xiv, 63, 65.
Newminster*	12th-13th cent.	*Chart. N.*, pp. 3, 18, 78, 132, 135, 200.
	1537	Ibid., 308; *Mon. Angl.*, 5: 401.
Quarr*	ca. 1200	S. F. Hockey, *Quarr Abbey* (1970), p. 52.
Rievaulx	1539-40	*Chart. R.*, p. 312.
Sallay	ca. 1240	*Chart. S.*, 2: 30.
Stanley	1189-90	*Mon. Angl.*, 5: 565.
Stoneleigh	1376	*Ledger S.*, p. 163.
	1537	*Mon. Angl.*, 5: 450.
Thame	1197	*Chart. T.*, p. 71.
Tintern	1291	*Mon. Angl.*, 5: 265.
Vale Royal	1341	*Ledger, V.R.*, p. 177.
Warden	1535	*V.C.H.* (*Bedfordschire*, 1908), 2: 283.
Whalley	1538	*Mon. Angl.*, 5: 651.
Whitland	1535	Ibid., p. 592.

* Fulling mill(s) on property described as a grange before 1300.

Appendix 6

TOLL EXEMPTIONS

Monastery			
Basingwerk	1285	restricted	*C.Ch.R.*, AD 1257-1300, p. 290.
Biddlesden	1155-8		E. Berger, *Recueil des Actes de Henri II*, 1: 161.
Bordesley	1156-9		Ibid., p. 223.
	1205		*Rot. Ch.*, p. 145.
Bruern	1205		Ibid., p. 146.
Byland	1154-89		*Mon. Angl.*, 5: 343.
	1196-1222	restricted	*E.Y.C.*, 2: 26.
	1190-1210	Helmsley	Ibid., 10: 147.
Cleeve		restricted	*Mon. Angl.*, 5: 732.
Coggeshall	ca. 1150		Ibid., p. 451.
Combe	1154-89		Ibid., pp. 582-83.
Combermere	1130-3	Chester	Ibid., p. 325.
	1232		*C.Ch.R.*, AD 1226-57, p. 153.
Conway	ca. 1186	restricted	*Mon. Angl.*, 5: 673.
[Rhedynog-felen, Aberconway]	1202		*Reg. Con.*, pp. 10, 19; *C.P.R.*, AD 1232-1247, p. 504; *Mon. Angl.*, 5: 674.
Croxden	1206		*Rot. Ch.*, p. 162.
	1250	Leek	*Chart. D.*, p. 358.
Cwmhir	1214		*Rot. Pat.*, p. 125; *Rot. Ch.*, p. 206; *C.Ch.R.*, AD 1226-57, p. 155.
Cymmer		restricted	E. A. Lewis, *Mediaeval Boroughs of Snowdonia* (1912), p. 181.
Darnhall	1275		*C.Ch.R.*, 1257-1300, p. 197; *Mon. Angl.*, 5: 711 (Vale Royal, 1299).
Dieulacres	1217-32	restricted	*Chart. D.*, p. 353.
Dore	1189-99		*C.Ch.R.*, AD 1257-1300, p. 55, AD 1327-41, p. 14; *C.A.D.*, 5: A 10443.
Fountains	1155		*E.Y.C.*, 1: 72; *Mem. F.*, 2: 3, 6; *Rot. Ch.*, p. 18.
	1155	Boroughbridge	*E.Y.C.*, 1: 72.
Furness	1154-89		*V.C.H. (Lancashire)*, 2: 119. *Rot. Ch.*, p. 41.
Hailes	1262		*C.Ch.R.*, AD 1257-1300, p. 43; *Cart. Ant.*, p. 121.
Holm Cultram	1189-90		*V.C.H. (Cumberland)*, 2: 167; *Pipe Roll*, AD 1200-1 (P.R.S.), p. 254; *Rot. Oblat.*, p. 118; *Rot. Ch.*, p. 89; *C.Ch.R.*, AD 1226-57, p. 32.
Jervaulx	1165-73		*E.Y.C.*, 5: 325; *Mon. Angl.*, 5: 568.

Monastery			
Kirkstall	1166-94	restricted	*Mon. Angl.*, 5: 353.
	1154-89		*Coucher K.*, pp. 216-17; *Mon. Angl.*, 5: 536; *Rot. Ch.*, p. 149.
Llantarnam	ca. 1216	Bristol	*C.M.I.*, AD 1212-1307, no. 125.
Louth Park	1155-6		*Chron. L.P.*, pp. 52-53; Berger, *Recueil*, 1: 181.
	1276-81	restricted	*Chron. L.P.*, p. 48 (exemption questioned).
Margam	1147-83	restricted	*Cartae Glam.*, 3: 176, 573.
	1205		*Rot. Oblat.*, pp. 269-70; *Rot. Ch.*, p. 167.
Meaux	1155-6		*E.Y.C.*, 3: 100; *Chron. M.*, 1: 209-10; *Rot. Ch.*, p. 146.
Merevale	1154-89		*Mon. Angl.*, 5: 483.
Neath	1147-57	restricted	D. Lewis, *Arch. Camb.*, 5th ser., 4 (1887): 95.
	1154-89		*Cartae Glam.*, 3: 98; *Mon. Angl.*, 5: 260; *Rot. Ch.*, 174.
Newminster	ca. 1165		Berger, *Recueil*, 1: 389.
Pipewell	1235		*C.Ch.R.*, AD 1226-57, p. 198.
Quarr	1193-1216	restricted	*C.A.D.*, 3: D 942.
Revesby	1155		Berger, *Recueil*, 1: 145.
Roche	1377-99		*Mon. Ebor.*, p. 323.
Rievaulx	1135		*Chart. R.*, pp. 127, 129-30, 141, 146, 310; *Rot. Ch.*, p. 94.
Rufford	1155		T.A.M. Bishop, *Lincs. Archit. and Archae. Soc. Reps.*, n.s., 4 (1952): 102; *C.P.R.*, AD 1461-67. p. 139; *Mon. Angl.*, 5: 519.
	1316	Nottingham	*C.P.R.*, AD 1461-67, p. 139.
Sallay	1154		*Chart. S.*, 1: 35.
Stanlaw	1178	restricted	*Mon. Angl.*, 5: 641.
Stanley	1189-90	Bristol	Ibid., p. 565.
Stoneleigh	1204		*Rot. Ch.*, p. 131; *Mon. Angl.*, 5: 444.
Strata Florida	1200		*Rot. Ch.*, p. 44; *C.Ch.R.*, AD 1226-57, p. 172.
Strata Marcella	1200	restricted	*Rot. Ch.*, p. 44.
Swineshead	1189-99		*Mon. Angl.*, 5: 338.
Thame	1155		*Chart. T.*, 2: 123; *C.Ch.R.*, AD 1226-1257, p. 14.
Tintern	ca. 1131	restricted	*Mon. Angl.*, 5: 268.
	1155-6		Berger, *Recueil*, 1: 96.
	1216-72	Bristol	F. B. Bickley, ed., *Little Red Book of Bristol* (1900), 2: 199.
Warden	1189		*Chart. W.*, pp. 288-89.
Waverley	1205		*Rot. Ch.*, p. 161.
Whalley	ca. 1256	Warrington	G. H. Tupling, *Trans. Lancs. Chesh. Ant. Soc.*, (1934-5): 134.
Whitland	1214		*Rot. Pat.*, 125.
Woburn	1155-6		Berger, *Recueil*, 1: 180.

Appendix 7

TRANSPORT OF WOOL

References to monasteries delivering, or with licence to deliver, or under obligation to deliver wool to Boston etc.; and wool belonging to monasteries at Boston etc.

Monastery				
Basingwerk	1277	London	6 loads	*C.P.R.*, AD 1272-81, pp. 227, 242.
Bordesley	1224	London	13 sacks	*C.P.R.*, AD 1216-25, p. 471.
Combermere	1283	Boston		*C.C.R. (V), Welsh Rolls*, p. 272.
Darnhall	1275-6	London	12 sacks	*C.Cl.R.*, AD 1272-9, p. 254.
Dore	1216	Windsor	7 loads	*C.P.R.*, AD 1216-25, p. 3.
Fountains	1276	Boston		*C.P.R.*, AD 1272-81, p. 141.
	1277-80	Clifton	62 sacks	*C.Cl.R.*, AD 1272-79, p. 354.
Furness	1224	Beverley		*Rot. Cl.*, 2: 7.
Holm Cultram		Newcastle		*Mon. Angl.*, 5: 614.
Louth Park	1275	Boston	ca. 15 sacks	*C.Cl.R.*, AD 1272-79, p. 321.
Meaux	1347	London		*C.Cl.R.*, AD 1346-49, p. 382.
	1275	Boston	129 sacks	*Rot. Hund.*, 1: 105; *Chron. M.*, 2: 156.
	1287	Hull	11 sacks	R. J. Whitwell, *Vierteljahrschrift für Sozial- und Wirtschaftsgeschichte*, 2 (1904): 33 n.i.
Roche	1224	Beverley		*Rot. Cl.*, 2: 7.
Stanlaw	1283	Boston		*C.P.R.*, AD 1281-1292, p. 68.
	1284	Boston		Ibid., p. 122.
Vaudey	1275	Boston		*Rot. Hund.*, 1: 390.
Woburn	1265	London		*C.P.R.*, AD 1258-66, p. 461.

APPENDIX 8

SHIPS IN THE SERVICE OF CISTERCIAN MONASTERIES

MONASTERY		
A. *Sea-going ships and vessels not specifically river-craft*		
Beaulieu	1213	*Rot. Cl.*, 1: 149.
	1233	*C.L.R.*, AD 1226-40, p. 228.
	1254	*C.P.R.*, AD 1247-58, p. 364.
	1254	*C.Cl.R.*, AD 1253-4, p. 25.
	1267	*C.P.R.*, AD 1226-72, p. 177.
	1268	Ibid., p. 192.
	1269-70	*Account B.*, pp. 170-71.
	1272	*C.P.R.*, AD 1226-72, p. 308.
	1281	*C.P.R.*, AD 1272-81, p. 457.
	1303	*C.Cl.R.*, AD 1302-7, pp. 78-79.
	1321	*C.Cl.R.*, AD 1318-23, p. 531.
Boxley	1225	*C.P.R.*, AD 1216-25, p. 505.
Buildwas	1292	*Mon. Angl.*, 5: 357.
Conway	1284	Ibid., p. 674; *Reg. Con.*, p. 21.
	1332	*C.Ch.R.*, AD 1327-41, p. 268.
Furness	1258	*C.P.R.*, AD 1247-58, p. 624.
	1333	*C.Cl.R.*, AD 1333-7, p. 105.
Holm Cultram	1300	*C.P.R.*, AD 1292-1301, p. 554.
Margam	1229	*C.Cl.R.*, AD 1227-31, p. 203.
	1234	*C.Cl.R.*, AD 1231-4, p. 360.
Meaux	1221-35	*Chron. M.*, 1: 421.
	1249	Ibid., 2: 65.
	1249-69	Ibid., p. 75.
Neath	1234-5	*C.P.R.*, AD 1232-47, pp. 69, 108.
Netley	1271	*C.P.R.*, AD 1266-72, p. 577.
Newminster	1429	*Chart. N.*, p. 302.
Quarr	1252	*C.Cl.R.*, AD 1251-3, p. 298.
	1254	*C.Cl.R.*, AD 1253-4, p. 59.
	1254	*C.P.R.*, AD 1247-58, p. 364.
	1339	*C.Cl.R.*, AD 1339-41, p. 33.

Monastery			
B. *Houses trading with Ireland (principally licences to buy provisions)*			
Conway	1283		*C.C.R. (V)*, p. 268.
Furness	1213		*Rot. Cl.*, 1: 157.
	1227		*C.P.R.*, AD 1225-32, p. 172.
	1231		Ibid., p. 457.
	1232		Ibid., AD 1232-47, p. 4.
	1233		Ibid., p. 27.
	1246		Ibid., p. 483.
	1252		Ibid., AD 1247-58, p. 147.
	1258		Ibid., p. 624.
	1277		Ibid., AD 1272-81, p. 198.
	1278		Ibid., p. 250.
	1283		Ibid., AD, 1281-92, p. 59.
Holm Cultram	1226		Ibid., AD 1225-32, p. 13.
	1228		Ibid., p. 226.
	1248		*C.Cl.R.*, AD 1247-51, p. 32.
	1282		*C.P.R.*, AD 1281-92, p. 51.
	1291		Ibid., p. 426.
	1301		Ibid., AD 1292-1301, p. 579.
	1302		Ibid., AD 1301-7, p. 38.
	1303		Ibid., p. 138.
	1305		Ibid., p. 316.
	1306		Ibid., p. 415.
Stanlaw	1283		*C.C.R. (V)*, p. 268; *C.P.R.*, AD 1281-92, p. 59.
Vale Royal	1278		Ibid., AD 1272-81, p. 265.
C. *River-craft*			
Beaulieu	1205	Thames	*Chart. Bl.*, p. 3.
Buildwas	1292	Severn	*C.Ch.R.*, AD, 1257-1300, p. 419.
Byland	1329	Ouse-Ure	*Mon. Angl.*, 5: 354.
Combermere	1266 *conf.*	Dee	Ibid., p. 324.
Dieulacres		Dee	*Chart. D.*, p. 331.
Flaxley	1270	Severn	*C.M.I.* AD 1212-1307, no. 383.
Fountains	1199-1216	Ouse-Ure	*Chart. F.*, 2: 725.
	1332	Derwent	*C.M.I.*, AD 1307-49, no. 1312.
Hailes	1262	Thames	*C.Ch.R.*, AD 1257-1300, p. 43.
Jervaulx	1236	Ouse-Ure	Ibid. AD 1226-57, p. 223.
Louth Park	1314	Ouse-Don	Ibid., AD 1300-26, p. 254.
Meaux	1310-39		*Chron. M.*, 2: 308.
Medmenham	1245	Thames	*C.Cl.R.*, AD 1242-7, p. 325.
Rievaulx	1332 *conf.*	Ouse	*Chart. R.*, p. 237.
Roche		Trent	*Mon. Ebor.*, p. 320.
Sawtry	12th cent.		*V.C.H. (Huntingdon)*, 3: 203, 256.
Tintern	1268	Wye	*C.M.I.*, AD 1227-1307, no. 354.

Appendix 9

EXPORT OF WOOL

Monastery				
Bordesley	1224	13 sacks		*C.P.R.*, AD 1216-25, p. 471.
Byland	1225		Flanders	Ibid., p. 509.
Fountains	1224	ship-load		*Rot. Cl.*, 1: 608; *C.P.R.*, AD 1216-25, p. 449.
	1229		Flanders	Ibid., AD 1225-32, p. 220.
Furness	1418-23		Zeeland	*Rot. Parl.*, 4: 251.
Garendon	1225		Flanders	*C.P.R.*, AD 1216-25, p. 522.
Holm Cultram	1224	ship-load		Ibid., p. 457.
Jervaulx	1225		Flanders	Ibid., p. 509.
Kirkstall	1224			*Rot. Cl.*, 1: 608; *C.P.R.*, AD 1216-25, p. 449.
Kirkstead	1224			*Rot. Cl.*, 1: 609, 634.
Meaux	1224	ship-load		*C.P.R.*, AD 1216-25, p. 461.
Melrose (Scotland)	1225	ship-load	Flanders	Ibid., p. 515.
Newminster	1225	ship-load	Flanders	Ibid., p. 538.
Roche	1224			Ibid., p. 461.
Strata Florida	1213-16			*Rot. Pat.*, p. 92.
Thame	1224	ship-load		*C.P.R.*, AD 1216-25, p. 457.
	1225	ship-load		Ibid., p. 519.

Appendix 10

CONTACTS WITH FOREIGN MERCHANTS

Monastery		Debt or Obligation*	Merchant of	Source	Note
Basingwerk	1294		Florence		1
Beaulieu	1272	50 m.	Flanders	*C.P.R.*, AD 1266-72, p. 700.	
	1294		Florence		1
Biddlesden	1272	20 m.	Flanders	*C.P.R.*, AD 1266-72, p. 700.	
	1284-5		Florence		2
	1334	£28	Lucca and Florence	*C.Cl.R.*, AD 1333-37, p. 329.	
Bindon	1294		Lucca		1
	1334	£200	Lucca and Florence	*C.Cl.R.*, AD 1333-37, p. 320.	
	1334	£80	Lucca and Florence	Ibid., p. 329.	
	1335	£100	Chieri	Ibid., pp. 530-31.	
	1335	£60		Ibid.	
Bordesley	1278	300 m.	Florence	*Rot. Parl.*, 1: 1.	
	1294		Florence		1
Boxley	1325	50 m.	Florence	*C.Cl.R.*, AD 1323-27, p. 518.	
Bruern	1264		Flanders	Ibid., AD 1264-68, p. 84.	
	1294	150 m.	Florence	Ibid., AD 1288-96., p. 383.	
	1294		Florence		1
	1305	150 m.	Florence	*C.Cl.R.*, AD 1302-7, p. 319.	
	1320	£400	Florence	Ibid., AD 1318-23, p. 241.	
	1321	£200	Florence	Ibid., p. 371.	
	1321	£160	Florence	Ibid., p. 490.	
	1321	120 m.	Lucca	Ibid., p. 491.	
	1321	100 m.	Genoa	Ibid., p. 502.	
	1324	£160	Florence	Ibid., AD 1323-27, p. 316.	
	1325	120 m.	Lucca	Ibid., p. 345.	
Buildwas	1264		Flanders	Ibid., AD 1264-68, p. 84.	
Byland	1294		Lucca and Florence		1
	1303	116 m.	Florence	*C.Cl.R.*, AD 1302-7, p. 104.	
Calder	1294		Florence		1

* To the nearest mark or pound sterling.

[1] T. H. Lloyd, *The Mouvement of Wool Prices in Medieval England*, Economic History Review, supplement no. 6. Table 5.

[2] G. F. Pagnini della Ventura, *Della decima e di varie altre gravezze imposte dal comune di Firenze* ... (Lisbon and Lucca, 1765), 2: 324-26.

Monastery		Debt or Obligation*	Merchant of	Source	Note
Cleeve	1294		Lucca		1
Coggeshall	1294		Florence		1
Combe	1294		Florence		1
Combermere	1294		Florence		1
	1313		Ypres	*C.Cl.R.*, AD 1313-18, p. 68.	
Conway [Aberconway]	1277			*C.P.R.*, AD 1272-81, p. 235.	
	1344	£200	Florence	*C.Cl.R.*, AD 1343-46, p. 251.	
Cymmer	1343	£80	Florence	Ibid., p. 244.	
Darnhall	1275		Cambrai	Ibid., AD 1272-79, p. 254.	
	1275		Florence	Ibid., p. 255.	
Dieulacres	1294		Lucca and Florence		1
Dore	1212		St. Omer	*Statuta* 1: 401.	
	1294		Florence		1
Flaxley	1277			*C.P.R.*, AD 1272-81, p. 200.	
Forde	1294		Lucca and Florence		1
Fountains	1212		St. Omer	*Statuta*, 1: 401.	
	1275		Flanders	*C.P.R.*, AD 1272-81, pp. 86-87.	
	1275		Lucca	Ibid., p. 95.	
	1276		Florence	*C.Cl.R.*, AD 1272-79, p. 354.	
	1284-5		Florence		2
	1294		Lucca		1
Furness	1212		St. Omer	*Statuta*, 1: 401.	
	1294		Florence		1
Garendon	1294		Florence		1
Hailes	1294		Lucca		1
Holm Cultram	1294		Florence		1
	13th cent., ?		Italy	*Reg. H.C.*, p. 86	
Hulton	1294		Florence		1
Jervaulx	1294		Florence		1
Kirkstall	1292		Lucca	*Coucher K.*, pp. 226-27.	
	1294		Lucca		1
Kirkstead	1274-5		Flanders	*Rot. Hund.*, 1: 317.	
	1294		Florence		1
	1340	£170	Lucca	*C.Cl.R.*, AD 1339-41, p. 492.	
Kingswood	1212		St. Omer	*Statuta*, 1: 401.	
	1264		Flanders	*C.Cl.R.*, AD 1264-68, p. 84.	
	1272	£60	Flanders	*C.P.R.*, AD 1266-72, p. 700.	
	1294		Florence		1
	1318		Florence	*C.Cl.R.*, AD 1313-18, p. 606.	
	1335		Florence	Ibid., AD 1333-37, p. 468.	
Louth Park	1274-5		Flanders	*Rot. Hund.*, 1: 317.	
	1294		Florence		1
Margam	1250		Ghent	*C.Cl.R.*, AD 1247-51, p. 304.	
Meaux	1264		Flanders	Ibid., AD 1264-68, p. 84.	
	1270-80		Lucca	*Chron. M.*, 2: 156.	
	1275-6			*Rot. Hund.*, 1: 105.	
	1294		Lucca		1

Monastery		Debt or Obligation*	Merchant of	Source	Note
Merevale	1264		Flanders	*C.Cl.R.*, AD 1264-68, p. 84.	
	1294		Florence		1
	1295	£37	Lucca	*C.Cl.R.*, AD 1288-96, p. 447.	
Neath	1294		Florence		1
Netley	1294		Florence		1
Newminster	1264		Flanders	*C.Cl.R.*, AD 1264-68, p. 84.	
	1272	40 m.	Douai	*C.P.R.*, AD 1266-72, p. 648.	
	1294		Lucca and Florence		1
Pipewell	1264		Flanders	*C.Cl.R.*, AD 1264-68, p. 84.	
	1272	100 m.	Flanders	*C.P.R.*, AD 1266-72, p. 700.	
	1290		Cahors	*C.Cl.R.*, AD 1288-96, pp. 192-194.	
	1310		Cahors	Ibid., AD 1307-12, p. 289.	
	1334	£100	Lucca	Ibid., AD 1333-37, p. 329.	
Quarr	1294		Florence		1
Revesby	1264		Flanders	*C.Cl.R.*, AD 1264-68, p. 84.	
	1274-5		Flanders	*Rot. Hund.*, 1: 317.	
	1294		Florence		1
Rievaulx	1280	144 m.	Florence	*Chart. R.*, p. 490.	
	1285	106 m.		*C.Cl.R.*, AD 1279-88, p. 353.	
	1294		Lucca and Florence		1
	1301	100 m.	Florence	*C.Cl.R.*, AD 1296-1302, pp. 475, 478.	
Robertsbridge	1284-5		Florence		2
	1294		Florence		1
	1320		Florence	*C.Cl.R.*, AD 1318-23, 319.	
Roche	1279	£300	Florence		3
	1284-5		Florence		2
	1294		Florence		1
Rufford	1294		Florence		1
Sallay	1294		Florence		1
Sawtry	1294		Lucca		1
	1320	£100	Pistoia	*C.Cl.R.*, AD 1318-23, p. 324.	
Sibton	1334	£100	Lucca and Florence	Ibid., AD 1333-37, p. 329.	
Stanlaw	1294		Florence		1
Stanley	1264		Flanders	*C.Cl.R.*, AD 1264-68, p. 84.	
	1318	100 m.	Genoa	Ibid., AD 1313-18, p. 601.	
	1325	100 m.	Florence	Ibid., AD 1323-27, p. 523.	
Stoneleigh	1294		Florence		1
	1324	£150	Genoa	*C.Cl.R.*, AD 1323-27, p. 180.	

[3] N. Denholm-Young, *Seignorial Administration in England* (London, 1937), p. 55, n. 8.

Monastery		Debt or Obligation*	Merchant of	Source	Note
Stratford Langthorn	1294		Florence		1
Thame	1284-5		Florence		2
	1294		Florence		1
Tilty	1288	340 m.	Lucca	*C.Cl.R.*, AD 1279-88, p. 548.	
	1294		Lucca and Florence		1
Tintern	1275-6		Flanders	*Rot. Hund.*, 1: 176.	
	1294		Florence		1
Vale Royal	1288	£172	Lucca	*C.Cl.R.*, AD 1288-96, p. 29.	
Vaudey	1274-5			*Rot. Hund.*, 1: 390.	
	1275-6		Montpellier	Ibid., p. 259.	
	1294		Lucca and Florence		1
	1321	200 m.	Florence	*C.Cl.R.*, AD 1318-23, p. 361.	
	1322	200 m.	Florence	Ibid., p. 687.	
	1323	£113	Lucca	Ibid., p. 704.	
	1323	£150	Bordeaux	Ibid.	
	1323	£60	Lucca	Ibid.	
	1323	£70	Lucca	Ibid., AD 1323-27, p. 146.	
	1323	500 m.	Florence	Ibid., p. 136.	
	1325	£70	Florence	Ibid., p. 372.	
	1325	£60	Lucca	Ibid.	
	1326	£27	Lucca	Ibid., p. 572.	
	1332	£122	Lucca and Florence	Ibid., AD 1330-33, p. 527.	
	1332	£120	Lucca and Florence	Ibid., p. 579.	
	1332	£100	Chieri and Genoa	Ibid., p. 562.	
	1336	£150	Lucca and Florence	Ibid., AD 1333-37, p. 705.	
	1338	£60	Lucca	Ibid., AD 1337-39, p. 407.	
	1338	£200	Florence	Ibid., p. 538.	
Warden	1294		Florence		1
	1323	£330	Florence	*C.Cl.R.*, AD 1318-23, p. 317.	
	1340	£500	Florence	Ibid., AD 1339-41, p. 638.	
Waverley	1294		Florence		1
	1320	£20	Florence	*C.Cl.R.*, AD 1318-23, p. 242.	
	1321	100 m.	Florence	Ibid., p. 497.	
	1324	£270	Chieri and Genoa	Ibid., AD 1323-27, p. 306.	
	1325	£180	Pistoia	Ibid., p. 489.	
	1329	£100	Lucca	Ibid., AD 1327-30, p. 566.	
	1334	£48	Lucca and Florence	Ibid., AD 1333-37, p. 330.	
	1340	£80	Lucca	Ibid., AD 1339-41, p. 494.	
	1341	£67	Lucca	Ibid., AD 1341-43, p. 278.	
Woburn	1294		Lucca		1

Appendix 11

MARKETS AND FAIRS

'G' indicates a grant and 'C' a confirmation of a grant. Col. A: date of the grant or the first reference to a market or fair. Col. B: the day on which the market was held: Monday (M), Tuesday (Tu), Wednesday (W), Thursday (Th), Friday (F), Saturday (S), Sunday (Su). Col. C: the number of fair days. Col. D: the month(s) in which the fair was held: March (M), April (A), May (Ma), June (Ju), July (Jl), August (Au), September (S), October (O), November (N).

Monastery		A	B	C	D	
Basingwerk	G Glossop	1290	W	3	Ju	*C.Ch.R.*, AD 1257-1300, p. 372.
			M	3	Jl	Ibid.
	G Holywell	1292	F	3		Ibid., p. 423; vigil, feast and morrow of Holy Trinity.
	G Charlesworth	1328	W	3	Jl	Ibid., AD 1327-41, p. 68.
Beaulieu	G Faringdon	1218	M			*Rot. Cl.*, 1: 354; *C.Ch.R.*, AD 1300-26, p. 203.
		1313	Tu			*V.C.H. (Berkshire)*, 4: 492.
	G Faringdon	1222		2	O	*Rot. Cl.*, 1: 486; *C.Ch.R.*, AD 1226-57 (1227), p. 60; *Chart. Bl.*, p. 9 (1227).
	Faringdon	1260		1[1]		
	Beaulieu	1468	Th			*C.Ch.R.*, AD 1427-1516, p. 234.
Biddlesden	G Biddlesden	1315				*Cal. Rot. Ch.*, p. 147: market and fair.
Bindon	G Wool	1280	M	3	Ma	*C.Ch.R.*, AD 1257-1300, 236.
Boxley	C Hoo	1189-90				*Mon. Angl.*, 5: 461: a market.
Buckfast	Cheristow	1275-76	F			*Rot. Hund.*, 1: 91: "nesciunt quo warranto."
	G Buckfastleigh	1353	Tu			*C.Ch.R.*, AD 1341-1417, p. 130.
	G Brent	1353		3	S	Ibid.
	G Kingsbridge	1460	S	3	Jl	Ibid., AD 1427-1516, p. 136.
	G Buckfastleigh	1460		3	Au	Ibid.
Buckland	G Buckland	1318	Tu	3	Ju	Ibid., AD 1300-26, p. 373.
	G Cullompton	1318	Tu	3	A	Ibid.
Cleeve	G Cleeve	1466	W	4	Jl	*C.P.R.*, AD 1461-7, p. 527.
	G Cleeve	1466		4	S	Ibid.

[1] On Trinity Sunday, possibly by prescription (*V.C.H. (Berkshire)*, 4: 493). *C. Ch. R.*, AD 1427-1516 (1468), p. 234, mentions a fair at Faringdon on the Monday, Tuesday and Wednesday after Whitsunday.

MONASTERY		A	B	C	D	
Coggeshall	G Coggeshall	1250		8	Jl-Au	*C.Ch.R.*, AD 1300-26, p. 480.
	G Coggeshall	1256	S			Ibid.
Combe	G Wolvey	1326	W	3	A	Ibid., p. 484.
Combermere	G Drayton	1245	W	3	S	Ibid., AD 1226-57, p. 289.
Dieulacres	Leek	1293	W	10	Jl	*Chart. D.*, p. 310; *Plac. Quo Warr.*, p. 714; *Abb. Plac.*, p. 231.
Dunkeswell	G Buckland Brewer	1290	W	3	Au	*C.Ch.R.*, AD 1257-1300, p. 371.
	G Broadhembury	1290	W	3	Au	Ibid.
Forde	G Charmouth	{1278	M	3	Jl-Au	Ibid., p. 213.
			W	3	S	Ibid.
	G Thorncombe	1312	W	6		Ibid., AD 1300-26, p. 204: fair on the Tuesday of Easter week and the five following days.
	Ford	1410	Su			*C.P.R.*, AD 1408-13, p. 222.
Furness	G Dalton	1239		3	O-N	*C.Ch.R.*, AD 1226-57, p. 243.
	G Dalton	{1246		3	O	Ibid., p. 295.
		{1292		3	O	*Plac. Quo Warr.*, p. 370; *Coucher F.*, 1: 135: market *ab antiquo*.
Holm Cultram	G *Wavermouth*	1300	Th	17	Ju-Jl	*C.Ch.R.*, AD 1257-1300, 488.
	G *Skinburness*	1301	Th	17	Ju-Jl	Ibid., AD 1300-26, p. 2.
	Kirkby Johannis	1305	Th	17	Ju-Jl	Ibid., p. 55, *Rot. Parl.*, 1: 161.
Jervaulx	G E. Witton	1307	M	8		*C.Ch.R.*, AD 1300-26, p. 81.
	G E. Witton	1307		2	N	Ibid.[2]
Meaux	G *Wyk*	1279	Th	15		Ibid., AD 1257-1300, p. 214: fair on the vigil, feast and morrow of Holy Trinity and the twelve following days.
	Pocklington	1300	S	3	O-N	*C.P.R.*, AD 1292-1301, p. 550; *York. Arch. Soc. Rec. Ser.*, 81 (1931): 27.
Netley	G Hound	1251	M			*C.Ch.R.*, AD 1226-57, p. 354.
	G Wellow	1251		2	Jl	Ibid.
	G Wellow	1251	W			Ibid., p. 371.
Newenham	G Pelynt	1356		3	Ju	Ibid., AD 1341-1417, p. 153.
Revesby	C Mareham	1384	Tu	3	O	*C.P.R.*, AD 1381-5, p. 383; *cf. C.Ch.R.*, AD 1300-26, p. 25.
Robertsbridge	G Robertsbridge	1225	W	3	Au	*Rot. Cl.*, 2: 14.
Rufford	C Rotherham	1285	M	8	N	*C.Ch.R.*, AD 1257-1300, p. 291; *Plac. Quo Warr.*, p. 206 (1293); *C.Ch.R.*, AD 1300-26 (1316), p. 291.
Sallay	G Gisburn	1260	M	3	S	Ibid., AD 1257-1300, p. 32.
	G Bolton	1354	W	3	Ju	Ibid., AD 1341-1417, p. 140.
Stoneleigh	G Stoneleigh	1284	Th	8	Ju	*Mon. Angl.*, 5: 444; *Ledger S.*, pp. 56-57.

[2] According to this, the fairs at East Witton were held (a) on the vigil and feast of the Assumption and the six following days, and (b) on the feast and vigil of St. Martin in winter. But *C.Ch.R.*, AD 1341-1417 (1400), p. 388 gives (a) the vigil and day of the Assumption, and (b) the seven days preceding the feast and the feast of St. Martin in winter.

Monastery		A	B	C	D	
Stratford						
Langthorn	G Burstead	1253	Tu	3	Jl	*C.Ch.R.*, AD 1226-57, p. 433.
	G Billericay	1476	W	3	Jl	*C.P.R.*, AD 1476-85, p. 17.
	G Billericay	1476		3	Au	Ibid.
Swineshead	G Swineshead	1298		5		*C.Ch.R.*, AD 1257-1300, p. 471: on the vigil, feast and morrow of Holy Trinity and the two following days.
Vale Royal	G Over	1280	W	3	S	Ibid., p. 237.
	G Kirkham	1287	Th	5	Ju	*C.P.R.*, AD 1399-1401, p. 508.
Waverley	G Wanborough	1512		3	Au	*C.Ch.R.*, AD 1427-1516, p. 276.
Whalley	G Hardhorn	1348	Th	3	O	Ibid., AD 1341-1427, p. 96.
Woburn	G Woburn	1245	F	3	S	Ibid., AD 1226-57, p. 282.
	G Woburn	1530		2	M	*Letters and papers: Henry VIII*, 4 (3): 6187.
	G Woburn	1530		2	Jl	Ibid.

BIBLIOGRAPHY

[Adam of Eynsham.] *Magna Vita S. Hugonis Episcopi Lincolniensis*. Ed. James F. Dimock. Rolls Series, 37. London, 1864.

Arbois de Jubainville, [Marie] Henry d'. *Etudes sur l'état intérieur des abbayes cisterciennes, et principalement de Clairvaux au XIIe et au XIIIe siècle*. Paris, 1858.

Arnold, Thomas. See Simeon of Durham.

Astle, Thomas, S. Ayscough, John Caley, eds. *Taxatio ecclesiastica Angliae et Walliae auctoritate P. Nicholae IV circa AD 1291*. London: Record Commission, 1802.

Atkinson, John C., ed. *Cartularium abbathie de Rievalle Ordinis cisterciensis*. Surtees Society Publications, 83. Durham, 1889.

——, and John Brownbill, eds. *The Coucher Book of Furness Abbey*. 6 vols. Remains ..., n.s., 9, 11, 14, 74, 76, 78. Manchester: Chetham Society, 1886-1919.

Aubert, Marcel. "Existe-t-il une architecture cistercienne?" *Cahiers de civilisation médiévale X^e-XIIe siècles*, 1 (1958): 153-158.

——. "La 'grange d'eau' d'Hautecombe en Savoie." *Bulletin monumental*, 112 (1954): 89-94.

Baildon, William P. *Notes on the Religious and Secular Houses of Yorkshire*. 2 vols. Yorkshire Archaeological Society, Record Series, 17, 81. London, 1895-1931.

Bain, Joseph. See Great Britain. Public Record Office.

[Balducci Pegolotti, Francesco.] *La Practica della Mercatura*. Ed. Allan Evans. Cambridge, Mass.: Mediaeval Academy of America, 1935.

Ballard, Adolphus. *British Borough Charters 1042-1216*. Cambridge: University Press, 1918.

Barley, M. W. "Cistercian land clearances in Nottinghamshire: three deserted villages and their moated successor." *Nottingham Mediaeval Studies*, 1 (1957): 75-89.

——. "Lost Villages in Nottinghamshire". *The Listener*, 5 May 1955, pp. 795-96.

Barnes, Frederic R. "The taxation of wool, 1327-1348." In *Finance and Trade under Edward III*, ed. George Unwin, pp. 137-177. Manchester: Manchester University Press, 1918.

Bell, Walter G. *Fleet Street during Seven Centuries*. London: Pitman, 1912.

Beresford, Maurice W. "The deserted villages of Warwickshire." *Trans. Birm. Arch. Soc.*, 66 (1945-46 [printed, 1950]): 49-106.

——. *The Lost Villages of England*. London: Lutterworth Press, 1954.

——. "The lost villages of Yorkshire". *Yorks. Arch. Jour.*, 37 (1951): 474-491; 38 (1952-54): 44-70, 215-240, 280-309.

Berger, Elie, ed. *Recueil des actes de Henri II*. Revised ed. 3 vols. Paris, 1916-1927.

Bernard, John H. and Constance M. Butler, eds. "The charters of the Cistercian abbey of Duiske." *Royal Irish Academy, Proceedings*, 35, sect. C, no. 1 (Dublin 1918): 1-188.

Bickley, Francis B., ed. *The Little Red Book of Bristol*. 2 vols. Bristol, 1900.

Bilson, John N. "Wyke-upon-Hull in 1293." *Trans. East Riding Ant. Soc.*, 26 (1926-28): 37-105.

Bishop, Terence A. M. "Assarting and the growth of the open fields." *Eco. Hist. Rev.*, 6 (1935-36): 13-29.

——. "A Cistercian customs exemption." *Lincs. Archit. and Archaeol. Soc., Reports and Papers*, n.s., 4 (1951-52): 102-108.

——. "Monastic granges in Yorkshire." *Eng. Hist. Rev.*, 51 (1936), 193-214.

——. "The Norman settlement of Yorkshire." In *Studies in Medieval History Presented to F. M. Powicke*, ed. Richard W. Hunt, et al., pp. 1-14. Oxford: Oxford University Press, 1948.

Blaauw, William H. "Letters of Ralph de Nevill, Bishop of Chichester." *Sussex Arch. Coll.*, 3 (1850): 35-76.

Boissonade, Prosper. *Life and Work in Mediaeval Europe*. London: K. Paul, Trench, Trubner, 1927.

Bond, Edward A. See Thomas de Burton.

Boyle, John R. *The Lost Towns of the Humber*. Hull, 1889.

Brewer, J. S. See Giraldus Cambrensis.

Britton, Charles E. *A Meteorological Chronology to AD 1450*. London: HMSO, 1937.

Brown, Elisabeth A. R. "The Cistercians in the Latin Empire of Constantinople and Greece, 1204-1276." *Traditio*, 14 (1958): 63-120.

Brown, William, ed. *Yorkshire Lay Subsidy ... Collected 30 Edward I (1301)*. Yorkshire Archaeological Society, Record Series, 21. Leeds, 1897.

——, and A. Hamilton Thompson, eds. *The Register of William Greenfield, Lord Archbishop of York, 1306-1315*. 5 vols. Surtees Society Publications, 145, 149, 151, 152, 153. London, 1931-1940.

Brownbill, John, ed. *The Ledger-Book of Vale Royal Abbey*. Record Society for Lancashire and Cheshire, publs., 68. [London and Manchester], 1914.

Bucher, François. "Cistercian architectural purism." *Comparative Studies in Society and History*, 3 (1960-61): 89-105.

Buffault, P. "Les forêts de l'Europe pendant le moyen âge." *Revue des eaux et forêts*, 74 (1937): 140-150.

Buhot, Jacquelin. "L'abbaye normande de Savigny, chef de l'ordre et fille de Cîteaux." *Le Moyen Age*, 3e sér., 7/vol. 46 (1936): 1-19, 104-121, 178-190, 249-272.

Burton, John, ed. *Monasticon Eboracense*. York, 1758.

Butler, H. E. See Jocelin de Brakelond.

Caley, J., ed. *Calendarium rotulorum chartarum et inquisitionum ad quod damnum.* London: [Record Commission], 1803.

Canivez, Joseph Marie. See Cistercian Order.

Carsten, F. L. "The Slavs in north-eastern Germany." *Eco. Hist. Rev.*, 11 (1941): 61-76.

Carus-Wilson, Eleanora M. "An industrial revolution of the thirteenth century." *Eco. Hist. Rev.*, 11 (1941): 39-60.

——. "The overseas trade of Bristol." In *Studies in English Trade in the Fifteenth Century*, ed. Eileen Power and Michael M. Postan, pp. 183-246. London: Routledge, 1933.

——, and Olive Coleman. *England's Export Trade, 1275-1547.* Oxford: Clarendon Press, 1963.

Carville, Geraldine. "The Cistercian settlement of Ireland (1142-1541)." *Studia Monastica*, 15 (1973): 23-41.

Cate, James L. "The church and market reform in England during the reign of Henry III." In *Mediaeval and Historiographical Essays in Honor of James Westfall Thompson*, ed. James L. Cate and Eugene N. Anderson, pp. 27-65. Chicago: University of Chicago Press, 1938.

Cateland, M. "La forêt domaniale de Cîteaux." *Revue du bois*, 10, no. 2 (1955): 10-12.

Champier, L. "Cîteaux, ultime étape dans l'aménagement agraire de l'Occident." In *Mélanges Saint Bernard. 24e Congrès de l'Association Bourguignonne des Sociétés Savantes*, pp. 254-261. Dijon, 1953.

Chapman, Alice B. Wallis, ed. *The Black Book of Southampton.* 3 vols. Southampton Record Society, Publications, 13, 14, 17. Southampton, 1912-15.

Chew, Helena M. *The English Ecclesiastical Tenants-in-Chief and Knight Service.* London: Oxford University Press, 1932.

Chibnall, Marjorie. See Ordericus Vitalis.

[Cistercian Order.] *Statuta capitulorum generalium Ordinis cisterciensis ab anno 1116 ad annum 1786.* Ed. Joseph Marie Canivez. 8 vols. Bibliothèque de la Revue d'histoire ecclésiastique. Louvain: Bureaux de la Revue, 1933-1941.

Clapham, Alfred. W. *English Romanesque Architecture After the Conquest.* Oxford: Clarendon Press, 1934.

Clark, George T., ed. *Cartae et alia munimenta quae ad dominium de Glamorgan pertinent.* 4 vols. Dowlais, 1885-93.

Clay, Charles T. "Bradley, a grange of Fountains." *Yorks. Arch. Jour.*, 29 (1929): 97-106.

Cole, Henry, ed. *Documents Illustrative of English History in the Thirteenth and Fourteenth Centuries Selected from the Records ... of the Exchequer.* London: Record Commission, 1844.

Constable, Giles. *Monastic Tithes from their Origins to the Twelfth Century.* Cambridge: University Press, 1964.

Cooke, Alice M. "A study in twelfth century religious revival and reform." *Bulletin of the John Rylands Library*, 9 (1925): 139-176.

Cooper, George M. "Notices of the Abbey of Robertsbridge." *Sussex Arch. Coll.*, 8 (1856): 141-175.

Cottineau, L. H. *Répertoire topo-bibliographique des abbayes et prieurés*. 2 vols. Mâcon, 1935-39.

Coulton, George G. *Five Centuries of Religion*. 4 vols. Cambridge: University Press, 1927-1950.

——. *The Mediaeval Village*. Cambridge: University Press, 1925.

Cowley, F. G. "The Cistercian economy in Glamorgan, 1130-1349." *Morgannwg*, 11 (1967): 5-26.

Crawley-Boevey, Arthur W., ed. *The Cartulary and Historical Notes of the Cistercian Abbey of Flaxley, Otherwise Called Dene Abbey*. Exeter, 1887.

Crossley, Frederick H. *Timber Building in England, from Early Times to the End of the Seventeenth Century*. London: Batsford, 1951.

Davies, James C. "An assembly of wool merchants in 1332." *Eng. Hist. Rev*, 31 (1916): 596-606.

[Davis, Henry W. C.] *Regesta Regum Anglo-Normanorum*, 2: *Regesta Henrici Prima, 1100-1135*. Ed. by Charles Johnson and Henry A. Cronne. Oxford: Clarendon Press, 1956.

Davis, Ralph H. C., ed. *The Kalendar of Abbot Samson of Bury St. Edmunds, and Related Documents*. Camden Society Publications, 3rd ser., 84. London: Royal Historical Society, 1954.

Deffontaines, Pierre. *L'homme et la forêt*. Paris, 1933.

d'Elboux, Raymond H., ed. *Surveys of the Manors of Robertsbridge, Sussex* ... Sussex Record Society, Publications, 47. Lewes, 1944.

Delisle, Léopold. "On the origin of windmills in Normandy and England." *Jour. Brit. Arch. Assoc.*, 6 (1851): 403-406.

Denholm-Young, Noël "The merchants of Cahors." *Medievalia et Humanistica*, 4 (1946): 37-44.

——. *Seignorial Administration in England*. London, 1937.

Denney, Anthony H., ed. *The Sibton Abbey Estates: Select Documents. 1325-1509*. Suffolk Record Society, publs., 2. Ipswich, 1960.

Desmond, L. A. "The statute *De Viris Religiosis* and the English monks of the Cistercian affiliation." *Cîteaux: Commentarii Cistercienses*, 25 (1974): 137-55.

Dimier, Anselme. "Cîteaux et les emplacements malsains." *Cîteaux in de Nederlanden*, 6 (1955): 89-97.

——. "Grange." *Dictionnaire de droit canonique*. Paris, 1953. 5: col. 987-993.

Dimock, James F. See Adam of Eynsham.

Donkin, R. A. "Cattle on the estates of medieval Cistercian monasteries in England and Wales." *Eco.Hist.Rev.*, ser. 2, 15 (1962-63): 31-53.

——. "Changes in the early Middle Ages." In *A New Historical Geography of England*, ed. Henry Clifford Darby, pp. 75-135. Cambridge: University Press, 1973.

——. *A Check-List of Printed Works Relating to the Cistercian Order* ... Documentation Cistercienne, 2. Rochefort, Belgium: Abbaye N.D. de S. Remy, 1969.

——. "The Cistercian grange in England in the twelfth and thirteenth centuries." *Studia Monastica*, 6 (1964): 95-144.

——. "The Cistercian settlement and the English royal forests." *Citeaux: Commentarii Cistercienses*, 11 (1960): 39-55, 117-132.

——, "The English Cistercians and assarting, c. 1128-1350." *Analecta Sacri Ordinis Cisterciensis*, 20 (1964): 49-75.

——. "The growth and distribution of the Cistercian order in medieval Europe." *Studia Monastica*, 9 (1967): 275-286.

——. "The urban property of the Cistercians in medieval England." *Analecta Sacri Ordinis Cisterciensis*, 15 (1959): 104-131.

Donnelly, James S. "Changes in the grange economy of English and Welsh Cistercian abbeys, 1300-1540." *Traditio*, 10 (1954): 399-458.

——. *Decline of the Medieval Cistercian Laybrotherhood.* Fordham University Studies, History Series, 3. New York: Fordham University Press, 1949.

Dubled, Henri. "Aspects de l'économie Cistercienne en Alsace au XIIe siècle." *Revue d'histoire ecclésiastique*, 54 (1959): 765-782.

Dugdale, William. *The Antiquities of Warwickshire Illustrated.* 2nd ed. 2 vols. London, 1730.

——. *Monasticon Anglicanum.* New enlarged ed. by John Caley, et al. 6 vols. in 8. London 1830.

Duvivier, Charles. "Hospites: défrichements en Europe et spécialement dans nos contrées aux XIe, XIIe et XIIIe siècles." *Rev. d'hist. et d'archéologie*, 1 (1859): 74-90, 131-175.

Easson, David E., ed. *Charters of the Abbey of Coupar Angus.* 2 vols. Scottish Historical Society, publs., 3rd ser., 40, 41. Edinburgh, 1947.

Ellis, Henry, ed. "Register and chronicle of the abbey of Aberconway." Camden Miscellany, vol. 1, no. 1: 1-23. Camden Society Publications, 39. London, 1847.

——. See Johannes de Oxenedes.

Espinas, George. *La draperie dans la Flandre française au moyen-âge.* 2 vols. Paris, 1923.

——. *La vie urbaine de Douai au moyen âge.* 4 vols. Paris, 1913.

Evans, Allan. See Balducci Pegolotti, Francesco.

Farrer, Wm., ed. *The Lancashire Pipe Rolls.* Liverpool, 1902.

——, et al., eds. *Early Yorkshire Charters.* Yorkshire Archaeological Society, Record Series, Extra Series, 1-(1914-).

Finberg, H.P.R. "An early reference to the Welsh cattle trade." *Ag. Hist. Rev.*, 2 (1954): 12-14.

Flach, Jacques, "Les villages créés dans les forêts et sur les terres désertes." In his *Les origines de l'ancienne France* (Paris, 1893). 2: 139-157.

Fletcher, Joseph S. *The Cistercians in Yorkshire.* London: SPCK, 1919.

Flower, Cyril T., ed. *Public Works in Mediaeval Law.* 2 vols. Selden Society Publications, 32, 40. London, 1915-1923.

Focillon, Henri. *The Art of the West in the Middle Ages.* 2 vols. London: Phaidon Press, 1963.

Forbes, R. J. "Power." In *A History of Technology*, ed. Charles Singer, et al., 2: 589-622. Oxford: Clarendon Press, 1956.

Fossier, Robert. "Les granges de Clairvaux et la règle cistercienne." *Citeaux in de Nederlanden*, 6 (1955): 259-266.

Foster, Charles W. and Thomas Langley, eds. *The Lincolnshire Domesday and the Lindsey Survey.* Publications of the Lincoln Record Society, 19. [Horncastle], 1924.

Fournier, Gabriel. "La création de la grange de Gergovie par les Prémontrés de Saint-André." *Le Moyen Age*, 4ᵉ sér., 5/vol. 56 (1950): 307-355.

Fowler, G. Herbert. *The Cartulary of the Abbey of Old Wardon.* Bedfordshire Hist. Rec. Soc. Publications, 13. Aspley Guise, 1930.

Fowler, John T., ed. *Chartularium abbathie de Novo Monasterio Ordinis cisterciensis.* Surtees Society Publications, 66. Durham, 1878.

Franklin, Thomas B. *A History of Scottish Farming.* London: Nelson, 1952.

Frost, Charles. *Notices Relative to the Early History of the Town and Port of Hull.* London, 1827.

Gaffney, Victor. "Summer shealings." *Scottish Historical Review*, 38 (1959): 20-35.

Gilchrist, John T. *The Church and Economic Activity in the Middle Ages.* London: Macmillan, 1969.

[Giraldus Cambrensis]. *Opera.* Ed. J. S. Brewer. 8 vols. Rolls Series, 21. London, 1861-1891.

Goblet, Felix. *Histoire des bois et forêts de Belgique.* 3 vols. Paris, 1927.

Godber, Joyce, ed. *The Cartulary of Newnham Priory.* Beds. Hist. Rec. Soc. Publications, 43. Bedford, 1963.

Gowland, Thomas S. "The honour of Kirkby Malzeard and the chase of Nidderdale." *Yorks. Arch. Jour.*, 33 (1938): 349-396.

Graham, Rose. *English Ecclesiastical Studies.* London: Macmillan, 1929.

——. "Excavations on the site of Sempringham Priory." *Jour. Brit. Arch. Assoc.*, 3rd ser., 5 (1940): 73-101.

Grainger, Francis, and W. D. Collingwood, eds. *The Register and Records of Holm Cultram.* Cumberland and Westmorland Antiquarian and Archaeological Society, Record Series, 7. Kendal, 1929.

Grandmottet, Odile. "Aspects du temporal de l'abbaye d'Auberive des origines à la fin du XIIIᵉ siècle." *Les Cahiers Haute-Marnais*, 52 (1958): 1-13.

Gras, Norman S. B. *The Evolution of the English Corn Market from the Twelfth to the Eighteenth Century.* Cambridge, Mass.: Harvard University Press, 1915.

Graves, Coburn V. "The Economic activities of the Cistercians in medieval England (1128-1307)." *Analecta Sacri Ordinis Cisterciensis*, 13 (1957): 3-60.

Gray, Thomas. "Notes on the granges of Margam Abbey." *Jour. Brit. Arch. Assoc.*, 2nd ser., 9 (1903): 161-181; 11 (1905): 11-29.

[Great Britain.] Ministry of Agriculture. *Markets and Fairs in England and Wales.* 5 vols. Economic Series, 13, 14, 19, 23, 26. London: HMSO, 1927-30.

——. [Parliament.] *Reports from Commissioners, Inspectors, and Others*: 1875. Vol. 27: *The Thirty-Sixth Annual Report of the Deputy Keeper of the Public Records.* London, 1875.

——. ——. *Rotuli parliamentorum.* 6 vols. London: Record Commission, 1767-77.

——. [Public Record Office.] *Calendar of the Close Rolls ... Preserved in the Public Record Office.* London, 1902-.

——. ——. *Calendar of Documents Relating to Scotland Preserved in Her Majesty's Public Record Office, London.* Ed. by Joseph Bain. 4 vols. Edinburgh, 1881-88.

——. ——. *Calendar of Entries in the Papal Registers Relating to Great Britain and Ireland. Papal Letters.* Public Record Office. London: HMSO, 1893-.

——. ——. *Calendar of Inquisitions Miscellaneous (Chancery) Preserved in the Public Record Office.* London, 1916-.

——.——. *Calendar of Inquisitions Post Mortem and Other Analogous Documents Preserved in the Public Record Office.* 14 vols. London, 1904-54.

——. ——. *Calendar of the Charter Rolls Preserved in the Public Record Office.* 6 vols. London, 1903-27.

——. ——. *Calendar of the Fine Rolls Preserved in the Public Record Office.* London, 1911-.

——. ——. *Calendar of the Liberate Rolls Preserved in the Public Record Office.* London, 1916-.

——. ——. *Calendar of the Patent Rolls Preserved in the Public Record Office.* London, 1891-.

——. ——. *Calendar of the Various Chancery Rolls ... Preserved in the Public Record Office.* AD *1277-1326.* London, 1912.

——. ——. *Curia Regis Rolls ... Preserved in the Public Record Office.* London, 1922-.

——. ——. *A Descriptive Catalogue of Ancient Deeds in the Public Record Office.* 6 vols. London, 1890-1915.

——. ——. *Register of Edward, the Black Prince Preserved in the Public Record Office.* 4 vols. London, 1930-33.

——. Royal Commission on Market Rights and Tolls. *Reports and Minutes of Evidence.* 16 vols. London, 1888-91.

——. Royal Commission on the Ancient and Historical Monuments and Constructions in Wales and Monmouthshire. *An Inventory of the Ancient Monuments in Wales and Monmouthshire.* 3. *County of Radnor* (London, 1913); 4. *County of Denbigh* (London, 1914).

Griesser, Bruno. "Walther Map und die Cistercienser." *Cistercienser-Chronik*, 36 (1924): 137-141, 164-167.

Guignard, Philippe. *Les monuments primitifs de la règle cistercienne publiés d'après les manuscrits de l'abbaye de Cîteaux*. Analecta Divionensia, 10. Dijon, 1878.

[Guiot de Provins.] *Les œuvres de Guiot de Provins*. Ed. John Orr. Manchester: University Press, 1915.

Hall, Hubert, ed. *Select Cases Concerning the Law Merchant*. Vols. 2, 3. Selden Society Publications, 46, 49. London, 1930-1932.

Hall, James, ed. *The Book of the Abbot of Combermere*. Record Society for ... Lancashire and Cheshire Publications, 31 [London and Manchester], 1896.

Hardy, Thomas D., ed. *Rotuli chartarum in Turri Londinensi asservati*. London: Record Commission, 1837.

——. *Rotuli de oblatis et finibus in Turri Londinensi asservati*. London: Record Commission, 1835.

——. *Rotuli litterarum clausarum in Turri Londinensi asservati*. 2 vols. London: Record Commission, 1833-44.

——. *Rotuli litterarum patentium in Turri Londinensi asservati*. London: Record Commission, 1835.

Heins, A. and Victor Fris. "Les granges monumentales des anciennes abbayes des Dunes et de Ter Doest dans la Flandre maritime." *Bulletijn der maatschapij van Geschied. en Oudheidkunde te Gent*, 13 (1905): 65-109.

Higounet, Ch. "Cisterciens et Bastides." *Le Moyen Age*, 4e sér., 5/vol. 56 (1950): 69-84.

——. "Les types d'exploitation cisterciennes et prémontrées du XIIIe siècle et leur rôle dans la formation de l'habitat et des paysages ruraux." *Géographie et histoire agraires. Annales de l'Est*, mémoire no. 21 (Nancy, 1959): 260-271.

Hill, James W. F. *Mediaeval Lincoln*. Cambridge: University Press, 1948.

Hilton, Rodney H., ed. *The Stoneleigh Ledger Book*. Dugdale Society Publications, 24. Oxford, 1960.

Hockey, S. F., ed. *The Account Book of Beaulieu Abbey*. Camden Fourth Series (Royal Historical Society), 16. London, 1975.

——. *The Beaulieu Cartulary*. Southampton Record Series, 17. Southampton, 1974.

——. *Quarr Abbey and its Lands, 1132-1631*. Leicester: Leicester University Press, 1970.

Hofmann, Konrad. "Grangien." *Lexikon für Theologie und Kirche* (Freiburg, 1932), 4: col. 646-647.

Hofmeister, Philipp. "Grangien." *Die Religion in Geschichte und Gegenwart: Handwörterbuch für Theologie und Religionswissenschaft*. 3rd ed. (Tübingen: J. C. B. Mohr, 1958), 2: col. 1825.

Honeybourne, Marjorie B. "The abbey of St. Mary Graces, Tower Hill." *Trans. London and Middlesex Arch. Soc.*, n.s., 11 (1952): 16-26.

——. *The Extent and Value of the Property in London and Southwark Occupied by the Religious Houses ... Before the Dissolution of the Monasteries*. M.A. thesis, University of London, 1929-30.

——. "The extent and value ... ." [Summary of thesis.] *Bull. Inst. of Hist. Research*, 9 (1931-32): 52-57.

Hoppe, Willy. *Kloster Zinna*. Leipzig, 1914.

Horn, Walter and Ernest Born. *The Barns of the Abbey of Beaulieu at its Granges of Great Coxwell and Beaulieu-St Leonards*. Berkeley and Los Angeles: University of California Press, 1965.

Hoskins, William G. *Essays in Leicestershire History*. Liverpool: Liverpool University Press, 1950.

——. *The Making of the English Landscape*. London: Hodder and Stoughton, 1955.

[Hoveden, Roger of.] *Chronica magistri Rogeri de Hovedene*. Ed. William Stubbs. 4 vols. Rolls Series, 51. London, 1868-71.

Hudson, William and John C. Tingey, eds. *Records of the City of Norwich*. 2 vols. Norwich, 1906-10.

Hugo, Thomas. "On the charters and other archives of Cleeve abbey." *Proc. Somerset Arch. Nat. Hist. Soc.*, 6 (1856): 17-74.

Hulbert, N. F. "A survey of the Somerset fairs." *Proc. Somerset Arch. Nat. Hist. Soc.*, 82 (1936): 83-159.

Hulton, William A., ed. *The Coucher Book, or Chartulary, of Whalley Abbey*. 4 vols. Remains ..., 10, 11, 16, 20. Manchester: Chetham Society, 1847-49.

Hunter, Joseph, ed. *Fines, sive pedes finium, sive finales concordiae in curia domini regis ... AD 1195-1214*. 2 vols. London: Record Commission, 1835-44.

Illingworth, William, ed. *Placita de quo warranto temporibus Edw. I, II et III*. London: Record Commission, 1818.

——. *Placitorum in domo capitulari Westmonasteriensi asservatorum abbreviatio. Temporibus regum Ric. I, Johann., Henr. III, Edw. I, Edw. II*. London: Record Commission, 1811.

——. *Rotuli hundredorum* ... . 2 vols. London: Record Commission, 1812-18.

Inama-Sternegg, Karl Theodor von. "Sallandstudien." In *Festgabe für Georg Hanssen zum 31 Mai 1889*, pp. 73-118. Tübingen, 1889.

Innes, Cosmo, ed. *Liber Sancte Marie de Melros*. 2 vols. Edinburgh: Bannatyne Club, 1837.

——. *Registrum S. Marie de Neubotle*. Bannatyne Club publs., 89. Edinburgh, 1849.

Introduction to the Study of the Pipe Rolls. P.R.S. Publ. 3. London, 1884.

Janauschek, Léopold. *Originum Cisterciensium*. Vienna, 1877.

Jenkinson, Hilary. "William Cade, a financier of the twelfth century." *Eng. Hist. Rev.*, 28 (1913): 209-27.

[Jocelin de Brakelond.] *The Chronicle of Jocelin of Brakelond*. Ed. H. E. Butler. London: Nelson, 1949.

[Johannes de Oxenedes.] *Chronica Johannis de Oxenedes*. Ed. Henry Ellis. Rolls Series, 13. London, 1859.

Johnson, Charles. See Davis, Henry W. C.

Jones, Morris C. "The Abbey of Ystrad Marchell (Strata Marcella)." *Collections Historical and Archaeological Relating to Montgomeryshire*, 4 (1871): 1-34, 293-322; 5 (1872): 109-148; 6 (1873): 347-386.

Kershaw, Ian. "The great famine and agrarian crisis in England, 1315-1322." *Past and Present*, no 59 (1973): 3-50.

Knowles, David. *The Monastic Order in England*. 2nd ed. Cambridge: University Press, 1963.

——, and R. Neville Hadcock. *Medieval Religious Houses, England and Wales*. 2nd ed. London: Longmans, 1971.

Koebner, Richard. "The settlement and colonization of Europe." In *The Cambridge Economic History of Europe*, 2nd ed., ed. by Michael M. Postan, 1: 1-91. Cambridge: University Press, 1966.

Krasoń, Jósef. *Uposażenie Klasztoru Cystersów w Obrze w Wiekach Srednich*. Posnań, 1950.

Krausen, Edgar. "Les particularités de l'Ordre cistercien en Bavière et en Franconie dans l'organisation agricole et l'art de ces pays." In *Mélanges Saint Bernard. 24ᵉ Congrès de l'Association Bourguignonne des Sociétés Savantes*, pp. 297-298. Dijon, 1953.

Lancaster, William T., ed. *Abstracts of the Charters and Other Documents Contained in the Chartulary of the Cistercian Abbey of Fountains*. 2 vols. Leeds, 1915.

——. *Abstracts of the Charters and Other Documents Contained in the Chartulary of the Priory of Bridlington*. Leeds, 1912.

——, and William P. Baildon, eds. *The Coucher Book of the Cistercian Abbey of Kirkstall*. Publications of the Thoresby Society, 8. Leeds, 1904.

Landon, Lionel, ed. *The Cartae antiquae*. 1: *Rolls 1-10*. P.R.S. Publications, 55; n.s., 17. London, 1938.

Leadam, I. S. "The Inquisition of 1517: inclosures and evictions." *Trans. Roy. Hist. Soc.*, 2nd ser., 6 (1892): 167-314; 7 (1893): 127-292.

Lees, Beatrice A., ed. *Records of the Templars in England in the twelfth century; the inquest of 1185*. Records of the Social and Economic History of England and Wales, 9. London: British Academy, 1935.

[Leland, John.] *The Itinerary of John Leland*. Ed. Lucy T. Smith. Vol. 5, pts. ix-xi. London, 1910.

Lennard, Reginald V. "The composition of demesne plough-teams in twelfth-century England." *Eng. Hist. Rev.*, 75 (1960): 193-207.

——. "Early fulling mills: additional examples." *Eco. Hist. Rev.*, 2nd ser., 3 (1950-51): 342-343.

——. *Rural England, 1086-1135*. Oxford: Clarendon Press, 1959.

Lewis, D. "Notes on the charters of Neath Abbey." *Archaeologia Cambrensis*, 5th ser., 4 (1887): 86-115.

Lewis, Edward A. "The development of industry and commerce in Wales during the middle ages." *Trans. Roy. Hist. Soc.*, 2nd ser., 17 (1903): 121-173.

——. *Mediaeval Boroughs of Snowdonia*. London, 1912.

Lindley, E. S. "Kingswood Abbey, its lands and mills." *Trans. Bristol and Glouc. Arch. Soc.*, 73 (1955): 115-191.

——, ed. "A Kingswood abbey rental." *Trans. Bristol and Glouc. Arch. Soc.*, 22 (1899): 179-256.

Lloyd, T. H. "The medieval wool-sack: a study in economic history." *Textile History*, 3 (1972): 92-99.

——. *The Movement of Wool Prices in Medieval England.* Economic History Review, Supplement, 6. Cambridge: University Press, 1973.

Lopez, Robert S. "The trade of medieval Europe: the south." In *The Cambridge Economic History of Europe.*, ed. by Michael M. Postan and E. E. Rich, 2: 257-354. Cambridge: University Press, 1952.

Luard, Henry Richards, ed. *Annales Monasterii de Waverleia.* In his *Annales Monastici,* Rolls Series 36, 2: 127-411. London, 1865.

——. See Paris, Matthew.

Lynam, Charles. *The Abbey of St. Mary, Croxden, Staffordshire.* London, 1911.

Lyon, Bryce. "Mediaeval real estate developments and freedom." *Amer. Hist. Rev.*, 63 (1957-1958): 47-61.

Maas, Walter. *Les moines-défricheurs.* Moulins, 1944.

Madox, Thomas. *Formulare Anglicanum.* London, 1702.

——. *History and Antiquities of the Exchequer of the Kings of England.* 2 vols. London, 1769.

Map, Walter. *De nugis curialium.* Trans. Montague R. James, ed. E. Sidney Hartland. Cymmrodorion Record Series, 9. London: Society of Cymmrodorion, 1923.

Map of Monastic Britain. Southampton: Ordnance Survey, 1954.

Martène, Edmond and Ursin Durand. *Thesaurus novus anecdotorum.* 5 vols. Paris, 1717.

Martin, Charles. See Peckham, John.

Martin, E. J. "The Templars in Yorkshire and a list of Templar lands in Yorkshire, 1185-1308." *Yorks. Arch. Jour.*, 29 (1929): 366-385.

Mason, W. A. Parker. "The beginnings of the Cistercian Order." *Trans. Roy. Hist. Soc.*, 2nd ser., 19 (1905): 169-207.

Matthew Paris. See Paris, Matthew.

McCrank, Lawrence J. "The Cistercians of Poblet as landlords: protection, litigation and violence on the medieval Catalan frontier." *Cîteaux: Commentarii Cistercienses*, 26 (1975): 255-283.

McGuire, Brian P. "Property and politics at Esrum Abbey, 1151-1251." *Mediaeval Scandinavia*, 6 (1973): 122-150.

McNulty, Joseph, ed. *The Chartulary of the Cistercian Abbey of St. Mary of Sallay in Craven.* 2 vols. Yorks. Arch. Soc., Record Series, 87, 90, 1933-34.

——. "Sallay Abbey, 1148-1536." *Trans. Lancs. and Chesh. Ant. Soc.*, 54 (1939): 194-204.

Morgan, J. L. *The Economic Administration of Coupar Angus Abbey.* 3 vols. Doctoral thesis, University of Glasgow, 1929.

Muggenthaler, Hans. *Kolonisatorische und wirtschaftliche Tätigkeit eines deutschen Zisterzienserklosters im XII und XIII Jahrhundert.* Munich, 1924.

Mullin, F. A. *A History of the Work of the Cistercians in Yorkshire (1131-1300).* Washington: Catholic University of America, 1932.

Nigellus Wireker. *Speculum stultorum.* In *The Anglo-Latin Satirical Poets and Epigrammatists of the Twelfth Century*, ed. Thomas Wright, vol. 1. Rolls Series, 59. London, 1872.

Notebaart, Jannis C. *Windmühlin.* Den Haag: Mouton, 1973.

[Nottingham, Eng.] *Records of the Borough of Nottingham.* Vols. 1-. London: Quaritch, 1882-.

Oliver, George. *Historic Collections, Relating to the Monasteries in Devon.* Exeter, 1820.

[Ordericus Vitalis.] *The Ecclesiastical History of Orderic Vitalis.* Ed. and trans. Marjorie Chibnall. Vols. 2-. Oxford: Clarendon Press, 1969-.

Orr, John. See Guiot de Provins.

Oschinsky, Dorothea. "Notes on the Lancaster estates in the 13th and 14th centuries." *Trans. Hist. Soc. Lancs. and Ches.*, 100 (1949): 9-32.

Owen, David E., et al. *Kirkstall Abbey Excavations, 1950-1954.* Thoresby Soc. Publs. 43. Leeds, 1955.

Pagnini della Ventura, Giovanni F. *Della decima e di varie altre gravezze imposte dal comune di Firenze ....* 4 vols. Lisbon and Lucca, 1765-66.

Palgrave, Francis, ed. *The Parliamentary Writs and Writs of Military Summons.* 2 vols. London: Record Commission, 1827-34.

[Paris, Matthew.] *Chronica majora.* Ed. Henry R. Luard. Rolls Series, 57. 7 vols. London, 1872-83.

[Peckham, John.] *Registrum Epistolarum Fratris Johannis Peckham.* Ed. Charles Martin. 3 vols. Rolls Series, 77. London, 1882-85.

Pegolotti, Francesco Balducci. See Balducci Pegolotti, Francesco.

Pelham, R. A. "The early wool trade of Warwickshire and the rise of the merchant middle class." *Trans. Birm. Arch. Soc.*, 63 (1944): 41-62.

——. "Medieval foreign trade: eastern ports". In *An Historical Geography of England Before AD 1800*, ed. Henry Clifford Darby, pp. 298-329. Cambridge: University Press, 1936.

Perkins, V. R., ed. "Documents relating to the Cistercian monastery of St. Mary, Kingswood." *Trans. Bristol and Gloucestershire Archaeological Society*, 22 (1899): 179-256.

Pierce, T. Jones. "Strata Florida abbey." *Ceredigion*, 1 (1950): 18-33.

Pike, Luke O. *A Constitutional History of the House of Lords.* London, 1894.

Plaisance, G. "Les caractères originaux de l'exploitation ancienne des forêts." *Rev. de Géog de Lyon*, 28 (1953): 17-26.

——. "Les Cisterciens et la forêt." *Revue du bois*, 10, no. 7/8 (1955): 3-8.

Platt, Colin. *The Monastic Grange in Medieval England: a Reassessment.* London: Macmillan, 1969.

[Playford and John Caley,] eds. *Rotulorum originalium in curia scaccarii abbreviatio.* 2 vols. London: Record Commission, 1805-10.
Pollard, Albert F. *The Evolution of Parliament.* 1st ed. London, 1920.
Poole, Austin L. *From Domesday Book to Magna Carta.* Oxford: Clarendon Press, 1951.
Postan, Michael M. "Glastonbury estates in the twelfth century." *Eco. Hist. Rev.*, 2nd ser., 5 (1952-53): 358-367.
——. "The trade of medieval Europe: the north." In *The Cambridge Economic History of Europe*, ed. by Michael M. Postan and E. E. Rich, 2: 119-256. Cambridge: University Press, 1952.
Potter, Thomas R. *The History and Antiquities of Charnwood Forest.* London, 1842.
Powicke, Frederick Maurice. *The Thirteenth Century, 1216-1307.* 2nd ed. Oxford: Clarendon Press, 1962.
[Public Record Office.] See Great Britain. Public Record Office.
Purvis, John Stanley, ed. *Monastic Chancery Proceedings: Yorkshire.* Yorks. Arch. Assoc., Record Series, 88. Huddersfield, 1934.
Raine, Angelo. *Mediaeval York.* London: J. Murray, 1955.
[Ralph of Coggeshall.] *Chronicon Anglicanum.* Ed. Joseph Stevenson. Rolls Series, 66. London, 1875.
Rees, William. *South Wales and the March, 1284-1415.* London: Oxford University Press, 1924.
Reich, Aloyse M. *The Parliamentary Abbots to 1470.* University of California Publications in History, vol. 7, no. 4. Berkeley and Los Angeles: University of California Press, 1941.
[Robertsbridge Abbey.] *Calendar of Charters and Documents Relating to the Abbey of Robertsbridge ... Preserved at Penhurst among the Muniments of Lord de Lisle and Dudley.* London, 1873.
Roehl, Richard. "Plan and reality in a mediaeval monastic economy: the Cistercians." *Studies in Medieval and Renaissance History*, 10 (1972): 83-113.
Roger de Hoveden. See Hoveden, Roger de.
Rogers, Charles, ed. *Rental Book of the Cistercian Abbey of Coupar Angus or Cupar-Angus, with the Breviary of the Register.* 2 vols. London: The Grampian Club, 1879-80.
Roskell, R. S. "The problem of the attendance of the lords in medieval parliaments." *Bull. Inst. of Hist. Research*, 29 (1956): 153-204.
"Rotuli collectorum subsidii regi a laicis ... ." *Yorkshire Arch. and Top. Jour.*, 5 (1879): 1-51, 241-266, 417-432; 6 (1881): 1-44, 129-171, 287-342: 7 (1882): 6-31, 145-186.
Roupnel, Gaston. *Histoire de la campagne française.* Paris, 1932.
Rowntree, Arthur. *The History of Scarborough.* London: J. M. Dent, 1931.
Russell, Josiah C. "The clerical population of medieval England." *Traditio*, 2 (1944): 177-212.

Rymer, Thomas. *Foedera, conventiones, litterae, et cujuscunque generis acta publica.* 4 vols. Ed. by A. Clarke, et al. London: Record Commission, 1816-1869.

Salter, Herbert E. "The city of Oxford in the middle ages." *History*, n.s., 14 (1929-30): 97-105.

——, ed. *The Thame Cartulary.* 2 vols. Oxfordshire Record Society, record series, 25-26. Oxford, 1947-48.

Saltzman, L. F. "The legal status of markets." *Camb. Hist. Jour.*, 2 (1926-28): 204-212.

"Sancti Bernardi Abbatis Clarae-Vallensis Vita et Res Gestae." Migne, *Pat. Lat.*, 185: coll. 226-468.

Savin[e], Aleksandr N. *English Monasteries on the Eve of the Dissolution.* Oxford Studies in Social and Legal History, 1. Oxford: Clarendon Press, 1909.

Schaube, Adolf. "Die Wollausfuhr Englands vom Jahr 1273." *Vierteljahrsschrift für Sozial- und Wirtschaftsgeschichte*, 6 (1908): 39-72.

Schmoller, Gustav F. von. *Die Strassburger Tucher- und Weberzunft.* Strassburg, 1879.

Schulze, Eduard O. *Die Kolonisierung und Germanisierung der Gebiete zwischen Saale und Elbe.* Leipzig, 1896.

Sclafert, Th. "A propos du déboisement des Alpes du Sud." *Annales de Géographie*, 42 (1933): 266-277, 350-360.

Sebicht, R. "Die Cistercienser und die niederländischen Kolonisten in der *goldnen Ave.*" *Zeitschrift des Harz-Vereins für Geschichte und Altertumskunde*, 21 (1888): 1-74.

Segogne, Henri de and Geneviève A. Maillé. *Abbayes Cisterciennes.* Paris, 1943.

Sellers, Maud, ed. *The York Mercers and Merchant Adventurers*, 1356-1917. Surtees Society Publications, 129. London, 1918.

[Simeon of Durham.] *Symeonis monachi opera omnia.* Ed. Thomas Arnold. 2 vols. Rolls Series, 75. London, 1882-85.

Skaife, R. H., ed. *A Survey of the County of York Taken by John de Kirkby, Commonly Called Kirkby's Inquest. Also Inquisitions of Knights' Fees. The Nomina Villarum for Yorkshire.* Surtees Society Publications, 49. Durham, 1867.

Smith, Lucy T. See Leland, John.

Smith, Reginald A. L. *Collected Papers.* London: Longmans, Green, 1947.

Spruner von Merze, Karl. *Spruner-Menke Hand-Atlas für die Geschichte des Mittelalters und der Neueren Zeit.* 3rd ed. by Th. Menke. Gotha, 1880.

Spufford, Peter. *Origins of the English Parliament.* London: Longmans, 1967.

Stansfield, John, ed. "A rent-roll of Kirkstall abbey." *Miscellanea*, pp. 1-21. Thoresby Society, publs., 2. Leeds, 1891.

Stenton, Frank M. *Documents Illustrative of the Social and Economic History of the Danelaw from Various Collections.* Records of the Social and Economic History of England and Wales, 5. London: British Academy, 1920.

——, ed. *Facsimiles of Early Charters from Northamptonshire Collections.*

Publications of the Northants. Record Society, 4. Lincoln and London, 1930.

[Stephen Harding, *Saint.*] *Exordium coenobii et ordinis cisterciensis.* Migne, *Pat. Lat.*, 166: col. 1501-1510.

Stevenson, Joseph. See Ralph of Coggeshall.

Stevenson, William H. *Calendar of the Records of the Corporation of Gloucester.* Gloucester, 1893.

Stuart, John, ed. *Records of the Monastery of Kinloss.* Edinburgh: Society of Antiquaries of Scotland, 1872.

Stubbs, William. See Hoveden, Richard de; William of Malmesbury.

Tait, James, ed. *The Domesday Survey of Cheshire.* Remains ..., n.s. 75. Manchester: Chetham Society, 1916.

Talbot, C. H. "The account book of Beaulieu Abbey." *Cîteaux in de Nederlanden*, 9 (1958): 189-210.

——. *The Cistercian Abbeys of Scotland.* London: Burns, Oates and Washbourne, 1939.

——. "Two opuscula of John Godard, first abbot of Newenham." *Analecta Sacri Ordinis Cisterciensis*, 10 (1954): 208-267.

Tanner, Thomas. *Notitia Monastica.* London, 1787.

[Thomas de Burton.] *Chronica monasterii de Melsa.* Ed. by Edward A. Bond. Rolls Series, 43. 3 vols. London, 1866-68.

Thompson, James Westfall. "The Cistercian Order and colonization in mediaeval Germany." *Amer. Jour. Theol.*, 24 (1920): 67-93.

——. *Economic and Social History of the Middle Ages.* New York: Century, 1928.

Thompson, Pishey. *The History and Antiquities of Boston.* London, 1856.

Thorpe, Benjamin, ed. *The Anglo Saxon Chronicle.* 2 vols. Rolls Series, 23. London, 1861.

Trenholme, Norman M. *The English Monastic Boroughs.* University of Missouri Studies, vol. 2, no. 3. Columbia: University of Missouri Press, 1927.

Trow-Smith, Robert. *A History of British Livestock Husbandry to 1700.* London: Routledge and Paul, 1957.

Tupling, George H. "Early Lancashire markets and their tolls." *Trans. Lancs. Chesh. Ant. Soc.*, 50 (1934-35): 107-137.

——. *The Economic History of Rossendale.* Manchester: Manchester University Press, 1927.

Turnbull, W. B. D. D., ed. *The Chartularies of Balmerino and Lindores.* Abbotsford Club, publs., 22. Edinburgh, 1841.

Turner, William H., ed. *Calendar of Charters and Rolls Preserved in the Bodleian Library.* Oxford, 1878.

Turton, Robert B., ed. *The Honor and Forest of Pickering.* North Riding Record Society, Publications, n.s., 1-4. 1894-1897.

Venables, Edmund, ed. *Chronicon Abbatie de Parco Lude.* Lincs. Rec. Soc., publs., 1. Lincoln, 1891.

Walbran, John Richard, and J. T. Fowler, eds. *Memorials of the Abbey of St. Mary of Fountains*. 3 vols. Surtees Society publs., 42, 67, 130. Durham, 1863-1918.

Waller, William Chapman. "An account of some records of Tilty Abbey preserved at Easton Lodge." *Trans. Essex Arch. Soc.*, 9 (1903-06): 118-121.

——. "Records of Tilty Abbey: an account of some preserved at Easton Lodge." Ibid., 8 (1900-03): 352-361.

Wallis Chapman, Alice B. See Chapman, Alice B. Wallis.

Webb. Geoffrey. *Architecture in Britain: The Middle Ages*. Pelican History of Art. Harmondsworth: Penguin Books Ltd., 1956.

Wellstood, Frederick Christian, ed. *Warwickshire Feet of Fines*, vol. 1 (AD 1195-1284). Dugdale Society Publications, 11. London, 1932.

Whitaker, Thomas D. *The History and Antiquities of the Deanery of Craven*. 3rd ed. London, 1878.

——. *An History of the Original Parish of Whalley* ... . 2nd ed. London, 1806.

White, Lynn. *Medieval Technology and Social Change*. Oxford: Clarendon Press, 1962.

Whitwell, Robert J. "English monasteries and the wool trade in the thirteenth century." *Vierteljahrschrift für Sozial- und Wirtschaftsgeschichte*, 2 (1904): 1-33.

——. "Italian bankers and the English Crown." *Trans. Royal Hist Soc.*, 2nd ser., 17 (1903): 175-233.

Willard, James F. "Taxation boroughs and Parliamentary boroughs, 1294-1336." In *Historical Essays in Honour of James Tait*, ed. John G. Edwards, et al., pp. 417-435. Manchester, 1933.

[William of Malmesbury.] *De gestis regum Anglorum libri quinque*. Ed. William Stubbs. 2 vols. Rolls Series, 90. London, 1887-89.

William of Newburgh. *Historia rerum Anglicarum*. In *Chronicles of the Reigns of Stephen, Henry II, and Richard I*, ed. Richard Howlett, vols. 1, 2. Rolls Series, 82. London: 1884-1885.

Williams, David H. "The Cistercians in Wales: some aspects of their economy." *Archaeologia Cambrensis*, 114 (1965): 2-47.

——. *The Welsh Cistercians*. Pontypool: Griffin, 1969.

Williams, Watkins W. *Saint Bernard of Clairvaux*. Manchester: University Press, 1935.

Winter, Franz. *Die Cistercienser des nordöstlichen Deutschlands*. 3 vols. Gotha, 1868-71.

Wiske, Dorothy, B. "The attitude of the English clergy in the thirteenth and fourteenth centuries towards the obligation of attendance on convocations and parliaments." In *Essays in History and Political Theory in Honor of Charles Howard McIlwain*, ed. Carl F. Wittke, pp. 77-108. Cambridge, Mass.: Harvard University Press, 1936.

Wolff, Philippe. "Le problème des Cahorsins". *Annales du Midi*, 62 (1950): 229-238.

Wood, Susan. *English Monasteries and their Patrons in the Thirteenth Century.* London: Oxford University Press, 1955.

Wroot, Herbert E. "The Pennines in history." *The Naturalist*, February-March 1930, pp. 45-60, 105-115.

——. "Yorkshire abbeys and the wool trade." In *Miscellanea*, Thoresby Society Publications, 33 (Leeds, 1935 [first printed, 1930]), pp. 1-21.

Wrottesley, George, ed. "The chartulary of Dieulacres." In *Collections for the History of Staffordshire,* ed. for the William Salt Archaeological Society, n.s., 9 (London, 1906): 291-365.

Youings, Joyce A. "The city of Exeter and the property of the dissolved monasteries." *Reps. Trans. Devonshire Assoc.*, 84 (1952): 123-141.

——, ed. *Devon Monastic Lands: A Calendar of Particulars for Grants, 1536-58.* Devon and Cornwall Record Society, n.s., 1. Torquay, 1955.

Young, Charles R. "English Royal Forests under the Angevin Kings." *Journal of British Studies*, 12 (1972-73): 1-14.

GENERAL INDEX

INDEX OF PLACES

See also the Index of Cistercian Houses and the Index of Forests.

INDEX OF CISTERCIAN HOUSES

* Entries marked with an asterisk are in England and Wales. Place-names in parentheses are earlier sites.

INDEX OF FORESTS

R: Royal forest or park
P: Private forest or chase